THE STRUCTURAL APPROACH TO DIRECT PRACTICE IN SOCIAL WORK

THE STRUCTURAL APPROACH TO DIRECT PRACTICE IN SOCIAL WORK

A SOCIAL CONSTRUCTIONIST PERSPECTIVE

THIRD EDITION

Gale Goldberg Wood and Carol T. Tully

COLUMBIA UNIVERSITY PRESS   NEW YORK

COLUMBIA UNIVERSITY PRESS
Publishers Since 1893
New York   Chichester, West Sussex

Library of Congress Cataloging-in-Publication Data
Wood, Gale Goldberg.
    The structural approach to direct practice in social work: a social constructionist
    perspective / Gale Goldberg Wood and Carol T. Tully. —3rd ed.
        p.   cm.
    Includes bibliographical references and index.
    ISBN 978-0-231-13284-8 (alk. paper)
    1. Social service. 2. Social service—United States. 3. Social workers. 4. Social workers—
United States. I. Tully, Carol Thorpe, 1946– II. Title.
    HV40.W66   2006
    361.3'2—dc22   2006006271

∞

Columbia University Press books are printed on permanent
    and durable acid-free paper.

Printed in the United States of America
c 10 9 8 7 6 5 4

To my loving husband, David F. Wood
and our family
Maxine, Richard, Kate, and Nicholas Pribyl
Patricia and David Webb
Susan, Steve, and Olivia Grace Loftus

—*Gale Goldberg Wood*

To my co-vivant, E. Jean Walker

—*Carol T. Tully*

CONTENTS

Acknowledgments   XI

Introduction   1

PART I   INFRASTRUCTURE

1. The Frame of Reference for Social Work Practice   7
    Two Dimensions that Define the Profession   9
    Four Categories of Social Work Activity   10
    Research Value   12
    Beyond Research   12

2. The Philosophical Base for Structural Social Work Practice   14
    The Practice Context   14
    The Philosophical Stance   16
    Postmodernism   17
    Deconstruction   17
    Postmodern Perspectives on Power   18
    Social Constructionism   19
    The Structural View   21
    Specialization   22
    Movement Through the Quadrants   24
    Conclusion   25

3. Ethics and Structural Social Work Practice   27
    Getting Grounded: Defining Ethics   27
    The NASW Code of Ethics   29

Ethical Principles for the Structural Approach   31

Conclusion   39

PART II **PRINCIPLES AND PROCESSES**

4. Basic Principles of the Structural Approach   43

    The Principle of Accountability to the Client   43

    The Principle of Following the Demands of the Client Task   49

    The Principle of Maximizing Potential Supports in the Client's
        Environment   55

    The Principle of Least Contest   68

    The Principle of Helping the Client Deconstruct Oppressive Cultural Dis-
        course and Reinterpret Experience from Alternative Perspectives   72

    The Minimax Principle   77

5. Intervention Principles and Procedures: A Process Model   80

    The Contract Phase   80

    The Task Phase   88

    The Flow of Initial Intervention in the Task Phase   91

    The Termination/Recontracting Phase   98

    Why Two Types of Paradigms   101

    Conclusion   101

PART III **ROLES**

6. The Conferee   105

    Translating Pressures into Tasks   106

    Facilitating Decision Making   109

    Concluding the Work   111

    Conclusion   113

7. The Broker   115

    The Tasks of the Broker   116

    The Broker in Quadrants A, B, and C   120

    Conclusion   126

8. The Mediator   127

    The Tasks of the Mediator   127

    The Mediator in Quadrants A and C   137

    Conclusion   138

9. The Advocate   139
   What Advocacy Is   140
   The Tasks of Advocacy   142
   The Advocate in Quadrants A, B, C, and D   153
   Conclusion   154

10. The Therapist   155
    The Tasks of the Therapist   155
    Radical Listening   156
    Externalizing the Problem   157
    Deconstructing Oppressive Discourse   160
    Seeking Counteracts   163
    Anchoring in History   165
    Conclusion   168

11. The Case Manager   169
    The Evolution of Case Management   169
    Tasks for Working as a Case Manager   171
    The Case Manager as Advocate   187
    Determining the Work   187
    The Case Manager in Quadrants A, B, and C   190
    Conclusion   191

12. The Group Worker   192
    The Basic Group   193
    Types of Groups   193
    Tasks for Working with Groups   196
    The Group Worker in Quadrants A, B, and C   209
    Conclusion   215

13. The Community Organizer   216
    What Is Community Organizing?   216
    The Tasks of the Community Organizer   217
    The Community Organizer in Quadrants B and C   226
    Conclusion   226

PART IV CONTEXT

14. Learning the Organization   229
    The Structures of Organizations   229
    Learning the Formal and Informal Arrangements of the Organization   234

Choice Points in the Organization: Getting from Point A to Point B   242

Conclusion   247

15.   Working in the Organization   249

The Self Principle   249

Processes for Carrying Out the Self Principle   250

Connecting the Conscious Use of Self with the Deliberate Use of Self   253

Changing the Organization from Within   254

The Metawork   257

Time Management   261

Time-Management Strategies   263

Conclusion   264

16.   A Paradigm Dilemma   265

References   269

Index   275

ACKNOWLEDGMENTS

THE CRAFT OF BOOK WRITING is an arduous one that takes tenacity and a good sense of humor. As with any adventure, many people are involved, all of whom are deserving of our thanks. We are indebted to those who helped with the actual production of the text.

First, thanks must go to John Michel at Columbia University Press, who insisted that a new edition of this book was needed. Sadly, he made his transition from this life before this edition was completed. Shelley Reinhardt, our editor at Columbia University Press, guided us through the quagmire of regulations and, although new, did a fine job. Gregory McNamee, our copyeditor, is a special guy with a good heart and a sharp blue pencil. His edits were extremely helpful, since we both have trouble knowing where commas actually belong.

We deeply value the suggestions, involvement, and willingness to help make this book better of those who read and responded to the manuscript draft, Susan Roche and Richard L. Edwards. We especially want to recognize Susan for her enormously helpful comments on our first draft.

Laura Gibson and Peggy McGuire computerized many of the figures from which the final versions were derived, and they both deserve no small amount of thanks for all their work. Both, we believe, now have a better understanding of how demanding the creation of a text is.

Finally, we thank our students. You may have no idea what a profound impact you have on us and on our writing.

—GALE GOLDBERG WOOD AND CAROL T. TULLY

Creating the structural approach and continuing to develop it have been part of my life for more than thirty years, and I am enormously pleased that this book has survived the test of time. Sadly, Ruth R. Middleman, my longtime friend and writing partner, was not able to participate in this, the most extensive shift in the theory's evolution to a postmodern, social constructionist epistemology. Ruth's health was rapidly declining, and she died almost a year before the book went to press. I still miss her.

I would like to thank Carol Tully for her willingness to learn a new set of ideas and adopt a new perspective on old ones in order to tackle the new thinking with me that the radically revisioned practice described in this edition required. I needed someone to challenge my thinking so I would not be limited by the boundaries of my own mind. We wrote this together and often jointly rewrote portions line by line.

I also want to thank my sweet husband David for supporting me throughout this process and reminding me that there is more to life than this text.

—GALE GOLDBERG WOOD

Although I have written and edited other books, reworking an existing text that has long been a classic in social work education was a new adventure for me. To my coauthor, Gale Goldberg Wood, who was gracious in letting me work with her on the revisions, I owe a huge debt. We chewed on words, discussed syntax, laughed at ourselves, and through it all never had an argument. Although I never met Ruth Middleman, her work is evident across the text, and I thank her for helping to make this book the classic it has become. She did not live to see the completion of this new edition, but I hope she would have been pleased.

I thank all those who helped keep me smiling as I wrote and rewrote. My partner, Jean Walker, deserves special recognition. She helped maintain everything in proper perspective by keeping me centered on the present moment. She is a constant reminder of the good in everyone. An especially warm thanks to David Wood, who knows that the path to greatness is through food. His lunches were always appreciated. As this book goes to press, many of my friends in New Orleans are still struggling with the aftermath of Hurricane Katrina. I thank them for helping me realize what is important.

—CAROL T. TULLY

THE STRUCTURAL APPROACH TO DIRECT PRACTICE IN SOCIAL WORK

INTRODUCTION

ALTHOUGH REALITY IS socially constructed and socially reproduced, the forces these social constructions generate and the institutional acts they spawn are real. *Poverty* is real, a function of a social construction, capitalism. A larger percentage of people of color are poor, a function of socially constructed *racism*. *Violence against women*—battering, rape, sexual harassment—is real, a function of patriarchy. The relationships in each instance are power relations; that is to say, they are political.

In most instances, those who benefit from the oppression of others are hidden from ordinary scrutiny, as are the dynamics of power and the connections of the personal to the political. Social constructionism and deconstruction can help us understand the roots of these problems and unmask the power dynamics involved in creating and sustaining them, but it takes political action to contest them and their consequences.

This third edition of the book attempts to apply both ideas—the social construction of reality and the political realities that social constructions generate. The structural practice principles now include one that is explicitly devoted to the deconstruction of taken-for-granted social discourse, as well as a chapter on narrative therapy and the role of the therapist. Deconstruction and narrative practice fit nicely within a direct practice model geared toward meeting social need through social change, promoting social justice, alleviating oppression, and increasing people's options in life. An additional chapter to guide grassroots community organizing also bolsters the practitioner's ability to help clients confront the oppressive political realities created by reification of social constructions.

In the more than thirty years since the first edition of *The Structural Approach to Direct Practice in Social Work* was published, the world has changed in dramatic ways. Having shifted focus from Vietnam to Iraq, we are once again involved in war; the terrorist attack on the World Trade Center in Manhattan on September 11, 2001, set the scene for new perspectives on homeland security; the 2004 holiday tsunami that devastated Asia awakened compassion from the global community; and the rapid technological advances of the past three decades herald a new age. What has not changed is the continuing despair of large numbers of people in not only the United States but also the entire world, and the continuing worldwide need for well-trained, compassionate social workers.

The social work profession continues to ebb and flow in relation to public opinion and political agendas as well as its own internal shifts of priorities as the dialectics of the times fluctuate. Social work and other professions have changed, as they cannot be divorced from the economic and political zeitgeist in which all thrive or try to survive. Since the 1970s, social work has shifted from a philosophy of changing the system to meet the needs of people back to a system of changing people to meet socially constructed norms. This is a continuous philosophical dance that had its genesis in the divergent philosophies of the Charity Organization Societies (changing people) to the settlement house movement (changing society). It continues to shift, depending upon the ideology of the times. With the epistemological shift from modernism to the postmodern worldview, and the rise of social constructionism and deconstruction, perhaps we are again at a point where system change will be considered more important than changing people. This is the hope of the structural approach.

WHAT MATTERS

Social workers have traditionally valued human dignity and have fought for the disenfranchised populations in society. Some of the values of social work are not popular in the dominant culture (a concern for those who have no voice). Social workers tend to see as important members of society who may *cost* society (for example, welfare recipients, the mentally ill) rather than those who provide a *gain* for society. There is, and will always be, a tension between human rights and profit.

Social work has been seen by some as a "foreign body" within mainstream capitalism (Farris and Marsh 1982). A foreign body is an irritant. A grain of sand in the eye must be quickly washed out. Yet the same grain of sand in an oyster can, over time, become a pearl—a thing of value. Such a stance has characterized social work's value base, norms, ethical imperatives, and traditions. It is a mentality concerned with social costs and human loss. Social work must continue to evolve and fulfill its historical imperatives.

It matters that the social work profession continue to attend to oppressed people. No other profession has held this societal mandate. By oppressed, we do not mean merely the poor—we mean all the disenfranchised populations. We mean minorities of color, disabled persons, women, gays, lesbians, bisexuals, transgender persons, raped and molested persons, battered women and children, and the many other strugglers who have the pressures of life's circumstances stacked against them. Oppressed persons and social workers are well known to each other.

It matters to this profession that the real income of many in this country has decreased in the past thirty years, that children born in the 1960s may not have a more financially secure life for themselves and their children than their parents, and that poverty continues to persist and grow at an alarming rate.

It matters that social workers continue to challenge and change the status quo by identifying deleterious discourses and hegemony. Social work has a mandate to question what is and work toward making society a better place for everyone.

It matters that diversity be honored. This means that social workers must operate from a perspective that recognizes there are multiple realities and respect each culture's and each person's frame of reference.

It matters that we be involved with persons different from ourselves and that we reach out to each other with compassion and humanness. The differences may be obvious (age, sex, race) or subtle (marital status, sexual orientation, spirituality), yet each difference is profound, and without awareness of and willingness to confront and discuss this, differences can obscure a meaningful working connection. The awareness of and use of process in working with others may be the component that makes the client/worker relationship "work."

It matters that social workers embrace the provision of goods and services as a major part of their work especially in eras when resources for the least powerful people are scare if existent at all.

It matters that all practitioners take seriously an obligation to work for social change. This mandate should not be left for macro-focused social workers, who are usually middle managers or administrators. Rather, it should be a central part of each direct practitioner's professional responsibility. It represents a structural approach mindset to the welfare both of one's clients and of oneself.

It matters, finally, that there never be an end to the "it matters" list. You need to add your own "it matters" to this list and check yourself from time to time to see if you are attending to what you have noted.

ORGANIZATION OF THE TEXT

The text is in four parts. The first, Infrastructure, comprises three chapters that set the stage for the remainder by providing the frame of reference for social work practice, describing the philosophical and theoretical bases for structural social work practice, and examining ethics in terms of structural social work practice. The second part, Principles and Processes, articulates the core concepts of structural social work practice by presenting both an analytical model and a process model. The third part, Roles, describes eight core social work roles (conferee, broker, mediator, advocate, therapist, case manager, group worker, and community organizer) in terms of how each is used by the structural social work practitioner. For this edition, each role has been rewritten to reflect current thinking. The fourth part, Context, includes some content previously not included that expands the direct practitioner's view of her organizational setting. The last chapter explores what we have called a paradigm dilemma that will allow practitioners an opportunity to ponder the future of our profession.

PART I

INFRASTRUCTURE

1

THE FRAME OF REFERENCE FOR SOCIAL WORK PRACTICE

THE HISTORY OF SOCIAL WORK has been characterized more by diversity than by unity. Practice has differed in accord with different fields of practice (medical social work, psychiatric social work, child welfare work, gerontological social work), different methods (casework, group work, community organization, administration), different schools of thought (psychosocial, functional, behavioral, task-centered, ecological, narrative), and different purposes (rehabilitation, socialization, resocialization, education, insight, behavior change, social action). So what, if anything, is there about social work's diverse practices that makes it a single profession? Subscription to a single set of ethics? Standing up for the needs and rights of oppressed peoples? While these similarities are significant, they are by no means sufficient to provide a clear and stable professional identity.

A profession is what it does; therefore, it should be defined by its actions. Thus, we must look to the activities of social work practitioners for the information from which to define the profession's boundaries. This chapter provides the frame of reference for examining, cataloging, and studying social work activities. The paradigm provides a foundation for social work practice in general and guides the practice of structural social work in particular.

Since the quadrant model was first introduced (Goldberg 1974, 1975; Middleman and Goldberg 1974), there has been increasing recognition that it connects the diverse activities of social work usefully and well. For example, Devore and Schlessinger developed one text devoted to ethnic-sensitive practice (1981) and another on social work in health care (1985), both of which make extensive use of the boundaries and divisions of the quadrant model. Anderson (1981) similarly used the model in his book on social work practice. The paradigm has been seen as valuable for helping workers identify where they are in any given instance of practice in terms of with whom and for whom they are performing an activity at a particular time. This helps workers keep their primary goals in mind despite "happy accidents," as when teenagers have good experiences providing recreation for disabled children. The social worker remains clear about the fact that the children are her intended beneficiaries and the teens are helping persons whom she engaged in behalf of the children. The worker, therefore, cannot inadvertently focus on the teenagers' having a good experience.

The quadrant model defines social work in terms of its actions. As Germain (1983) notes, it comes out of social work itself. It does not rely on theory or practice in psychology, biology, sociology, ecology, or theology. It derives from what the worker is doing, with whom, and for whose benefit. In her historical review of social work's technology, Germain describes the model as the most

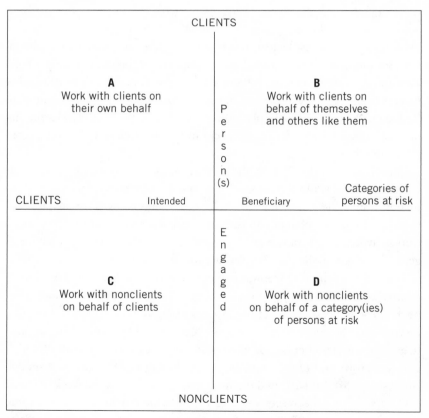

FIGURE 1.1 The frame of reference defining the profession of social work

promising framework "for knowledge-building activities and the means for sorting out social work objectives, processes and technologies" (50). The quadrant model consists of four categories of activity (that is, what the worker is doing), and is formed, as shown in figure 1.1, by the juxtaposition of two bipolar dimensions—Persons Engaged and Intended Beneficiary.

TWO DIMENSIONS THAT DEFINE THE PROFESSION

Two dimensions, when juxtaposed, define and set the boundaries for all of social work. The horizontal dimension, Intended Beneficiary, is the worker's locus of concern, which constitutes the only rationale for social work intervention. The first pole on this dimension is "Client(s)," a specific person or persons suffering in relation to particular facets of various problems. For example, a homeless woman cannot take a second-shift job because shelter beds are not available after 5:00 p.m., nor can she take a third-shift job because shelter beds are not available in the daytime. The opposite pole on this dimension is Categories of Persons at Risk, subpopulations of persons identified as sufferers by definition of a social problem. One example would be the working poor, those who earn minimum wage that is not sufficient for renting an apartment. Another example would be children without health insurance.

The vertical dimension transecting the horizontal one is Persons Engaged, which refers to the different people with whom the social worker does her work at various times, that is, clients, resource providers, community politicos, and others in accord with her rationale for intervention, which is *always* either specific clients or categories of persons at risk. The poles on this dimension are (1) Clients and (2) Nonclients. On one hand, the social worker may engage clients, that is, individuals, families, or community groups in helping themselves and each other to change the particular situations that limit their functioning and exacerbate their suffering. On the other hand, the social worker may engage nonclients, that is, resource providers, other social workers, neighbors, congressional representatives, local merchants, charitable organizations, or other professionals such as teachers, lawyers, or nurses to help an individual or a family, or a group, or a category of persons. The social worker may approach state legislators, for example, to amend archaic housing laws that protect landlords, not tenants. Local civic leaders may be mobilized to demand additional free daycare centers for single parents earning minimum wage or more accessible and affordable health centers. Or neighbors may be enlisted to provide special supports during a particularly trying time in the life of an individual or a family.

FOUR CATEGORIES OF SOCIAL WORK ACTIVITY

The four categories of social work activity bounded by these two coordinates (Intended Beneficiary and Person[s] Engaged) are labeled A, B, C, and D. Quadrant A (figure 1.2) designates all activity in which the social worker directly engages clients out of concern with their needs and problems. To illustrate, one worker at a community mental health center found isolation and loneliness to be the major recurrent themes expressed by her clients. To help alleviate this problem, she directly engaged the clients in forming a telephone network through which they communicated with each other every day. That is, Client 1 called Client 2, who then called Client 3. Client 3 called Client 4, who then called Client 1. (See chapter 4 for a description of the worker's process in developing this structure.) The creation of such a self-help network, comprising and for the sole benefit of the few, specific people engaged with the social worker, is typical of activity in Quadrant A. Quadrant A activity also includes therapy with families concerning problems various members are having with each other, and with individual persons who are having problems with themselves.

Quadrant B (figure 1.3) designates all activity in which the social worker directly engages specific clients out of concern for them and an entire category of people suffering from the same deleterious situation. Quadrant B activities include working with some tenants (clients) to press for home improvements for all tenants (a

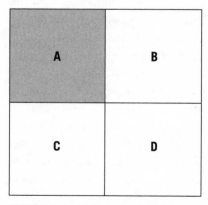

FIGURE 1.2 Activity in Quadrant A

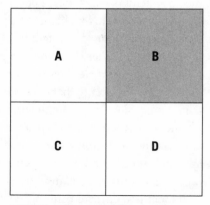

FIGURE 1.3 Activity in Quadrant B

category of persons at risk) or working with a committee of senior citizens to plan programs for a larger senior citizen population. In other words, the typical Quadrant B activity involves direct engagement of one or a few specific clients for the benefit of themselves and other persons in situations similar to theirs.

Quadrant C (figure 1.4) designates all activity in which the social worker works with others (nonclients) out of concern with the troubles effecting particular clients. For example, a social worker at a multiservice center found out that clients of hers who use mental health services were often spending a whole day waiting to get their prescriptions rewritten by the psychiatrist. She also found that others were on a long waiting list, unable to get needed prescriptions at all. The situation was largely due to the limited number of staff psychiatrists. In an effort to deal with the problem, the social worker sought to organize general practitioners and family physicians in the larger community to take on the prescription-writing and medication-monitoring functions for persons in their neighborhoods.

Had the social worker organized some of the people (clients) for purposes of pressuring the mental health service arm of the multiservice center to hire more psychiatrists, or pressuring the local physicians to extend their general practices to include supervision of people on medication, the worker's activity would be classified as Quadrant B activity. That is to say, organizing some clients to do something that will benefit both themselves and others besides themselves is a Quadrant B activity. But organizing others (nonclients) to do something that will benefit clients who are suffering is a Quadrant C activity. Other Quadrant C activities include supervision of line workers, direct practice consultation, and staff training.

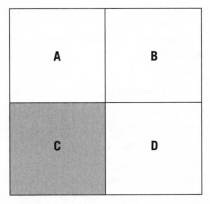

FIGURE 1.4 Activity in Quadrant C

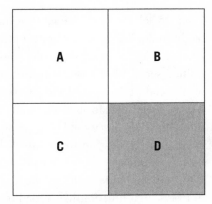

FIGURE 1.5 Activity in Quadrant D

Quadrant D (figure 1.5) designates all activity in which the social worker directly engages others (nonclients) out of concern with the plight of a category of persons. Examples include social policy analysis and development, social planning, fundraising, lobbying, and organizing scattered programmatic efforts to manage or alleviate a particular social problem into coordinated units for comprehensive service delivery.

RESEARCH VALUE

In addition to providing a classificatory scheme for ordering thoughts about social work practice, the four-quadrant paradigm has potential for guiding some research. For example, it can be used to track the activities of a given social worker at work in a particular instance, or to compare her activities across instances, thus providing a mechanism for determining the typical activity of a particular worker in different problematic situations. Holding the type of situation constant, it is possible to track the activities of different workers in order to determine typical social worker activity as a function of school of thought, field of practice, or methodology. In such ways as this, it is possible to collect data that will tell us what social workers do irrespective of differences in methods and settings for practice (generic activities), and what social workers do as a function of their different methods and practice contexts (specialized activities).

BEYOND RESEARCH

What social workers do might be quite different from what social workers ought to do. Research can contribute to knowledge of the former, and it can provide evidence to substantiate or disclaim the existence-in-action of a single, unified social work profession. But research cannot be permitted to dictate what social workers ought to do. *One cannot get ought from is.* If research findings were to indicate at a statistically significant degree that beating children improves their classroom behavior, surely school social workers would not be encouraged to beat unruly pupils. When the collectable data are in, we will have to decide whether we like all of it, part of it, or none of it—and that decision must be made quite independent of the data. In other words, findings from research function like a road map, illustrating where things are in relation to each other. The driver will decide where to go and which route to take.

Even an evaluative study that shows route X to be more effective (shorter, for example) than route Y does not, in and of itself, say "Use X!" although presumably the study was conducted for the purpose of making such a decision. The point is that research measures; it does not command.

Nevertheless, the frame of reference and the information collected and organized can focus attention on possible gaps in the range of approaches to social service delivery. Recognition of gaps can serve as a springboard for redetermining specializations and for developing new approaches to serving the heretofore unserved and underserved segments of the population frequently labeled "unreachable."

2

THE PHILOSOPHICAL BASE FOR STRUCTURAL
SOCIAL WORK PRACTICE

THIS CHAPTER discusses the philosophical base for structural social work practice. Structural social work will be seen as a strengths-based, collaborative practice, set in a postmodern context with a social constructionist epistemology.

THE PRACTICE CONTEXT

Toward the end of the twentieth century, the postmodern emphasis on calling all "givens" into question and the feminist exegesis of discourse and discourse-related beliefs and practices led to recognition of gender and cultural biases in practice theories and processes (Bertolino and O'Hanlon 2002; Brown 1994; Flax 1992; MacKinnon 1994; Smith 1987, 1990). At the same time, also largely as a result of the feminist critique (Brown 1994; Butler 1992), pathology-based and other victim-blaming systems that marginalize and silence the voices of women, people of color, lesbians, and gay men, as well as other disenfranchised groups, came under fire. During this time strengths-based social work practices rose to prominence. These include the strengths perspective (Saleebey 1992, 1997), empowerment approaches (Lee 1994), collaborative language systems (Anderson 1993; Anderson and Goolishian 1988), narrative therapy (Morgan 2000; White 1991; White and Epston 1990), and solution-focused practices (Christensen, Todahl, and Barrett 1999; DeJong and Berg 2002). These strengths-oriented methods are more consistent with the structural approach to social work that was first introduced in 1974 (Goldberg 1974a, 1974b; Middleman and Goldberg 1974) and elaborated in 1989 (Wood and Middleman 1989), 1991 (Wood and Middleman 1991), and 1997 (Wood and Middleman 1997).

Structural social work differs from other strength-based approaches in its embrace of conflict theory (Collins 1975; Crozier 1974; Dahrendorf 1959) and its consequent primary emphasis on meeting social need through social change, as opposed to consensus or systems theory (Craib 1992; Merton 1968; Parsons 1967). Social thought offers two views of society.

From a systems perspective, societies cohere as a function of a consensus of values among members, "which outweighs all possible or actual differences of opinion or interests" (Dahrendorf 1959:157). This is not to suggest that systems theory denies the existence of differences. Rather, this perspective regards differences as less important than agreements of value. When differences, or the pursuit of different vested interests by different groups of people, reach a critical point, resulting in general acknowledgment that particular conditions be defined as social problems—for instance, poverty or crime—these problems are thought to be the product of deviant individuals. That is to say, it is believed that some people are not adjusting as they should, not performing their legitimate social roles, and that these persons need to be controlled and changed in some way, made to conform. But sometimes conformity is impossible, as when the number of jobs that pay a living wage is severely limited and unemployment is rampant.

Dahrendorf (1959:161) summarizes the basic tenets of the systems view of how society coheres with the following propositions:

1. Every society is a relatively persistent, stable structure of elements.
2. Every society is a well-integrated structure of elements.
3. Every element in a society has a function—that is, renders a contribution to its maintenance as a system.
4. Every functioning social structure is based on a consensus of values among its members.

Dahrendorf goes on to note that "In varying forms, these elements of (1) stability, (2) integration, (3) functional coordination, and (4) consensus recur in all structural-functional approaches to the study of social structure" (1959:161).

From a conflict or coercion theory perspective (Collins 1975; Craib 1992; Dahrendorf 1959), social order is presumed to be based on power differentials among multiple vested interest groups. Groups with greater assets and voice are dominant, while those with fewer resources are subordinated and coerced to accommodate. Conflict theory does recognize agreements in values, but posits the primacy of difference. Conflict theorists hold that society is a political struggle between groups with opposing goals. Unlike in systems theory, the term *deviance* has no meaning within this framework, because difference just adds to the number of competing groups.

Given structural social work's base in conflict theory, it stands to reason that in any given instance of client suffering, structural social work directs the practitioner to first explore environmental pressures in order to see if environmental change would alleviate the suffering, and to see if it is possible to change the environment in the manner necessary to alleviate the suffering. If it is not possible to change the environment, or if it is possible and the change that is made still does not alleviate the person's suffering, then therapy for the individual may be indicated, a therapy that identifies and challenges the relevant environmental narratives oppressing that person. For example, an elderly man living on the third floor of a building in a gang's territory was afraid to go out to shop for food. As a consequence, he became malnourished and depressed. Because it was not possible to have police constantly patrolling the area, after treatment for malnourishment, the social worker arranged for the man to move into a safer neighborhood. By this time, however, his depression was so severe that he was loath to leave his apartment. Thus, therapy was indicated, and it eventually restored the man's interest in life and his ability to move about the neighborhood to meet his needs. To have provided therapy first would not have helped, for at that time the man was still subject to gang violence.

The primary rationale for considering the situation first is to avoid getting locked into a tautological and self-confirming system. To presume that the problem is psychological is to preclude proof that it is not. To presume that the problem is rooted in the social structure, however, allows for observable evidence to indicate that the assumption is fallacious if, in fact, it is.

THE PHILOSOPHICAL STANCE

The structural approach is a postmodern, social-constructionist, strength-based, narrative, and collaborative social work practice theory. Structures are intended to be understood as sets of narratives and their related sociocultural and local interactions that have persisted over time to the extent that they are considered to have become "institutionalized." The policies and practices seem to be givens — the only way, the way things have always been, and, most damnable, the way things should be.

The term *structural*, as it is used here, is not meant to convey essentialism. Social structures are socially constructed, even though, in many instances, they were constructed generations ago and handed down, through discourse and teachings, all the way to the twenty-first century (Gergen 1999). It is because these institutionalized "structures" were socially constructed that they can be changed. In other words, they can be deconstructed and reconstructed. This is a hopeful stance for social workers at all levels of practice.

POSTMODERNISM

A major function of postmodernism is "to de-naturalize some of the dominant features of our way of life; to point out those entities that we unthinkingly experience as 'natural' ([including] capitalism, patriarchy, liberal humanism) are in fact 'cultural'; made by us, not given to us" (Hutcheon 1989:2). It is in this regard that postmodernism calls all "givens"—including social work practice theories—into question. Postmodernism seeks to interrogate the way in which meaning is produced, to uncover the ideologies and vested interests that inform its generation (Chambon 1999; Foucault 1995). In some ways this task has its roots in the 1960s distrust of powerful social structures, ideologies, and presumed-universal theories that ignore context and diversity (for example, the developmental stage theories of Erik Erikson and Jean Piaget). As Hutcheon indicates, "Drawing its ideological grounding from a general 1960's challenging of authority...today's postmodernism is both interrogative in mode and 'detoxifying' in intent" (1989:10).

Postmodernism is also reflexive. It recognizes and calls into question its own complicity in its interrogation, due to the inextricable and ubiquitous presence of the analyst and her or his ideology in the analysis. Postmodernism abides no pretense of objectivity. The self is a subjective self, and all that self does is to a large degree subjective. A social worker cannot completely step outside of her beliefs and vested interests, and therefore the social worker's position is always somewhat compromised. Nothing can be taken to be politically neutral or theoretically innocent. Always, social work activity is both political and consequential. Always, social workers are complicit in their formulation of problems, their selection of diagnoses, and their choice of practice modalities.

DECONSTRUCTION

Deconstruction (Derrida 1976; White 1991; Wood and Roche 2001a, 2001b, 2001c) is a postmodern tool for seeking out and exposing hidden power relationships in cultural and local discourses (Foucault 1995), power relationships that explain, sustain, and reproduce current, inadequate, and reluctantly provided social resources, marginalizing social practices and controlling, pathology-based social work. A discourse is a set of ideas, beliefs, and practices that circulate in society and generate a social reality that is experienced as real. That is to say, discourses—talk, text, and their related patterns of activity—are constitutive (White 1991; Wood and Roche 2001a, 20001b, 2001c).

Discourses involve the social construction and maintenance of sets of social arrangements and relationships among people in which some groups of persons have more power than others. The latter are said to be "marginalized," which means that their voices are peripheral in social decision-making. In our society, for example, men have more of a say-so than women do, and white people have a greater voice than do members of racial and ethnic minorities. Deconstruction is further elaborated in terms of work with clients in chapter 10.

POSTMODERN PERSPECTIVES ON POWER

A postmodern perspective on the social construction and operation of power relations focuses attention on the way in which interpersonal behavior reflects and reproduces broader sociocultural discourses (Derrida 1976; Foucault 1980, 1995). This knowledge of the relationship between local actions and the larger political context opens new windows of opportunity for changing oppressive social arrangements ordinarily seen as institutionalized—part of the system—*and* unchangeable.

Modern perspectives on power focus on its functioning at the societal level to limit and marginalize persons based on such ascribed criteria as race, gender, sexual orientation, or disabilities. While at times ascribed categories of persons are helpful, as for group consciousness-raising and for challenging oppressive cultural discourse in the process of therapy, it does not explain the ways in which people are conscripted into self-subjugating, as if they *should be* marginalized or denied voice. Without understanding this, the social worker's ability to change existing social arrangements is severely hindered. The hidden, the all-important means, the how-it-happens, through which persons become unwitting partners in their own oppression are critical to creating needed change in the everyday actions and interactions that wreak havoc in clients' lives. By highlighting ways in which individual human beings self-subjugate (Foucault 1978, 1985, 1986, 1995) in accord with oppressive sociocultural discourses and interact in ways consistent with these cultural messages, the postmodern power analysis emphasized in this text assists structural social workers in their efforts to bring about needed social changes through advocacy, group work, and community organizing.

SOCIAL CONSTRUCTIONISM

Social constructionism is an epistemology, a theory of knowing, that recognizes the social construction of meaning and the consequent idea of multiple realities (Berger and Luckmann 1967; Bruner 1990; Gergen 1999; von Glasersfeld 1984). As discussed earlier, it offers possibilities, whereas essentialism, the "naturalizing" or giving of concrete, "entity" status to communication-based structures that have come to be taken for granted sets obstacles to justifiable provision of goods and services in mental stone, quashing hope for change in social arrangements, professional practices, and self-representations—that is, identities. A constructionist approach loosens the grip of taken-for-granted "realities" such as policies and procedures in both social agencies and sociopolitical economic arrangements for service delivery. For example, through a social constructionist approach, mediation and advocacy may become possible, whereas essentialism would preclude them because of the way a problem has come to be defined and accepted as such over time. If one defines a presenting problem as psychological rather than interpersonal or societal, then some form of psychotherapy becomes the only logical option. Because problems are socially constructed, however, they can be defined in many different ways. Essentialism serves to freeze social workers' critical thinking skills into rigid, often defeatist, habits of thought consistent with taken-for-granted definitions.

As suggested earlier, definition of a problem is a highly potent force in determining action to alleviate it, for the way in which the problem is formulated places constraints on the range of alternatives from which solutions can be chosen. For example, if male violence against women is defined as "her nagging" in the instance of battering, or "her seductive clothing" in the instance of rape, efforts to alleviate the problem would be directed toward changing the behavior of the woman. On the other hand, if the problem is defined as men beating and raping women, attention would go toward changing the men and altering the patriarchal system that enables them, indeed relies on them, and reproduces violence at the local level. Similarly, if the problem of unemployment is defined as lack of motivation, resolution efforts would be (and have been) directed toward motivating the unemployed. Defining unemployment as a lack of jobs, on the other hand, or systematic biases in the structure of opportunity, means that efforts to resolve the problem would be focused in a very different, environmentally based direction.

While it is obviously ridiculous to define a psychological problem such as fear of heights in social terms (are buildings too tall?), the tendency to define social problems in psychological terms is a more subtle version of the same fallacy. And it is this fallacy—defining social problems in psychological terms—that has made some social workers with good intentions unwitting parties to the mounting conspiracy against the poor, people of color, women, lesbians and gay men, and others.

The tendency to define social problems in psychological terms is a thinking habit rooted in the heinous doctrine of exceptionalism, which stems from the discourse on individual responsibility. This discourse comprises a set of personal deficit narratives that mask rampant institutionalized biases that privilege some (for example, white, heterosexual men) and marginalize others (for example, black people, gay people, women, elderly persons, persons with disabilities). The individual responsibility/personal deficit discourse was foisted upon us as children and reinforced throughout our further "education." We were taught to believe that an individual's economic limitations stem from her or his personal deficits, that she or he is an exception in an otherwise functional set of social arrangements, personally inadequate in some way, and that she or he needs to be changed—made more adequate via counseling, cognitive-behavioral practices, psycho-educational processes, socialization, acculturation, rehabilitation, and so forth—in order to hold her or his own in society. Operating from this perspective, the social worker is an agent of social control, maintaining the inequitable status quo by placating a potentially dangerous population of have-nots.

At this point, it seems important to note the word *inadequate*, which, when applied to people, leads to such goals for intervention as increased ego strength and can be insidiously tyrannical, for it is not merely a descriptive term. It refers to a disparity between the skills and resources of a given person and the demands of a given situation. If one believes that the person ought to be more skillful or resourceful, better able to meet the demands of a given situation, then the person will be labeled "inadequate." If, on the other hand, it is believed that the situation ought to place fewer demands on the person, then the situation will be labeled "inadequate." Thus, to say that a given person is inadequate is both a description of disparity between that person and a particular situation and a value judgment attributing blame for that disparity at one and the same time. For further discussion of this issue, see William Ryan's *Blaming the Victim* (1961).

THE STRUCTURAL VIEW

The structural view, an alternative perspective, considers most social problems to be predictable, deliberately built into the system for the benefit of some at the expense of a systematic population of "others." This line of thinking suggests that opportunities and resources are unequally distributed and that members of deprived populations are structurally victimized. Thus it appears that social workers ought to be changing oppressive situations and statuses, not the people trapped in them. That is to say, initially, and ultimately where needed, social workers should bring to bear, modify, or create resources to meet human needs. Social workers should be agents of social change, not "status quotitions." From this perspective, public, secular social services should be a human right of all women, men, and children who, for whatever reason, cannot provide for themselves.

Because problems are socially constructed, the issue of problem definition is always a choice. Critical thinking and the open-minded attitude that problems can be construed in many different ways provide social workers with choices, as opposed to habits. Structural social work is based on the decision to define social problems in the environment first, not in the client.

The practice theory presented in this text presupposes that sufferers are not necessarily the cause of their problems and therefore are not always the appropriate targets for change efforts. The point is that inadequate social arrangements may be responsible for many of the problematic situations that are frequently defined as products of those who suffer from them. Poverty, for example, was not created by the poor, nor was racism invented by people of color.

Consistent with this philosophy, we propose the following four-part professional assignment for the structural social worker in direct practice:

1. To help people connect with needed resources.
2. When feasible, to change social structures (including discourses) where existing ones limit human functioning or exacerbate human suffering.
3. To help people negotiate problematic situations.
4. To help people deconstruct sociopolitical discourse to reveal its connections to their daily struggles.

This professional assignment can and should hold across agency settings. The service delivered by a social worker is a professional social work service rather than the service of a particular agency. Much as an obstetrician delivers babies in the same way irrespective of which hospital employs her, the social worker should perform the same professional assignment irrespective of the employing agency. In both instances, the service that the professional renders is the service of the profession.

Agencies define client populations (for example, residents in a particular catchment area) and provide resources (for example, emergency financial assistance). They do not determine the professional practice of the professionals they employ, though they may try to do so. Thus social work professionals must be prepared to articulate and sustain their professional practice. They must also be willing and able to fight for policies that enable professional practice where agencies do not seem to respect professionals. This is not to deny that the way in which a worker implements the professional assignment must be modified in accord with the primary functions of different organizations. The point is that the basic thrust does not change, although the specific movements of the worker may. We elaborate on this in part IV.

SPECIALIZATION

Social work practice has always been divided in some way. But the specializations were not designated a priori in accord with a hypothetical construct of the whole. Rather, specializations evolved in the course of actual work, and partial theories to justify them appeared later.

One problem posed by evolutionary development, as opposed to a priori designation of specializations, is that of determining the amount and kind of additional specializations that are required. In other words, how will we know when we have arrived at the whole? Perhaps this partially accounts for social work's reluctance to either completely embrace or completely reject any innovation in practice. With no overall, orienting scheme, with no image of what the whole should look like, there is no basis for separating the relevant from the irrelevant.

Related to this is the problem of recognizing gaps in social work practice. The absence of a scheme that organizes and gives meaning to the various specializations suggests that each is a whole unto itself, and that the profession is a loose federation of functionally autonomous units. How can there be gaps when social work is so conceived? If there is a whole of social work practice

with an assigned or an assumed social function to perform, then specializations must be seen as parts in relation to other parts, each deriving its special
responsibilities from, and having meaning only in relation to, the whole.
Meaning does not exist outside of a context.

It should be noted that social work practice does not fall naturally into any
particular set of subunits as opposed to any other particular set of subunits.
Practice specializations must be arbitrarily defined, and in this sense, any
scheme for partitioning the whole is as logical as any other scheme. The
important issue is that there be some scheme, some theoretical framework
(albeit tentative) that represents the whole and specifies the relationship
among parts, irrespective of the particular way in which that whole is parti-
tioned.

Fulfillment of the professional assignment specified above demands performance of all four types of work defined by the quadrant model explicated in
chapter 1. And this is a tall order for any one social worker to carry out. Moreover, while the social worker is involved in D-type activities (lobbying, social
policy development), what happens to the people left behind in Quadrant A?
For example, who will help Mrs. Paul's eighth-grade general science classes
get updated textbooks while the social worker engages state legislators in efforts
to increase funding for public school materials? Conversely, who will work
toward alleviating the problem of out-of-date text and reference books in the
state's public schools while the social worker is engaging local benevolent
organizations in raising money for cutting-edge science texts for Mrs. Paul's
students? For pragmatic reasons at least, some division of labor is necessary.

The four-quadrant model presented in chapter 1 is one way to conceptualize the whole of social work practice. It guides our discussion of practice here
and serves as a point of origin for dividing social work practice into the two
complementary areas of specialization diagramed in figure 2.1. Since specialization is necessary for pragmatic reasons, so too the overlap in Quadrants B
and C is necessary for pragmatic reasons. The overlap is intended to prevent
built-in gaps in service that hound theorists, confound practitioners, and frus-
trate clients.

Quadrants A, B, and C can be used to describe the *micro*-practice of social
work, while Quadrants B, C, and D can be used to describe the *macro*-prac-
tice. Since Quadrant A is presumably specific to micro-practice and Quadrant
D is presumably specific to macro-practice, Quadrants A and D should be
considered the exclusive categories of activity that provide the needed division
of labor. With respect to the example cited earlier, the social worker doing
micro-practice would help Mrs. Paul's eighth graders get updated science

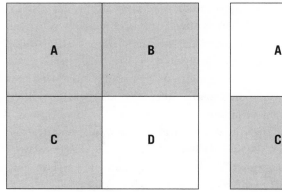
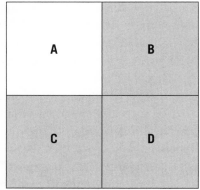

Micro practice   Macro practice

FIGURE 2.1 Specializations

books, while the social worker doing macro-practice would lobby legislators for increased funding for textbooks in the state's public schools. Both micro and macro practitioners would operate in Quadrants B and C, however, so these should be considered the mutual categories of activity that provide the overlap to control for gaps between areas of specialization.

MOVEMENT THROUGH THE QUADRANTS

Given the preceding, it seems reasonable to assume that every instance of micro social work would begin in Quadrant A, with the expressed needs and struggles of particular persons, and extend to Quadrants B and C, in accord with requisite tasks to meet the needs and alleviate the struggles. Requisite tasks are defined as activities designed to ease the deleterious aspects of problems impinging on the client. Every instance of macro social work, on the other hand, would begin in Quadrant D, and extend to Quadrants B and C in accord with the demands of the social task. The social task is defined as activities designed to eliminate a social problem. In other words, the objectives of macro social work would grow out of the social problem itself, while the objectives of micro social work would grow out of the expressed needs and struggles of a particular client, whether individual, family, group, or community.

Since both specializations would operate in Quadrants B and C, their respective activities might at times look alike. In terms of Quadrant B, for example, either specialist may organize a group of tenants to press for improved maintenance and repairs for themselves and others living in the same housing project. As the specialists proceed from different loci of concern, however, their work manifests certain important differences.

The social worker in macro-practice can organize tenants in various housing projects in an effort to bring about broader social change, such as a bill of tenants' rights that includes the right to safe and functional physical facilities in government housing projects. Their concern would be with a category of sufferers—all residents of public housing projects—rather than with any single instance within that category, for example, the stopped-up toilets and the stove that does not work in the home of Mrs. Banks and her daughters at the Glenhills Housing Estate. Thus their organizing job is not finished when a tenants' association is organized at Glenhills, but their work with the tenants of Glenhills is finished. The macro workers move on to organize residents of other housing projects with unsafe or nonfunctional physical facilities.

Social workers doing micro-practice, on the other hand, organize the tenants at a particular housing project in response to specific tenants expressed needs for and struggles with the declining physical conditions of their homes. The worker's concern is with the plight of these particular tenants. When these tenants, with the help of the worker, have organized and accomplished the requisite task—reached an agreement with the Housing Authority to improve the physical facilities of their homes—the worker is out of the tenant-organizing business. She may still be involved with these particular tenants in any number of other problematic situations they encounter, such as the prejudice to which their children are subjected at school or increases in food prices beyond that attributable to inflation at the only store within walking distance.

CONCLUSION

This chapter has discussed the philosophy underlying structural social work. We defined the term *structure* as a set of narratives and their related sociocultural and local interactions that have persisted so long that they have become "institutionalized." We compared and contrasted structural social work with other strength-based methods and elaborated on its postmodern and social constructionist roots. We explained deconstruction as a tool for identifying power relationships important to the practice of social work, and we identified discourse as an often elusive social structure that deconstruction brings to light. We emphasized the importance of problem definition and presented the structural view of social-problems causation and relevant targets for change, heavily influenced by conflict theory. Consistent with this, we posited a four-part professional assignment and delineated two specializations, macro and micro, in terms of the quadrant model introduced in chapter 1. We described and illustrated differential movement through the quadrants as a function of specialization.

To specify a professional assignment and designate areas of specialization in terms of activity provides an orientation to practice, but it does not describe practice itself. In other words, such a formulation, while essential to a coherent, systematic practice, is too abstract to guide intervention. Elaboration of a practice requires specification of a set of principles, process definitions of the principles, the functional roles that derive from those, and the explicit acts that the worker should perform. This will be done in chapters 4 and 5, where we will specify the practice in detail and illustrate it with real-world examples.

3

ETHICS AND STRUCTURAL SOCIAL WORK PRACTICE

THIS CHAPTER provides an overview of the philosophies and theories that underpin social work ethics (Dolgoff, Loewenberg, and Harrington 2004; Freeman 2000; Reamer 1993). We define the term *ethics* and analyze the NASW Code of Ethics (1996) in terms of its application with the structural approach to social work practice. Herein we call certain aspects of the NASW Code into question, in keeping with postmodernism, and we demonstrate the basic principles and processes of the structural approach (Wood and Middleman 1989). This chapter provides the fundamental components of social work ethics and the structural approach to practice that are further developed in subsequent chapters.

GETTING GROUNDED: DEFINING ETHICS

The word *ethics* has a long and impressive pedigree. Coming from the Greek word *ethika*, meaning "custom" or "character," ethics is generally defined as having to do with principles or standards of human conduct. But it is also considered to be a study of these principles and is thought of as "moral philosophy." As a branch of philosophy, ethics is defined as a normative science, that is, the way society constructs and perceives what is right and wrong, and is thus a social construction. Though some sources consider it a social science, more pragmatically, the *Oxford English Dictionary* (1995) and *Webster's Ninth New Collegiate Dictionary* (1988) define ethics as related to what is good or bad and, perhaps more important, as related to ideal of human character and the ideal ends of human action (moral values). Linzer (1999) also sees ethics as related to morals and values as well as ways of exploring the right thing to do in terms of our interactions with others; Bosanquet (1916) views ethics as specifically related to a caring for people with an emphasis on integrity, cordiality, and even good manners. Dolgoff, Loewenberg, and Harrington (2004) explore differences between general ethics, professional ethics, and social work ethics, but they see all of these as related to prevailing social values and morals. Reamer (1995, 1998, 2001a) perceives professional ethics as interwoven with societal values and morals and supported by six social work ethical principles that are actualized through personal values. He further sees the term *ethics* as relating to the immune system of both society in general and the profession of social work in particular (Reamer 2001b). That is, while norms and mores are elastic, they may be stretched only so far before a countermovement forms. Virtually every author who writes about ethics defines the term somewhat differently, yet all agree that it is related to ideal standards of human conduct, to what is good or right, and to what is in the best interest of public welfare (Bosanquet 1916; Dolgoff, Loewenberg, and Harrington 2004; Johnson 1955; Reamer 1995, 1998, 2001a, 2001b). In other words, the concept is socially defined and intended to benefit society as a whole by controlling individuals.

From this generalized view, various professions have developed their own codes of ethics; some of these professions include social work, medicine, law, nursing, and psychology (CASRO 1999–2004). While differing in scope, professional codes tend to provide either general or specific guidelines for what is considered ethical demeanor within the profession—professional behavior to be used when providing professional services (Dolgoff, Loewenberg, and Harrington 2004). Complicating the issue, some professions have more than one professional code. There are at least three professional codes of ethics in social work, including separate codes for the National Association of Black Social Workers, the Clinical Social Work Federation, and the National Association of Social Workers. Additionally, there are ethical codes that tend to reach across professions. For example, there are various codes of ethics that can be used when doing social science research irrespective of the discipline (CASRO 1999–2004). Because this chapter addresses ethics in the social services, the operational definition of the concept will be drawn from the National Association of Social Workers (NASW) Code of Ethics (1996). Nonetheless, it is important to realize that ethical behavior has its antecedents and currency in prevailing philosophy and theory. More simply stated, ethics is a social construction, and the way a social worker, or any professional, applies her ethical standards has a great deal to do with the way she views the world and her personal belief systems.

In social work, in a very general sense, there are two prevailing philosophical views related to ethics. Reamer (2000) defines these as *cognitivist* and *noncognitivist*; Dolgoff, Loewenberg, and Harrington (2004) see them as *ethical absolutism* and *ethical relativism*. Cognitivists believe that guidelines and criteria to assess and determine what is ethically correct or incorrect can be objectively defined. Ethical absolutism stresses the extreme importance of fixed moral rules. Thus, both cognitivists and absolutists have rigid perceptions of right and wrong irrespective of the context and consequences of any action taken. Both noncognitivists and ethical relativists believe that ethical judgments are the subjective opinion of the person making the judgments, and that ethical determinations must be made based on the context of the presenting situation and the consequences that may created by the decision (Dolgoff, Loewenberg, and Harrington 2004; Reamer 2000).

Structural social work embraces ethical relativism. Ethical behavior requires the social worker to consider the context and consequences of her or his actions. This is especially significant from a social constructionist position, which holds that behavior can have no meaning apart from the social context in which it is enacted, and that meanings attributed to behavior differ across contexts.

Ethics are not as clear as dichotomous variables; however, seldom are situations defined as simply ethical or unethical. While some situations (for instance, having a sexual relationship with a current client) are easily defined as unethical, others (having a sexual relationship with a former client) are murkier. Rather, all ethical decisions fall somewhere along a continuum between ethical and unethical and are best evaluated in terms of the social context and the prevailing situation in which the worker finds her or himself at a given point in time. This is consistent with the anthropological insight that social constructs such as good and bad are time- and culture-bound.

For example, many believe it is unethical under any circumstances to take the life of another human being (ethical absolutism). However, in some wartime situations, the taking of human life is seen as necessary, moral, and ethical (ethical relativism). To demonstrate the complexity of the ethics domain, consider that there are times when, even during a war, killing may be seen as immoral and unethical. In the Vietnam War or in the war in Iraq, many believed the fighting to be illegitimate, hence the killing unethical. This complex and relativistic view supports the six principles of structural social work delineated in chapter 4.

THE NASW CODE OF ETHICS

Although there are many codes of ethics by which social workers may be bound, given the limits of space, only the National Association of Social Workers 1996 Code of Ethics (revised in 1999) is explored here. This code is far more detailed than either of its two prior editions (NASW 1960–67, 1979–80), yet all three maintain a systems theory base and an ecological perspective. All three versions tend toward the idea of changing people, as opposed to structural social work's requirement to change systems for the benefit of people.

Moreover, the 1996–99 code is far more prescriptive and complex than its precursors. When one positions the 1996–99 code on the continuum between ethical absolutism and ethical relativism, the code can be seen to be far more absolute than relativistic. That is, good and bad (or ethical and unethical) tend to be perceived as dichotomous, a serious threat to critical thinking. Furthermore, this raises the question of whether the code itself is ethical because of its rigidity.

As currently written, the code comprises a preamble that defines the mission of social work, a second section that explores the purposes of the code, a third section that defines six ethical principles (service, social justice, dignity and worth of the person, importance of human relations, integrity, and competence), and a final section that discusses ethical standards. It is the final section that identifies three kinds of ethical issues: issues involving errors that social workers might make that would have ethical implications; issues associated with difficult ethical decisions; and issues related to social workers' misconduct. The code culminates in a segment related to six areas in which social workers have ethical responsibilities (to clients, colleagues, practice settings, the profession, the broader society, and as professionals).

The purpose of the code is generally seen as (1) to provide the identification of core values on which the profession is said to be based; (2) to establish a specific set of ethical standards that practitioners should use to guide their practice; (3) to provide a baseline on which practitioners can rely when faced with ethical uncertainties; (4) to define specific ethical standards by which society at large can hold the profession accountable; (5) to give new professionals a means by which to become acculturated to the profession's mission, values, and ethics; and (6) to articulate specific standards by which social workers' behaviors may be assessed. Although the code clearly notes that it has a specific commitment to enhancing human well-being, client empowerment, service to the oppressed, and the promotion of social justice in a culturally diverse society, it is far more biased toward the needs and interest of the agency rather than the needs, interests, and rights of the clients.

For example, a client in an inpatient psychiatric ward was upset and yelling at no one in particular. The cause for the outburst was related to the fact that his wife would not be able to visit him that week. The policies of the facility clearly state that a patient who becomes unruly must be placed in the time-out room. In this instance the social worker spoke with the man and was able to calm him. Once calmed, the patient requested a cigarette. Because of the policies, the social worker explained that he needed to ask his supervisor whether the patient could have one. The supervisor insisted that because of the patient's outburst he must be placed in the time-out room immediately and could not have a smoke. The worker, seeing that the patient had calmed down, did offer him a cigarette, knowing that the time-out room was intended to calm patients, not punish them, and that the patient was likely to become upset unnecessarily if placed there. Ultimately, the worker was disciplined for insubordination. The supervisor viewed the situation from the perspective of an ethical absolutist, the worker from a perspective of ethical relativism. The structural approach, which values context and consequences, would side with the social worker in this case.

The 1996–99 code tends to support the perspective of the ethical absolutist when it states, "Social workers generally should adhere to commitments made to employers and employing organizations" (NASW 1996–99:3.09a). Yet, it seems to contradict itself when it states, "Social workers should not allow an employing organization's policies, procedures, regulations, or administrative orders to interfere with their ethical practice of social work" (NASW 1996–99:3.09d). Section 3.09d of the code supports the worker if ethical determinations are based on the context of the presenting situation and the consequences that may be created by the decision. This latter view is the position taken by the structural approach. Ethical dilemmas such as the preceding are ever-present, and each social worker must decide what to do based on the specific set of circumstances and how best to meet the needs of the client. A review of various ethical principles supported by structural social work follows.

ETHICAL PRINCIPLES FOR THE STRUCTURAL APPROACH

There are numerous ethical principles to which various authors subscribe (Dolgoff, Loewenberg, and Harrington 2004; Mattison 2000; NASW 1996–99; Reamer 1993, 2000; Reid and Popple 1992), and there are a number of ethical domains defined by legal standards related to conducting research (for instance, the Nuremburg Code of 1948 and the National Research Act of 1974). This section defines six principles congruent with the structural approach that social workers must consider when practicing. These include the principles of respect for the individual, beneficence, confidentiality, informed consent, justice, and honesty.

RESPECT FOR THE INDIVIDUAL

Respect for the individual is the primary ethical principle that supports structural social work. It is the willingness of the worker to hear the client's elaborated story without judgment and then begin, with the client, to consider possible interventions and alternative story lines. Each client's story is unique, and that unique story defines the next step in the process. A social worker cannot have preconceived ideas about how the story should end, because each client and each situation is different and only the client has the right to decide how her or his life will be. Respecting uniqueness and choices includes the worker's recognition-in-action of the client's personal dignity, autonomy, and self-determination, from the initial handshake to the frequent question of whether the topic of conversation is what the client considers important. Accepting the client where she or he happens to be at the moment is key, and allowing the conversation to evolve in a nonjudgmental fashion is vital. The following example may be helpful in further defining this principle.

During a discussion about health care in the city, Mr. Thomas, a thirty-eight-year-old African American, tells the worker that he has been "barebacking" (having unprotected anal sex). He says he was tested for HIV/AIDS six months ago in San Francisco but, because of his recent sexual activities, he thought it necessary to be retested and asked where he could go for the test.

Even if the social worker is extremely religious and believes homosexuality to be a sin, she continues talking with the client in a respectful and ethically acceptable manner, treating her own beliefs as personal and not to be pressed onto others either verbally or nonverbally. The worker maintains a gentle, sincere concern for and empathic stance related to the client and his situation, tells Mr. Thomas where he can be tested, and provides additional information regarding health care in the city.

BENEFICENCE

The principle of beneficence requires that the social worker protect the client from harm by maximizing the benefits of all available services and minimizing all potential harm to the client. In other words, beneficence demands that a professional social worker has a duty to do no harm. This requires that the social worker have some notion of the construct of harm. Generally defined, harm means to inflict physical or psychological injury or damage. So, social workers have an ethical obligation not to harm clients either physically or psychologically. This may seem fairly straightforward (and probably should be), but there may be times when doing no harm is more complicated than it seems. Take, for example, the following scenario.

The Sangers are an elderly couple who have been married for decades. They have no children and no living relatives. Mrs. Sanger has been recently diagnosed with early-stage Alzheimer's disease, and Mr. Sanger has advanced rheumatoid arthritis that makes him totally dependent on his wife. Because both are in declining health and have always been proponents of death with dignity, they have agreed that whenever their health fails they will help each other die, neither wanting to live without the other. Their plan is for Mr. Sanger to kill his wife and then himself. The Sangers come to see a social worker in the local area agency on aging to ask that she take care of the necessary paperwork following their deaths.

The social worker first agrees to take care of the necessary paperwork following their deaths. Then she engages the Sangers in a discussion of their health, their plan, and alternatives they have considered. After listening to the couple at length, the worker decides that she will neither detain the Sangers nor report their plan. It seems to the worker that these people, in this situation, have come to a thoughtful decision, and she will not stand in the way of their self-determination despite the 1996–99 NASW Code of Ethics requirement that she do so. In her estimation, detention or reporting would cause serious psychological injury to both partners, particularly to Mrs. Sanger, who is very frightened of her mental destiny.

This is by no means the only way to approach the situation. The 1996–99 code would have us believe there is only one approach—to maintain the life of the client at all costs. But the costs are born by the client. This is again an extremely murky ethical area, one in which absolutism does not help. The decision to do no harm is based on the specific situation and the consequences of the worker's behavior. If the client were a troubled adolescent threatening suicide, the worker should have come to a very different decision.

CONFIDENTIALITY

Confidentiality has been proclaimed one of the cornerstones of the profession of social work. It means keeping the content of the client's conversations with the worker private in the client/practitioner relationship. It is a major standard of the 1996–99 NASW Code of Ethics (1.07). Such confidentiality is necessary

(1) when social workers deal with other social workers or other professionals on behalf of a client; (2) in determining what "documentation" is placed in administrative records and who can or can not access and read them; (3) in defining what aspects of client information are faxed to insurance companies or third-party payers and who has access to these faxes; and (4) in considering what, if anything, is shared with relatives of the client. It is the position of structural social work that the principle of confidentiality should not be used to protect worker and agency by keeping private what is said about the client. Rather, clients should have access to all information about themselves. The structural social worker does not keep secrets from the client. Often professionals are reluctant to give clients information that might upset them. But if the worker withholds information from the client, the worker violates the ethic of honesty, thereby sabotaging the client/worker relationship. Furthermore, such withholding of information makes it impossible for clients to participate fully in and make informed decisions about their treatment.

The construct of confidentiality is generally not viewed as a legal one. It is more often seen as an ethical one (Dolgoff, Loewenberg, and Harrington 2004) because there may be "compelling" (NASW 1996–99:1.07c) reasons for which client information may not be held in confidence. In this regard, confidentiality must be distinguished from another construct, privileged communication, a legal right that is granted by legislative statute. Privileged communication allows the client to limit the admissibility of statements made in confidence — in court or elsewhere (for example wives are not made to testify against their husbands). For the most part social workers do not have privileged communication in their relationships with clients; therefore, they must inform clients at the start of the relationship about the limits of confidentiality and under what circumstances a social worker has a legal responsibility to report confidential materials. Social workers must fight for the right accorded psychiatrists, priests, and lawyers. Clients should also be told that their records can be subpoenaed by the courts for various reasons. The following example should clarify this.

Claire Delacroix, a fifteen-year-old high school student, has come to the school social worker to ask his advice about an assignment she is doing for her English class. She has been asked to write a brief fictional account of what it is like to be a teenager in today's world. She is upset about the assignment because she wants to write about what is happening to her but is afraid to do so. During the worker's interview, he discovers that her mother's boyfriend is sexually abusing the girl. Ms. Delacroix begs the worker not to tell anyone because she is afraid her mother would blame her, and choose the boyfriend over her. She is afraid that she will wind up in foster care, or worse, in a group home. She is concerned that she will not be able to attend her same school, and consequently lose all her friends. She is also afraid that if she is removed from her mother's care, college will be out of the question.

The worker initially engages the teen in a full discussion of the circumstances of the sexual abuse (for example, how long has it been occurring, when and where it happens, and the like) and her experiences and feelings about the abuse. The social worker thinks about the consequences for the client—if confidentiality is breached, all the student's fears may become a reality (she may lose her mother, school, friends, and plans for college and be forced to enter the foster care system). By law, social workers do have an ethical responsibility to report child abuse, and, in this case, if confidentiality is not breached the sexual abuse may well continue. Thus, the social worker reluctantly tells Ms. Delacroix that he is required by law to report the abuse. He also says that when he does, he will also report the child's fears, placing a strong emphasis on the need for the mother to support the daughter rather than blame her.

This situation is also ethically murky because while social workers must obey the law, there may be other ways to stop the abuse without reporting it and risking serious interruption of the daughter's life, which is tantamount to victimizing her all over. For example, calling the mother in for an interview with the daughter and urging her to support the daughter and oust the boyfriend may have resolved the problem without further disrupting the daughter's life. Another possibility for the teenager could be housing with an aunt who lives in the neighborhood. While neither of these two moves assure that the boyfriend will be prosecuted, either one may do far less harm to the child than removal from her situated life, and it is worth noting that prosecution for sexual abuse is often hampered by the victim's recanting. It should be noted that two frequent and related reasons for recantation are (1) avoidance of blame for "tearing the household apart" and (2) trying to maintain as much of one's "normal" life situations as possible.

INFORMED CONSENT

Informed consent as an ethical principle means that the social worker and the agency must be granted permission by the client to use specific methodologies or interventions related to assessment, treatment, follow-up, and research before any work can legitimately be done (Barker 1995). This requires the worker to inform the client of all the facts related to worker behavior and treatment methods, possible side-effects of the proposed treatment (both negative and positive), possible outcomes of the treatment (both positive and negative), and various alternatives to the proposed plan so that the client can make a knowledge-based choice to participate in the process or decline to participate in all or any part of it (Barker 1995; Shulman 1992). Explaining the concept of informed consent to the client must come very early in the client/practitioner relationship because the client must be aware of all that is involved in this unique partnership. There are five general questions of concern when dealing with informed consent.

1. Did the worker fully inform the client of the purposes and types of services to be provided (including a discussion of benefits and risks) as well as possible alternative methods?
2. Did the client show that she or he understands the information that has been provided by the social worker?
3. Did the client demonstrate that she or he is competent to understand the information and thereby provide the requisite consent?
4. Was the client's consent totally voluntary and gained without coercion?
5. Was the decision to either receive or not receive services explicitly made by the client? (Barker 1995; Shulman 1992)

Often gaining informed consent is not as easy as it may seem. The following example illustrates this point.

Ai Nguyen, a refugee from Vietnam, arrived in the United States in the late 1970s. She was in her late fifties when she arrived in Louisville, Kentucky. As the eldest member of her family, she was sheltered by family members and never bothered to learn English. Now in her early eighties, she has only a minimal understanding of English, and relies, when necessary, on her family to translate for her. She rarely leaves the family's neighborhood, where others who speak her native language surround her.

Sadly, one afternoon Ms. Nguyen, who has been become increasingly forgetful and more likely to wander farther and farther from home, became totally disoriented and wandered a couple of miles outside her neighborhood. She became lost, and a Good Samaritan called the police, who picked her up and took her to adult protective services. There she was met by a social worker. The worker, who did not speak Vietnamese, tried to explain service options to the client in English but was not successful in gaining truly informed consent. The worker sought and found someone who spoke Vietnamese and could translate for them, thereby removing the language barrier. Nonetheless, the worker decided that the client's obvious mental impairment prevented her from truly consenting to treatment because voluntary consent is based on the ability of the client to make a well-informed decision. This is ethically murky because if a person has not been legally judged to be mentally incapable, then the assumption should be made that the person is able to make decisions in her own best interest even if it seems as though the person may not be able to do so. Therefore, in this instance, the worker should have assumed that Ms. Nguyen could make decisions on her own and that if she did consent to being assisted, the choice was hers to make. Although this is counterintuitive, it is the best way to protect client rights.

JUSTICE

The concept of justice is not one that is clearly defined in the social work professional literature. For example, it is not listed as a category in the 1995 *Encyclopedia of Social Work,* nor did it rate an entry in the 1995 *Social Work Dictionary.* The term is generally defined as being related to the moral rightness of an action or the upholding of what is thought to be correct (that is, fairness or justness). In the context of justice as an ethical principle, it must be understood as always doing what is just or fair in relation to the client's unique situation. However, fairness as a construct is tempered by the policies of the agency, the cost of services, and the conditions under which the agency is willing and able to provide services. For example, it may be neither fair nor just that a lesbian couple wanting to adopt a child is denied services by agencies whose policies discriminate on the basis of sexual orientation.

The idea of treating clients in a just and fair manner by doing what one thinks is correct is also difficult. Consider the reality that in the United States there are rural communities with no doctors or health facilities located nearby. This means that access to health care in some areas is severely reduced. As a consequence, people without transportation suffer or even die without receiving adequate treatment. This hardly seems either fair or just. Social workers in such communities may advocate for health professionals to move into the area or may broker services for some, but until there is ample funding and support for rural health care, the problem will persist.

HONESTY

The construct of honesty is seemingly indistinguishable from that of truth and integrity. When conceptualized in terms of an ethical principle, the idea of honesty is one that requires social workers to tell the truth to their clients. This honesty should include truthful information related to anything connected to the client and the client/practitioner relationship. It is the position of structural social work that such truthfulness is a client's right and that to withhold such information would prove harmful. Some social workers violate this ethical principle with impunity, often citing as their reason their own belief or the belief pressed onto them by other professionals (psychologists, psychiatrists, oncologists, and the like) that giving certain knowledge to particular clients would be harmful to them. It has also been argued that in some circumstances, to withhold truthful information might, in the long run, prove more beneficial than telling the truth (Reamer 1995, 2000). But this violation of the ethical principle of honesty precludes client participation in treatment. Consider the following example.

Harold Walker, a fifty-four-year-old Caucasian man, has been admitted to the cancer treatment ward of a local Veteran's Administration hospital. He has been diagnosed with terminal lung cancer, and while he knows he has cancer, he believes it to be no worse than a temporary inconvenience and is sure that he will enjoy a full recovery. The doctor has indicated to Mr. Walker's social worker that, based on his current condition, he has less than a week to live. When the worker saw the client, Mr. Walker's mood was ebullient. He indicated that he did not feel too well but would be better once out of the hospital. The doctor told the social worker not to tell Mr. Walker that he had only a few days to live because doing so would probably send Mr. Walker into a depression and hasten his demise.

This situation becomes an ethical quagmire because the principle of honesty requires that the worker inform the client of his condition irrespective of the doctor's request. However, there are some social workers who would honor the doctor's orders and not tell the client the truth about his situation. Sadly, by not telling Mr. Walker of his situation, the client/worker relationship is damaged, the client is unable to make informed decisions about available treatment options, and the client can not prepare himself for death. For example, Mr. Walker may need to write a will, engage in end-of-life life review, say good-byes, make apologies, or express previously unexpressed emotions. Structural social work demands that irrespective of the pain that might be caused, the social worker has an ethical obligation not to violate the ethical principle of honesty.

The six principles of respect for the individual, beneficence, confidentiality, informed consent, justice, and honesty form the basis for ethical decision making. They will be used throughout the remainder of the book as guides for the practice of structural social work.

CONCLUSION

This chapter has provided an overview of the philosophies and theories that underpin social work ethics and defined concepts generally associated with ethics. We analyzed the NASW Code of Ethics (1996) in terms of its relationship with the structural approach to social work practice. Specifically, we considered ethical principles in terms of their application to the structural approach. We questioned aspects of the NASW Code of Ethics in keeping with postmodernist skepticism regarding "givens" and the basic principles and processes associated with the structural approach. The chapter provided the fundamental components related to professional social work ethics and the structural approach to practice that will be developed in subsequent chapters.

PART II

PRINCIPLES AND PROCESSES

4

BASIC PRINCIPLES OF THE STRUCTURAL APPROACH

EVERY INSTANCE OF social work involves an intervention into the relationship between people and their social environment in order to improve the quality of that relationship. The ultimate target of change may be the people, the social environment, or the relationship itself. There are many conceptual models to guide people changing and relationship changing, but few to inform direct practice aimed at social change. In the structural model described here, the social environment is the primary target of change. The social worker intervenes to improve the quality of the relationship between people and their social environment primarily by bringing to bear, changing, or creating social structures.

The structural model rests on six practice principles:

1. The worker must be accountable to the client.
2. The worker must follow the demands of the client task.
3. The worker must maximize the potential supports in the client's environment.
4. The worker must proceed from an assumption of least contest.
5. The worker must help the client deconstruct oppressive cultural discourse and reinterpret experience from alternative perspectives.
6. The worker must identify, reinforce, and/or increase the client's repertoire of strategic behavior for minimizing pain and maximizing positive outcomes and satisfaction.

THE PRINCIPLE OF ACCOUNTABILITY TO THE CLIENT

The principle of accountability to the client translates the basic assumption of "adequate person v. inadequate social arrangements" into action. People suffering in relation to their social situations are presumed competent to describe the pressures upon them and to explain their need. Therefore, structural social work practice takes as its starting point the task confronting a particular client or set of clients as it is expressed in terms of their felt need. In other words, the pressures on the clients define the task, and the task is always to reduce those pressures. This task, explicitly understood by worker and client alike, constitutes one of two essential parts of the service contract.

The service contract operationalizes the principle of worker accountability to the client. A service contract may be said to exist when both worker and client explicitly understand and agree upon (1) the task to be accomplished and what the worker and client will do to help accomplish it. Thus, the service contract is a working agreement.

In creating the service contract, the client, with the help of the worker, describes the pressures on him (for example, poor housing conditions, job loss, or age discrimination). These pressures, in turn, define the task to be accomplished, what must be done to alleviate the pressures the client describes. In the instance of poor housing conditions—for example, a leaky roof or broken toilet in a rental unit—the task may be to obtain necessary repairs or find a different apartment. In the event that all possible efforts of worker and client do not accomplish the client task, worker and client may change the contract and work on an alternative task. If there is no alternative acceptable to the client, however, the contract may be terminated.

When a task acceptable to both client and worker has been determined, the worker defines the way in which she will help the client to accomplish it—the second part of the service contract. Should the worker's definition of her part be unacceptable to the client, either the worker or the client may suggest an alternative way for the worker to help. If the worker and client cannot agree on what the worker's part should be, then no contract can be made. Should worker and client agree, then the contract is established and the work can begin.

As changes in the definition of the task may occur as the work proceeds, so the definition of what the worker will do may also change. This change may be necessitated by changes in the task, or by the implications of additional information obtained in the course of working on the original contract. In any event, changes in the contract must be discussed and agreed upon before action continues.

The degree of detail in the terms of the service contract is less important than the social worker's being transparent. That is, the worker should not have goals or methods kept secret from the clients. The mandate to establish a service contract with each client or set of clients requires that workers explicitly state their intentions. This assures not only the client's right to decide whether the worker's intended behavior is acceptable, but also worker awareness of what she or he is about.

Because the contract openly specifies what worker and client have agreed upon as the task to be accomplished and the worker's part in helping to accomplish it, at least theoretically, the client is able to hold the worker to that task and the part they both agreed that the worker would play. That is, the client can hold the worker accountable for actions specified in the contract. While it is recognized that clients who feel powerless (because they frequently are) are unlikely to confront a worker who may be subverting the terms of the service contract, recognition of their right to do so sets a different tone for the worker/client relationship.

Social work by contractual agreement reduces the relative powerlessness of the client in a helping relationship. Rather than a dependent recipient of worker behavior, the client is a partner in determining, every step of the way, what will be done and how it will be done. In order to get help, the client is not called upon to trust blindly a person she or he hardly knows.

SALIENT SKILLS

To serve as an accountability device, the contract must be developed at the beginning of the worker/client relationship. Though necessary, this is unfortunate, for in the beginning it is very hard for many clients to talk openly about their private thoughts and feelings, to describe in detail, to a stranger, the nature of the situations that are causing them pain. Yet, this is exactly what is necessary for the contract to reflect the client's needs and problems. Thus, it is very important for the social worker to do everything possible to ease the way for clients to provide well-detailed, minimally distorted pictures of their plight. Eight key skills can facilitate the interaction at this early and vulnerable point in the helping process: (1) positioning, (2) attending, (3) reaching for feelings, (4) getting with feelings, (5) creating empathic connections, (6) checking out an inference, (7) reaching for information, and (8) giving feedback.

POSITIONING Positioning is intended to provide a social-emotional environment congenial to connection or rapport. It involves placing one's self physically at a right angle to the client (Myers 1969) approximately 29 to 36 inches away (Hall 1963). It also involves avoiding the desk, a potentially separating accoutrement that can be both a physical and cultural barrier to communication.

ATTENDING Attending is the interactional counterpart of listening. It includes a slightly forward lean, occasional head nods and unobtrusive "uh-huhs" that tell clients "I am following you," and good eye contact, which encourages clients to say more (Middleman and Wood 1990; Wood and Middleman 1987).

REACHING FOR FEELINGS Reaching for feelings (Shulman 1979) is significant throughout the work and critical at the outset. If the feelings that surround a description of pressures or an expression of need are not promptly and openly engaged, they become obstacles to the work, skewing perceptions and subtly distorting information that is sent and received. The social worker can reach for feelings that may be present but are not verbally expressed by verbalizing the client's nonverbal behavior in a statement such as, "You're frowning," or by suggesting feelings that the client's situation is likely to evoke such as, "That can be frightening."

GETTING WITH FEELINGS When the client does express affect in words, the worker can get with feelings by making a congruent statement such as, "That is exhausting," or a congruent noise, such as "Wow." Getting with feelings indicates to clients that the essence of their inner experience has been communicated, that what they feel is understandable and has been understood.

CREATING EMPATHIC CONNECTIONS To create an empathic connection the social worker asks if one or more persons can imagine what another person might be feeling or understand the feeling a person is experiencing. The idea is to invite people to step into another person's shoes for a moment in order to respond to that person with genuine feeling.

CHECKING OUT AN INFERENCE Checking out an inference the worker has drawn involves stating her connection or interpretation, then asking the client if that statement seems accurate. The worker's inferences are important because they can provide clients with new ways to construe events and feelings, or offer them new insights. If the worker does not check out her inferences with the client, however, the inferences are not only useless to the client, but incorrect ones can also mislead the worker in ways that are detrimental to the client and undermine the requisite transparency of the worker/client relationship.

REACHING FOR INFORMATION To reach for information is to ask the client for facts, opinions, values, and/or judgments that increase knowledge of a situation or event. The worker can reach for information using two different forms: open-ended questions, such as "What happened?" to explore, and close-ended questions, such as "Who went with you?" in order to clarify details.

GIVING FEEDBACK Giving feedback, another skill essential to the development of authentic contracts with clients, involves repeating the essence of what the client has said in a way that asks if the meaning received by the worker was, in fact, the meaning intended by the client. The worker's version of the client's statement can then be confirmed if it is accurate, or be corrected by the client if it is inaccurate.

In sum, the principle of accountability to the client translates the basic assumption of "adequate person" into action through the structural mechanism of the service contract, encompassed by the task, which is defined by the pressures on the client and the part the worker will play in helping to accomplish that task.

EXAMPLE OF THE PRINCIPLE OF ACCOUNTABILITY

The following episode illustrates the accountability principle and the way in which use of the preceding six skills facilitates the interaction process. Examples of skills are underscored in the practice excerpts.

One of the fifth-grade teachers stopped me in the hall to tell me that a girl in his class was having problems with some of the other children. He asked me if I would talk to her, and I said I would. A short while later, Debby came into my office and sat down without saying anything. *I moved to a nearby chair and angled it so we were knee-to-knee.* I waited several moments and then said, "I was talking with Mr. Taylor a little while ago, and he seemed concerned that you were having some problems with some of the other kids in class." I paused and waited to see if Debby would say anything. When she didn't, *I asked her if she thought that there was any problem.*

The social worker presumes that Debby is competent to describe the pressures on her. She does not act according to the teacher's perception that Debby has a problem, for it is quite possible that what may seem like a problem to the teacher may not be felt as a problem by Debby. And even if Debby does consider it a problem, she has a right to refuse the social worker's offer. But Debby does feel some pressure, and with the help of the worker's *positioning* herself to maximize the child's comfort and *reaching for information*, she begins to describe her situation.

Debby then replied that the other kids have been teasing her, and that she has been upset. *I said that teasing could make you feel pretty bad.* She nodded and began describing some examples of it. *I listened, nodding at points.* When she finished, I asked her if she'd like me to help her talk to the kids who tease her. She said that it seemed like a good idea, but from the look on her face I could tell that something was bothering her. *I said, "You don't look as if you think it's a good idea."*

The worker *gets with Debby's feelings*, then *attends* as the child tells more of her painful story. When the worker picks up a nonverbal clue that Debby is not really in agreement with her suggestion, she does not violate the intent of the contract by accepting Debby's verbal "yes" when her expression seems to indicate "no." Rather, the worker *reaches for her feelings* and invites her to voice her doubts. In response to the worker's use of empathic skill, Debby begins to describe a feared consequence.

Debby hesitated and then said that she was afraid the other kids might start a fight with her afterward. I told Debby that I had not thought of that and agreed that it could be a problem. *I said that I guessed that could really be upsetting* and pointed out that if she really wanted to get together with the kids who tease her, this could be one of the risks she would have to take. I asked Debby if she understood what I was saying, and she said she did.

The social worker does not try to convince Debby to take action. Rather, she *gets with the child's feelings*, confirming that such a consequence is possible, and encourages Debby to consider whether talking with the children who tease her is worth the risk. The choice belongs to Debby, for the consequences of the choice are hers to bear. Debby decides to wait until the children tease her again, and a service contract is established.

Debby was silent for a few moments and then said that she didn't want to do anything until the children started to tease her again. She said that when they did, she would tell me. *I asked her if she wanted me to wait until I heard from her again and at that time she would tell me if she wanted me to help her talk to the kids.* She said yes, and I agreed to her plan.

The terms of the service contract between Debby and the social worker were openly specified and agreed upon by both parties. The worker checked to be certain of this by *giving feedback* to Debby. When Debby acknowledged that the worker's formulation was accurate, it was clear that a contract had been established. No action would be taken unless another incident arose and Debby indicated to the social worker that she wanted help. Therefore, Debby possessed the power to determine when and under what circumstances she would want help.

THE PRINCIPLE OF FOLLOWING THE DEMANDS OF THE CLIENT TASK

The principle of following the demands of the client task requires the social worker to move from quadrant to quadrant as required by the work. For example, helping a Muslim child who suffers from the effects of racism at school talk with his teacher about it takes the worker from talking with the child in Quadrant A to helping the child talk to the teacher in Quadrant C. In addition, the worker may try to engage the faculty and administration in creating an atmosphere more congenial to the needs and struggles of Muslim children in today's world (Quadrant C). Or, if necessary, the worker may organize the parents of Muslim children at that school to confront teachers and administrators (Quadrant B). Notice that the direct service worker does not move to Quadrant D, which is reserved for macro social workers. This is not to suggest that the direct practitioner is not able to perform Quadrant D tasks. Rather, as described in chapter 1, the worker cannot be in two places at once. She cannot leave her clients in order to lobby federal legislators.

As workers move from quadrant to quadrant in pursuit of the client task, they engage both the client and others, in different configurations, at different times. Quadrant A activity may be carried out with an individual, with a family, or with a group. Similarly, in Quadrant C, the worker may engage one community person or a group of community people in behalf of client interest. In Quadrant B, the worker may engage an individual, a family, a group, or an entire community in behalf of themselves and others suffering from the same pressures.

Prerequisite to Quadrant B activity is the identification of others suffering in the same situation. If workers are to include Quadrant B activities among their alternatives, they must consistently and systematically look beyond the client to see if there are others facing the same tasks. For example, Quadrant B activity is not a viable alternative when only one Muslim family is suffering the effects of racism at the local school. When other Muslim families are also subjected to racism at that school, however, the need for structural change rather than an individualized plan that results from a case-by-case approach is more evident, and Quadrant B activity, by the social worker, becomes an alternative for accomplishing the desired change. The demand that the worker consistently look beyond the client to see if others are suffering in relation to the same phenomenon translates the essence of a structural approach to social work—meeting social needs through social change—into actual practice behavior.

In other words, the worker looks beyond the client to see if others are in the same deleterious situation, moves from quadrant to quadrant in accord with the demands of the client task, and also engages different configurations of people as the work requires. For example, when the worker agrees to help three residents of a public housing project to get needed home repairs, the client is this three-person group with the common task of getting the repairs done (Quadrant A activity with a group). In the course of working on this task the worker may engage the local representatives of the city housing authority (Quadrant C activity with an individual) or the housing authority representative along with representatives from related agencies (Quadrant C activity with a group) in an effort to get the repairs.

ROLES

Following the demands of the client task also implies the need for role flexibility. That is, the worker needs to use different sets of behaviors at different times, depending upon the nature of the task and the situation at any given point. Eight recognizable sets of behavior can be subsumed under the role names: (1) conferee, (2) broker, (3) mediator, (4) advocate, (5) case manager, (6) therapist, (7) group worker, and (8) community organizer.

THE CONFEREE The social worker takes the role of conferee for the purpose of determining, with clients, the task to be accomplished and the course of action to be pursued. The social worker confers with clients, providing information on alternative actions and the possible consequences of each, and encourages clients to decide which alternatives, if any, are congenial to their needs and life styles.

THE BROKER The role of broker is perhaps the most familiar one. The broker stands at the interface between client need and community resources, helping the former to connect with the latter. As brokers, social workers gather resources, update knowledge of them, create them, and build and maintain relationships with resource holders.

THE MEDIATOR Mediation presumes a common bond. The common bond may be a complementary one, as the bond between client need and agency service, or it may be an identical one, as the bond among construction workers who need each other in order to obtain wage increases. Consistent with this, conflict is viewed as a sign that one or more parties to the encounter have lost sight of the need each has for the other(s), and signals the worker to take the role of mediator.

The aim of the mediator is to help the parties in conflict to rediscover their need for each other, thereby freeing them to contribute to each other's welfare. Mediators position themselves between the conflicting parties to help each reach out to the other for their mutual self-fulfillment (Schwartz 1971). In other words, the basis for mediation in social work is to implement the identity or complementarity of individual and social interest where it breaks down or grows obscure.

THE ADVOCATE Advocacy is crucial to structural social work inasmuch as it seeks to create social justice and protect human rights. The advocate engages in consciousness raising, power balancing, bargaining, persuading and lobbying, always arguing in behalf of client interest.

The advocate's aims are always universal rather than individual, however. The idea is to obtain a concession so that the benefits to which the client is entitled are forthcoming, then to treat the conceder as a partner in outrage over the violation of client rights, thereby paving the way for cooperative action to modify or create structures by which all present and future clients can obtain entitlements without needing an advocate.

THE CASE MANAGER The role of case manager, often a combination of conferee, broker, therapist, and advocate, involves finding special resources and arranging for their provision. Sometimes this entails helping with decision making, obtaining goods and services at fair prices, and checking on the general welfare of clients at specific intervals. Case managers link clients with resource providers and monitor and assess services and their delivery.

THE THERAPIST The role of therapist is necessary when persons are plagued by psychological issues or have internalized troublesome identities attributed to them by oppressive social ideologies. The therapist engages persons in conversations to loosen the problem's grip on them and generate new ways of understanding themselves and their experiences.

THE GROUP WORKER The role of group worker involves a specialized set of tasks and skills for helping people interact with one another. As soon as the configuration of clients and/or others moves from one person to a family or a small group, the group worker role is required. The group worker role is essential when mediating and community organizing. Group workers organize groups, build groups, facilitate interaction, and develop cohesion.

THE COMMUNITY ORGANIZER The community organizer role involves group work and advocacy tasks as well as tasks for recruiting and maintaining large groups and lobbying. While sometimes thought of as an activity for middle managers or administrators, direct practitioners, too, may need to use the role of community organizer.

Each of the eight social work roles briefly outlined here is elaborated in separate chapters in part III of this book. To recapitulate, the principle of following the demands of the client task requires the worker to look consistently and systematically beyond the client to see if others are facing the same task, and to assume different roles at different times while performing different types of activities (Quadrant A activities, Quadrant B activities, and Quadrant C activities) with various configurations of people. The following episode illustrates the principle of following the demands of the client task.

EXAMPLE OF THE FOLLOWING THE DEMANDS OF THE CLIENT TASK

Mrs. Fuller had asked the Community Resource Center to help her sixteen-year-old son, Joe, who was experiencing difficulty at school. In response to her request, Mr. Rand, a social worker at the agency, visits Joe. He begins his activity in Quadrant A, and takes the role of conferee.

I met with Joe in his home one morning before he went to school. *We sat across from each other at the kitchen table.* I began by asking him if he had some idea about why I was there, and he said that he guessed so, that he had trouble with schoolwork. I told him that his mother had said as much and asked him if the difficulty in school was worrying him. He shook his head slightly in an affirmative way and, not looking directly at me, asked if I was going to get him into welding school. I said I didn't know and asked him if that's what he would like. He said he guessed so, but that he didn't know. He said he wasn't doing well in school. His speech was hesitant at this point. *I said, "You seem as if you're not too sure of yourself."* There was a long silence.

Joe broke the silence, saying that he knew some guys who were going to college and that's what he'd like to do but that it's impossible. *I asked him if he meant his grades would get in the way,* and he said that was partly it but it was mainly because he can't read. He spoke slowly and hesitantly, but articulately. I remained silent, nodding my head in acknowledgment. There was another silence.

Again Joe broke the silence. "I really can't read," he said. "I can't even understand some of the instructions in shop 'cause I can't read." He said that in school they don't care if you don't learn as long as you stay out of trouble. "You stay out of trouble, you pass."

We do not know what led Mr. Rand to sit across from Joe instead of using the preferable corner-to-corner arrangement. Perhaps in the Fuller kitchen there was no way to maneuver himself into a better position. Nevertheless, from Joe's allowing himself to be vulnerable by volunteering the information that he is not able to read, we can suppose that in this instance, the worker's position did not adversely affect the interaction process.

The statement, "You seem as if you're not too sure of yourself," demonstrates *checking out an inference,* a skill useful across the board, but especially important when the worker is trying to connect separate bits of information that have been generated while following the demands of the client task. It is at this time that the worker is most likely to draw consequential inferences. Therefore, it is at this time that the worker must be most careful to state all inferences aloud and ask the client if they are valid. When workers do not do this, there is danger that unfounded assumptions and interpretations could be acted upon—resulting in harm to the client.

In addition to increasing accuracy, checking out an inference often results in both worker and client becoming clearer about sometimes elusive elements of thought and feeling. This, too, is illustrated in the previous excerpt. In response to Mr. Rand's statement of the first inference he drew, Joe clarified what he would like, and when Mr. Rand checked out a second inference, Joe revealed the more basic nature of the problem he was facing.

Having something solid to go on, Mr. Rand *reaches for information* in order to look beyond the client to see if others are in a similar predicament.

We talked about needing to know how to read, whether for welding or for college, and *I asked Joe if he knew of other guys in a similar predicament.* He said that he did, and I wondered whether he could talk to them about getting a group together for reading or whatever. He said he would try, and we ended with the understanding that we would get together again.

While Joe contacted some of the others who shared his plight, Mr. Rand moved from Quadrant A to Quadrant C, and shifted his role from that of conferee to that of broker, exploring potential community resources.

I talked without success to the Educational Unit of the County Welfare-to-Work Program. This unit is set up to serve the educational needs of all TANF, or food stamp recipients in the county, a 50,000-plus population. The unit is supposed to deal with tutoring, and whatever other needs may develop in the area of education, but focuses on the parent's training needs in order for them to enter the workforce. The unit consists of one social worker with obviously not enough time even to consider extending the program to include poorly educated high school students in order to prevent them from needing TANF and food stamps after high school.

Later, I spoke with Joe's counselor at school. The counselor was not aware of the exact nature of Joe's difficulties but seemed interested in helping out. There was a class for improving reading, but it was, as a rule, not available to students as old as Joe and his friends. The counselor said he would look into making an exception, however. I said that I would talk further with Joe about it.

The word *exception* poses a dilemma, for it suggests that the needed service will not be available to everyone. In this instance it implies that, through the goodwill of this particular counselor at this particular time, Joe and his friends will be tutored in reading. But others, who have a different counselor, or who have the same counselor but do not find reading a problem until next month or next year, may have no place to turn. In addition to the need to address the structural problem of social promotion, especially in the early grades, which accounts for the presence of tenth graders who cannot read, a high school reading program should be consistently and systematically available to all students. A structure is needed, and this leads directly to a discussion of the third practice principle.

THE PRINCIPLE OF MAXIMIZING POTENTIAL SUPPORTS
IN THE CLIENT'S ENVIRONMENT

Maximizing potential supports in the client's environment requires connection of persons with existing structures, modification of existing structures, or creation of new structures to meet human needs, and this embodies the essential thrust of the structural approach to social work practice. The creation of structures makes it possible for people in need to access resources that were not previously available without the help of a social worker. This shifts the helping relationship from client/worker to client/community and neighbor/neighbor, and those relationships have the potential advantage of endurance over time. This is not true of a client/worker relationship, which, by its very nature must end. The professional helping relationship is a temporary one, and an emphasis on changing existing structures and creating new structures to meet human needs recognizes this. Workers should not occupy the central position in the helping process. Instead, they should change structures and create structures that can operate without them.

In accord with the principle of following the demands of the client task, the worker maximizes potential supports in the client's environment by working in various quadrants as necessary. Often workers must simultaneously work in two or three quadrants to help the same people. For example, the worker who notices that a few of her clients are sandwiched in crisis trying to provide care to their young children and their aging parents at the same time may involve them in a mutual support group (Quadrant A). She may also help these women to reach out to others in the same situation through a newsletter (Quadrant B). And the worker may go into Quadrant C to broker respite care, meals-on-wheels, visiting nurses, and daycare. In this example, the worker maximizes potential environmental supports by creating a new structure (Quadrants A), modifying an existing structure that she created (Quadrant B), and connecting persons with existing structures (Quadrant C).

In sum, the principle of maximizing potential supports in the client's environment tells the worker not to occupy the central position in the helping process. Rather, the worker is directed to change and create structures to reduce the pressures on clients—to meet social need through social change.

EXAMPLE 1: MAXIMIZING POTENTIAL SUPPORTS IN THE CLIENT'S ENVIRONMENT

QUADRANT A The first step in forming the self-help network to lessen somewhat the isolation and loneliness expressed by several clients of the Mental Health Center involved phone calls to potential candidates.

I called Mrs. Buterac and introduced myself as one of the social workers at the Mental Health Center. I said I wanted her to get involved in a kind of phone network where people call each other a few times a week to see how each other is doing. This would be a way of letting people feel that they have someone to talk to when things are on their minds. Mrs. Buterac said it sounded like a good idea. I said the first meeting would be November 9 at 1:00 p.m. She said she would come.

Not everyone responded as Mrs. Buterac did. Approximately half of the people whom the social worker called refused to get involved, and several others said they "would see." Eight people agreed to come to the first meeting to find out more details. The social worker took the role of group worker in Quadrant A.

At the first meeting, three people showed up. They all looked at me with suspicion. I welcomed them and explained briefly the thought behind the program. I invited them to share with one another what they thought of the idea. All three seemed to agree that it sounded like a pretty good idea and began to share tentatively with one another their feelings of loneliness and isolation. The meeting ended with an exchange of phone numbers.

After the meeting, I called all of those who said they were coming or made some tentative commitment to come, to find out what happened and to encourage them to attend the following week.

At the second meeting, two of the original three members showed up, plus Mrs. Buterac, who could not make it to the first meeting. I asked Mrs. Carmichael and Mr. Getz how things worked out for them this week. Mrs. Carmichael said that Miss Harrison (who was not present at this meeting) did call her last week, but she never got to return her call because so many things came up. I tried to get an empathic connection going by *asking Mrs. Carmichael how she thought Miss Harrison may have felt about not being called back.* She said she really did not know but that she would explain everything when she called her later today or tomorrow. I tried again, *saying that of course she cannot know for a fact how Miss Harrison may have felt, but if she were in Miss Harrison's shoes, how may she have felt?* She thought about this for a moment and said that she guessed she may have felt a bit hurt. I said yes, that could well be the case.

The worker's efforts to generate empathy are well founded. *Creating empathic connections* is an important skill for the social worker in the role of group worker, that is, any time she is working with more than one person at a time. It is especially useful when she is simultaneously in the role of broker, mediator, advocate, and/or community organizer. Empathic connections have a powerful impact on human behavior, and are often pivotal in bringing out the best in people, enabling them to interact with caring and compassion. The worker tries to *generate an empathic connection* again as the meeting continues. Later, she uses two empathic skills in a conversation with Mr. Getz—*reaching for and getting with feelings.*

We talked a bit more about telephoning one another, and I asked Mrs. Buterac how she felt about the program, especially since she thought it was a good idea, but she did not care for the idea of people calling each other a set number of times a week. She thought this would mean that some weeks she would call someone just to fill a "quota," and not because she really wanted to talk to that person. *I said I could see what she meant, but had she thought of it from the other person's point of view, the person expecting the call from her? Maybe the time she really does not feel like calling is the very time that person needs to get a call from her.* She thought about this for a while and said, "You have a point there." She added that she would like to have the telephone numbers of all the people so that she could call not only the one person she was responsible for but the others as well. I said that was a really good idea and that I would have them for her and anyone else who wanted a list next week.

I turned to Mr. Getz and said that I was glad to see him this week, especially since he did not know if he would come back, since his wife may object to his getting calls from other women. (Last week he said he may not be able to participate because of this.) He smiled and said he told his wife what the program was about and she did not seem to mind the whole thing. I said I was glad about that.

There was a short silence during which Mr. Getz looked pensive. He broke the silence by asking what was the "ultimate purpose" of this whole program and why did I start it in the first place? I reviewed the purpose as I saw it and asked Mr. Getz what purpose he saw in it for himself, since he is taking part in it. He thought for a while and it seemed to him that a program like this helps people to come out of their shell. He went on to say, with much feeling, that sometimes when he talks to other people for any length of time or over a period of a few days, they begin to look at him funny, or ask his family what's wrong with him. "So I just withdraw, and sit back and don't say nothing." *I said to Mr. Getz that it must be very upsetting to be afraid to talk to other people.* He said it certainly was. *I said it must also hurt to hear comments questioning whether there was something about him that was "not right."* He said, "You're damn right it does." I said, *"No wonder you withdraw."* I asked Mr. Getz how he felt talking right now. He said he felt okay, that he likes the idea of this group coming together and talking every week, but he is not ready yet to make phone calls. "Let me go at my own pace." Mrs. Buterac nodded. "We'll do that, and we'll be happy to have you just come to the group meetings for a while, now that we know how you feel about talking to other people." He seemed quite satisfied with this arrangement.

Mrs. Carmichael said she had called Miss Harrison to find out why she had not come to the last meeting, but was unable to reach her. She said she also called Mrs. Buterac and chatted with her for about an hour. She said that Mrs. Buterac even put her two-year-old son on the phone to talk. She said they both enjoyed the conversation.

Though the service contract had been developed quite a while ago and work on the task was well under way, when Mr. Getz spoke about his recurrent, emotion-laden experience, the worker appropriately *reached for his feelings*—both the fear and the hurt. And when he acknowledged that the feelings for which the worker reached were, indeed, the feelings inside of him, the worker *got with his feelings* with a precision that not only validated them but also connected them to his behavioral response as well ("No wonder you withdraw"). Such precision is not always possible, but where it is, the impact can be quite powerful.

The telephone network continued to operate. Members began to call each other on occasions other than those agreed upon and, as described below, some participants began getting together beyond group meetings and phone calls.

The participants in the telephone network have been connecting well with one another on the outside. While they do not call each other every day, they do call one another a couple of times a week. Two of the women have started sewing together, and the third one may join them. They do call one another when one of them does not show up for the Monday meeting. Around the Christmas holidays they exchanged cards, and one member called another on New Year's Eve to wish him and his family a happy new year. Attendance has been excellent on the whole, with members calling me when they cannot come for any reason. It is hard to say just what it is that is making them come to the meetings in rain, snow, and bitter cold.

As time went on, the members of the phone network extended their contact with each other from phone calls and weekly meetings to visits to each other's homes. The sense of isolation decreased markedly, and members attempted to come to grips with some of the social factors that fostered their isolation. In the process, the group worker *reaches for feelings*.

Mrs. Carmichael went on to say that she would like to invite Miss Harrison to her house but she is afraid she will be harmed coming into the project where she (Mrs. Carmichael) lives, being that Miss Harrison is white and whites often get hassled and robbed. *I said it must be difficult for her to want to reach out to a friend in such a nice way and to have such fears at the same time.* Mrs. Carmichael looked sad and said it was really a shame to have things like that get in the way of a friendship. I suggested that perhaps there was a way she could help insure Miss Harrison's safety so that she could visit her. She thought for a few minutes and said that she could tell Miss Harrison exactly at which entrance to be and she could meet her downstairs.

Miss Harrison had thought that perhaps she could meet her at the corner or at the bus stop. Mrs. Carmichael said that was a good idea and decided to invite Miss Harrison as soon as she speaks to her on the phone.

There were also differences that had to be confronted in the group. Obstacles to self-help had to be challenged by the worker even when the group would have preferred to deny their existence. To help the group talk about the issue, the worker tries to *create an empathic connection.*

Shortly after the meeting began, I informed the members of the group that the following week we would be joined by a new member, Mrs. Cook. Everybody seemed quite happy about this, and there was general agreement to the effect that it would be nice to have couple more members in the group. I told the group that I quite agreed and then turned to Mr. Getz and asked how he felt about having another woman in the group, since right now he was the only man, with three women members and a woman worker. He laughed and said he felt fine about that and that it would be all right to have another lady in the group. I turned to the women and asked if they had any thoughts or feelings about this. They agreed that they have felt very comfortable with Mr. Getz, that he was "open-minded," a nice person, and easy to talk to, that the fact that he was a man "made no difference."

Mrs. Buterac said, "We all have common problems; that's why we are here and can help each other; it makes no difference whether you are a man or a woman." The other two women agreed with this. I said that there was much to what they were saying and that it must be good for each of them to hear that they can be accepted and cared for simply because they are people with human problems. But could they now try to put themselves in Mr. Getz's place and *try to imagine how it would feel to be the only man in a group of five women* and Mrs. Carmichael said she would love it since it would bring a lot of attention to her. The other two agreed, and Mr. Getz said laughingly that there was something to that, although he would prefer to be thought of as "just another member of the group." The women assured him that he was and that they would treat him "exactly the same."

A bit later on I inquired as to how the telephone network was going. The three women told me who had called the other during the week. They seemed quite satisfied with the arrangement. I at this point asked if anybody had called Mr. Getz. There was a deafening silence and obvious discomfort. After a pretty long silence, Mr. Getz admitted that he was more than equally responsible for this. "I really have not made an effort to call any of the ladies, except once when I called Mrs. Carmichael." Mrs. Cook said that the women were just as responsible, since they have not called him. Miss Harrison said, "I guess we have not treated you as equally as we thought." Mr. Getz said he doesn't blame the women for not reaching out to him being that he has not really reached out to them. "Before I started coming here I was so withdrawn I did not want to talk to anybody. I feel different now and I think you have been very patient with me and let me go at my own speed. But I agree with the social worker that I can go a little faster now."

Mr. Getz did "go a little faster," as he said he would. With the support of the members of the telephone network who encouraged him, and who listened to his excited reports, Mr. Getz volunteered his services on the men's ward of the hospital, and was accepted as an official volunteer—complete with badge, which he wore to every meeting. It may be the first palatable label that has been tacked on him in years!

While the initial development of the telephone network took place in Quadrant A, it seemed possible to extend the benefits to additional persons who were lonely. Thus the worker moved to Quadrant B.

QUADRANT B The social worker talked with group members about how they feel about reaching out to other people who might be lonely and be interested in joining the telephone network.

Mrs. Carmichael said that maybe one or two more people could join in, but with more new people than that, the closeness that had developed with each other would get lost. I agreed that expanding their little group too much could be a threat to their cohesion. Mrs. Buterac asked me if I could start a second group if many other people were interested. I said that I could. Then Miss Harrison said she could post a note on some internet bulletin boards. Mr. Getz thought that was a wonderful idea. He said that he and his wife could put up signs in the two pharmacies near their house. Then Mr. Getz asked if they could specifically recruit people like themselves, "people who feel depressed or are afraid to talk to other people, not just anybody who might be lonely." I said that would be appropriate since this was a mental health center program.

He seemed to breathe easier and said his signs would say "Anybody who feels depressed or scared and lonely…" Miss Harrison said she would word her Internet postings the same way. Mrs. Buterac volunteered to put up signs in the park where she walks her dog, and maybe in the supermarket where she shops.

We talked some more about members' plans to get the word out, and I said I would talk to staff and see if they might refer some people. This seemed to be okay with the group.

In Quadrant B the social worker works with some clients for the benefit of themselves and others in a situation similar to theirs. In this instance, the worker engaged the clients in the telephone network in reaching out so that similar others might also benefit.

QUADRANT C Simultaneously, the social worker introduced the idea of including other people in the telephone network at a staff meeting.

I outlined the whole program at a staff meeting and asked other staff members to keep the network and its rationale in mind, to see if they come across any people who could benefit from this program. The announcement and request were met with the usual noncommittal silence and lack of interest, with an occasional, vague Mona Lisa smile on a few people's faces. The unit supervisor said the program sounded interesting and worthwhile, and that he was sure staff members would keep it in mind for possible referrals. I was not so sure at all, and I am certain that neither was he.

The worker's second attempt to involve other staff members in locating isolated persons and connecting them via the telephone network took the form of individual contacts.

I began approaching individual staff members, reminding them of my concern and asking them whether they had come across any persons who could benefit from the program. The answer was invariably, "No," but they each gave me a verbal pat on the back as if to say, "That's nice, dear." Only one person showed any real interest, and she has since referred one person to the telephone network.

Since both efforts to involve other staff members were unsuccessful, the worker stepped back to reassess the situation in order to determine yet a third strategy. She recognized that, except for herself, the staff was primarily oriented toward and engaged in providing therapy, and that she was proposing that therapists refer "their patients" to a nontherapy, albeit therapeutic, service. Perhaps the unspoken message they inferred was, "I have found a better way," which could be felt as a threat. Or perhaps she may have seemed to be asking other staff people to help her.

The social worker did have a continuing telephone network that was serving a useful function for its members and could be expanded to include other clients. Because staff time was limited and staff was not able to serve all persons in need, the telephone network actually could help the other staff by lightening the burden of attempting to see more clients than their time allowed. Thus, the worker could *give* something to other staff members—a resource to help remedy some of the isolation their clients were experiencing, and a service for people on the waiting list with whom they were concerned yet did not have sufficient time to engage in therapy. It was from this perspective that the social worker made her third attempt to obtain the cooperation of her colleagues to increase service to their clients.

In the staff meeting I reviewed the history of the telephone network and gave a very positive report. I said I knew how hard it was to serve the number of people each of them was trying to serve in their limited time, and that I knew how much they cared about providing service to as many people as possible. I said it was because of this that I wanted to tell them about this resource and make it available if they thought it could be helpful to any of their clients. There was much more interest this time.

One staff person wanted to know the criteria for joining—personality disorders, bipolar, schizophrenia, or something else. There was much amazement when I said the only criterion was the possession of a telephone, and that for people who couldn't afford a phone, the Department of Health could arrange for one to be installed since this was a mental health service. While there was surprise at the thought that clients could benefit from something other than therapy, staff seemed willing to try. Several people asked if they could refer clients they were seeing in therapy as well as those they were unable to see, and I said they could refer anyone they thought would benefit, that I respected their professional judgment.

Staff members did refer clients to the phone network and, combined with the outreach results of network members, there was a sufficient number of people to form an additional network.

EXAMPLE 2: WORKING WITH A CLIENT IN AN INSTITUTIONAL SETTING

The principle of maximizing supports in the client's environment is appropriately applied not only in instances where clients live in the community at large, as in the prior example, but also in instances where the client's environment is an institution. In fact, in an institution the need to maximize environmental supports for clients is often more urgent and more compelling than it is for clients whose surroundings are not as circumscribed.

QUADRANT A In the following example, the social worker at Rafferty Place, a nursing home, works to maximize supports in the institutional environment for Mrs. Brown, a seventy-eight-year-old widow who was admitted to Rafferty Place directly from the local hospital, where she had been treated for a stroke. Mrs. Brown had been living alone for the past ten years, had been in relatively good health, and had never planned to enter a long-term care facility.

The admissions material on Mrs. Brown said she is alert and oriented to person, place, and time, and that her memory has not been affected. It said she has minimal speech difficulty, but use of her left arm and leg is severely limited. She is in a wheelchair. It additionally notes that she is very unhappy to be here, but does realize she can't live alone right now. The social worker goes to her room to see her. He *positions* himself, and *reaches for feelings*.

I entered Mrs. Brown's doorway and knocked on the door. I saw that she was lying in bed with her back to me. She moved when I knocked, but she didn't say anything. I asked if I could come in, and she replied with a very weak "Yeah." I said, "Hi. My name is Sam Robinson. You can call me Sam. I'm your social worker and I work here at Rafferty Place. I pulled up a chair and *sat down near her bed at a right angle.* She looked at me but didn't say anything. I said, *"It can be lonely being in a room by yourself.* Mrs. Brown closed her eyes and pulled her legs up to her chest in a semi-fetal position. I waited a few moments, then reached for her feelings again. *"It can be scary to be in a new place, not knowing what to expect next."*

It is important to notice the respect the worker accords Mrs. Brown, knocking on the open door, waiting in the doorway, asking permission to enter, and calling her *Mrs. Brown*. In all too many instances, professionals and paraprofessionals alike feel free to walk right in on patients and call them by their first names, as if illness gives everyone a license to invade the sick person's territory and treat them with forced intimacy. It is also important to notice that as soon as the worker positions himself, he starts attending to the client's feelings, and he continues to engage her feelings as their work proceeds. In the interaction below, the worker *checks out his inferences* about the client's feelings, reaches for her feelings again, and reaches for information.

Mrs. Brown opened her eyes and looked at me. "My daughter brought me here. She said it was a good place. My ... my mother was in a nursing home. She died there." *"Are you afraid you'll die here?"* I asked her. "No, not really," she says, but she begins to cry. *"You're crying."* I say. "Oh, this is all so new to me," she says. A couple of weeks ago I was so active. I was involved with my church, my card groups, my gardening. I took care of my apartment and all of my affairs. Now look at me—I'm in a nursing home and my family doesn't think I'll be able to go back home." "Do you think you'll be able to go back home?" I ask. She says she hope so, and she wants to, but.... *"But you're afraid you won't be able to?"* I offer. "Yes; I'm afraid I won't be able to go back home. Oh, damn it, why did this have to happen to me? Why did I have to have this stroke? Why do I have to be here in this empty room? You know, I had a beautiful apartment. With all the comforts—my green easy chair, my magazine stand, my new wide-screen plasma TV. I asked her if she know she could bring things from her apartment here, to her room, while she stays. She seems surprised. "Can I really bring those things in?" "Yes," I tell her. "You can bring in your chair, your magazine stand, and your TV. You can also bring in some pictures to be hung, and those shelves over there, those are yours, too." Mrs. Brown sighs. "Well at least that might brighten things up a little. I'll talk to my daughter about bringing some things in."

The worker continues to be responsive to the client's feelings and begins to give immediately relevant information, but does not overwhelm her with a description of everything about the facility and its resources. In the helping process, information is important only when it is specifically relevant to the client's present concern, and when the client does not have it already. If too much is presented at once, or if it is not immediately pertinent, it can overwhelm and hinder rather than enlighten and empower. In the practice excerpt above, it is only when Mrs. Brown talks about missing her personal furnishings that Sam tells her which of them she may bring to Rafferty House. As the process continues below, he *reaches for information, reaches for feelings* several more times, then gives pertinent information about the Newcomers Club and Resident Sponsors precisely when Mrs. Brown is thinking about old friends and new ones.

"What about that empty bed over there—is someone coming in soon?" Mrs. Brown asks. I tell her I'm not sure who will be coming to this room. "*What kind of a roommate would you like?*" "Oh, I don't know," she says and takes a deep breath, sighs and closes her eyes for a minute, then opens them and looks at me. "Someone like me, I guess." "*And what would someone like you be like?*" I ask her. "Someone with all their marbles," she replies. "You know, I'm not crazy like some of these people." I tell her I'll do my best to get her a roommate with all her marbles. Then I say, "*It can be scary to think of getting someone who's confused for a roommate.*" "Yes, it is scary." she says. "I had a roommate in the hospital who cried all night for her mother. She was in her nineties. She never remembered my name and she made me nervous. I again say that I'll do my best to find her an appropriate roommate. "I'll introduce her to you if I can before she comes," I add. "Yeah, that would be nice," she says, sliding her knees down from her chest and smiling at me. "*You're smiling,*" I say. "Yeah," she says. "I am. I think I'm feeling better." She then closes her eyes again, takes another deep breath, and sighs. "You know," she says, "all my friends live on the other side of town, so I doubt I'll be able to visit with them." "*It can be sad to be separated from friends you've had for a long time.*" I say. "It is sad," she continues, "especially when I don't have any friends here." "*It can be lonely when you don't have any friends,*" I say. "Yeah, it can be lonely," she says. She starts to cry, but stops abruptly and wipes her eyes. She looks at me. "But I've always made friends rather easily before. In a few weeks or so I'll find a friend here," she says with more confidence than I think she has.

I ask her if she knows that we have a "Newcomers Club" here at Rafferty. "What's a Newcomers Club?" She asks. I tell her it meets twice a month, and all the new residents who are able to come, come to meet each other and get acquainted. I ask her if she would like to go to this group, and she says yes, she does, that it sounds like a good way to meet people. She asks me when it meets next and I tell her it meets tomorrow morning, in the lounge. I also tell her there are resident sponsors who'll take her on a tour of the building, when she wants to, that they'll show her some of the favorite activities she might like and introduce her to other residents. "In fact," I say, "one of the resident sponsors will be coming down to see you later today, and she'll tell you more about it. And they will come and get you after breakfast and take you to the meeting." She says that sounds good.

"Okay," I said, "Let me sum up a little. You were worried about the type of room-mate you might be getting, and I said I would try to find someone for you who isn't confused. I also said that I would introduce them to you if I could before they came. You said you're afraid you might not be able to go back home and that your room is empty looking, so you're going to talk to your daughter about bringing in some things from home while you're staying here. You also decided you wanted to meet other people and would attend the Newcomers Club tomorrow. And I told you a resident sponsor will come to see you later today." Then I asked her if this sounded like what we worked on together. She said, "Yes, it does," and she asked me when I'll be coming back to see her again. I said I'll stop in to see how she is getting along later tomorrow afternoon. Then I got up, put my chair back where it came from, said goodbye, and left the room.

At the end of the session, the worker recaps the facts and feelings of their transaction. This summary not only pulls the work together, but it also outlines the terms of the service contract as the worker understands them to be. Summarizing is also useful at the start of a session in order to (1) refresh memories about where work stopped at the end of the prior session and (2) lay a foundation for setting the focus of the session that is beginning. Also, if talk strays from the purpose of a meeting, summarizing can be used to help refocus.

Later the next day, after the Newcomers group, I went to see Mrs. Brown to see how she was doing, how the group went for her, and if she got to know any of the other residents. I knocked on her door and asked if I could enter. "Yeah, come on in. I've been waiting to talk to you!" She said in an angry voice. "*You sound angry,*" I said. "Yeah, I'm angry all right," she said. "Those snobs in that group you sent me to ignored me most of the time and then they made plans to go and play cards afterward. They didn't even ask me to go. Of course I couldn't play anyway—with my left hand hanging down limp like this." I say, "*It can be upsetting to be ignored.*" "You're right," she says. "I'm upset because I was ignored by those women. That one lady, Mrs. Sykes, she ignored me the whole time. I wonder what I did to her? Can you ask her what's going on?" I say, "No, I think that's something *you* need to talk to her about." "Well, I thought you were my social worker," she responds. I say, "I *am* your social worker, Mrs. Brown. However, I think you're able to ask Mrs. Sykes what's going on. I wasn't there to know what happened."

The worker *reaches for feelings* as Mrs. Brown describes her painful experience. Then she asks him to speak with another person for her. The worker refuses, not because he does not care, but because he cares very much that the client take her difficulty to the proper place where she may get results. By asking her to speak directly to the person for whom her message is intended, he conveys his belief that Mrs. Brown is competent to manage her interpersonal relationships even though it is sometimes difficult and uncomfortable to do. Although the "reason" the worker gives Mrs. Brown is somewhat misleading, his refusal to speak for her nonetheless implies recognition that it is through direct involvement that people can discover real and lasting resolutions to their struggles with each other. It is to this end that, a short while later, the worker offers to try and arrange an opportunity for direct talk between the two parties involved.

As the process continues below, Sam also provides accurate information to counter Mrs. Brown's partial, skewed, or otherwise distorted picture. The accurate information that the worker presents involves the existence of highly pertinent resources—potential environmental supports—that can be brought to bear in reducing the client's current limitations.

"Well, that's true," Mrs. Brown says. "You weren't there. I think I know why they ignored me anyway—it's because I had a stroke. You know, I can't do things for myself anymore like I used to. I can't tie my shoes, I can't play cards, I can't ... " (she stops talking and turns her head).

"No, Mrs. Brown," I say. "You may be not able to do those things now; however, you may be able to learn to do some of those things again. Are you aware of some of the adaptive devices you could order which would help you with those things?"

"No, I'm not. What are they?" She asks. "I know Jane, our physical therapist, has a catalogue she can order specific items from, such as a plastic card holder so you could play cards again. Would you like to talk to Jane?" I ask. Mrs. Brown looks interested and says, "Yes, I would like to talk to her." I say, "All right. I'll go down and talk to her after we're finished and let her know you'd like to talk to her about this." Mrs. Brown smiles and says, "that will be fine."

"Now, about the group," I say. "Did you meet any other people besides Mrs. Sykes?" "Yeah," she says. "There were a couple of nice people there, but I didn't catch their names." I ask, "will you go to the next meeting so you can learn who they are?" "No!" She says adamantly. I won't be going back to that group until I've had it out with Mrs. Sykes. I won't be ignored by her again!" "Would you be willing to meet with her and discuss how you were feeling, what happened, and what could be done to help the situation?" I ask. "Well, I'll meet with Mrs. Sykes if she'll meet with me," Mrs. Brown replies. "Then I'll talk with Mrs. Sykes and see if she'll be able to meet with you, and then I'll get back with you and let you know," I say. She says "That'll be fine."

"Now, back to your feeling that you were ignored because you've had a stroke," I say. "Can you tell me what leads you to think that was the reason." "Well, I know I look like a cripple, that I can't do things I used to do, that I can't get around too easily by myself anymore like I used to," she says. "*That can be frustrating to face.*" *I say.* "Especially when others don't understand!" She acknowledges. "*Yeah,*" *I say,* "*that is upsetting.*"

"Have you heard of the St. Louis Stroke Club?" I ask. "No. What's that?" She asks. "It's a group that meets once every month at the Senior Citizens Center downtown. They have outside speakers in to talk about issues that people who have had strokes have to face. They also have refreshments and a get acquainted time," I tell her. Then I ask if she'd like more information about the club. "Yes. Especially after that last group I went to," she says. I also tell her that another resident here at Rafferty, Mrs. Lynford, is a member of the Stroke Club. "In fact, she lives two doors down from you. Perhaps you've met her already." Mrs. Brown says that she hasn't met her. "Could I talk with her before I go to any meetings?" She asks. "I'm sure she'd be happy to talk to you," I say. "How about the next time you're up and about you go over to her room and ask her to tell you about the group," I suggest. Mrs. Brown says she'll give it a try. "And in the meantime," I say, "I'll call the Stroke Club and ask them to send out some literature for you and find out what the topic this month is or who is speaking." She says that's a good idea.

"Okay, Mrs. Brown," I say, "let me try to summarize. When I came to see you this afternoon, you were angry because you felt ignored by Mrs. Sykes. Now I'm going to speak to Mrs. Sykes and see if she'll meet with you and me to discuss what happened. Then we talked about some adaptive devices you might benefit from, and I'm going to talk to Jane so she can come up and discuss these items with you. Then we talked about the Stroke Club, and you're going to talk to Mrs. Lynford about it and I'm going to ask the Stroke Club sponsors to send some material about the club to you. Right?" I asked. "That's right. I need to talk to Mrs. Sykes; I'm going to go over to Mrs. Lynford's and talk about the Stroke Club, and I want to talk to Jane about the devices so I can do more for myself." She replies. "Okay," I say. I'll stop back tomorrow to see how things are going.

Initially, the worker took the role of conferee and kept in close contact with Mrs. Brown, but also, from the beginning, he took the role of broker and connected her with other residents, other staff persons, and other programs outside the nursing home. He did not borrow the physical therapist's catalogue in order to show her the adaptive devices he mentioned. Rather, he arranged for the physical therapist to get together with Mrs. Brown. He did not find out about the Stroke Club and give her the information. Rather, he suggested she talk with another resident who is a member. Thus, in accord with the principle of maximizing supports in the client's environment, the social worker was not occupying the central role in the helping process.

The principle of maximizing supports in the client's environment is as essential in work with clients in residential settings as it is with clients who live in the community. In doing so, the social worker brings to bear, modifies, and/or creates structures that can function without her or him.

THE PRINCIPLE OF LEAST CONTEST

The principle of least contest directs the worker to exert the least pressure necessary to accomplish the client task. In the first place, force tends to generate counterforce. The amount of pressure that the worker brings to bear on a target person, group, or organization is directly related to the amount of counterpressure that the target is likely to exert. And since low-pressure interventions tend to evoke minimum resistance on the part of the target, low-pressure interventions are more likely to result in successful task accomplishment. Moreover, when low-pressure interventions are not successful, greater pressure can then be exerted.

The initial use of forceful intervention behaviors precludes the use of less forceful behaviors. It can be likened to "putting all the eggs in one basket," for in the event that the forceful intervention does not result in task accomplishment, alternative interventions are severely limited. To maximize the probability of task accomplishment, the worker should not act so as to preclude alternative actions. This suggests that the worker should serially order the possible interventions along a power dimension, from the least forceful to the most forceful.

QUADRANTS OF ACTIVITY

With respect to quadrants of activity, when task accomplishment demands a change in a particular procedure in a given agency, such as a lengthy intake procedure, the worker should try Quadrant C activity (work with others in behalf of the client) prior to Quadrant B activity (work with some clients in behalf of themselves and others in their situation). For example, the worker should try to work with agency staff (Quadrant C activity) before organizing a client protest (Quadrant B activity). The worker's own efforts with agency staff are likely to be less threatening than a client protest, which could bring, for example, unwanted media attention, and therefore less likely to generate the counterpressure than the more threatening client protest is likely to evoke. Further, in the event that Quadrant C activity does not succeed, the worker can then move to Quadrant B. The reverse is not possible, however, for the worker who has organized a client protest is no longer credible as a person who wants to help the agency.

ROLE-TAKING BEHAVIOR

Role-taking behavior is governed by a rationale similar to that which guides movement through the quadrants of activity. The worker should take the role of broker prior to the role of mediator, and the role of mediator prior to the role of advocate, for brokerage is less threatening than mediation, and mediation is less threatening than advocacy. Moreover, the worker who has attempted to mediate the client/agency engagement can, in the event that complementarity of interest cannot be implemented, shift from the role of mediator to the role of advocate. Again, the reverse is not possible, for the worker who has taken the side of one of two parties to a conflict has lost credibility as a "neutral," or as a person equally concerned with both parties.

POINT OF INTERVENTION

The same rationale holds for selecting a point of intervention into a bureaucratic system. An issue is of less moment when it is raised, and remains, at lower levels of the hierarchy, and increases in importance as it moves upward in the hierarchy. Therefore, the worker should escalate issues slowly, initiating action at the lowest possible hierarchical level and proceeding upward until a concession is obtained. This process gives personnel at lower hierarchical levels an opportunity to contain the issue at the lower level by granting the concession that clients need, which personnel in the highly political public welfare agencies are likely to seize. And if personnel at lower levels cannot or do not grant the concession, the worker can then escalate the issue to the next hierarchical level.

The principle of least contest, then, directs the worker to rank possible interventions along a power dimension and to use less powerful interventions prior to using more powerful interventions. Specifically, the worker should engage in Quadrant C activity before Quadrant B activity, take the role of broker before taking the role of mediator and the role of mediator before the role of advocate, and escalate issues slowly by intervening at the lowest possible hierarchical level in a bureaucratic organization and proceeding upward until a concession is obtained.

EXAMPLE: PRINCIPLE OF LEAST CONTEST

After hearing the tremendous worry about the ever-rising costs of prescription drugs expressed by many of her elderly clients, the social worker invited her clients and others they knew who were also alarmed to gather in the meeting room of a high-rise retirement and personal care facility in order to share all of their concerns, set some priorities, and plan what to do about the problem. She started out in Quadrant A and took the roles of conferee and group worker as she met with the people to explore the extent and details of their problem situation.

People were already talking about their fears as they walked into the room. There were many more people than I expected, some even pushing others in wheelchairs so they would not have to miss the meeting. When they were finally all seated, there were so many private conversations about their personal situations going on all at once that I had to flick the lights to get their attention.

"It's hard to be old; I certainly don't have to tell you that. You could probably write books about it!" I began. "And one of the things I know from many of you is that you're on fixed incomes and the cost of prescription medicine is spiraling upward even as we meet here. So this is the main issue we'll be talking about this afternoon. The details of your concerns, your fears and other feelings, and your ideas about what we should do." *I viewed the whole group so everyone would see that I was interested in whatever each might have to say.* Then I opened the floor for discussion.

Mr. Yaeger, whom I know from my work with others in the building, talked about his anger at the AARP for endorsing the worthless discount cards many insurers are hawking. He said the applications are too long for old people to read and remember what to write where, and too complex for anybody who isn't a lawyer. He got a big round of applause, followed by Mrs. Robinson's comment that many of them can't write anyhow, because of arthritis. "And some old people can't read the small print," Mrs. Shipp said, then added, "And I'm sure there are some people who didn't get enough education to read at all." Mr. Yaeger took the floor again and said that even if the applications were easy, you have to pay for the cards, and the drug companies just raised their prices, which offsets the discount. "The AARP is supposed to look out for us," he continued. "How could they support such a cruel joke. They should have *demanded* that Medicare have the right, no—the responsibility—to make price deals with the drug companies, like Blue Cross and Aetna and Humana do." There was more applause and some shouts of agreement.

Mrs. Collins said she was so scared she'd have to pick and choose which medicines to buy, or take her pills once every two or three days. A woman I didn't know announced that her medicines cost almost $800.00 a month, so even with a card with a one-time $600 on it would be less than one month's supply if the prices stay like they are or go up. Many people agreed with her. After much more talk about feelings and personal plights, talk shifted to what we should do about it.

Some people wanted to sue AARP, or Medicare, or the state governor or the president. Others thought a delegation should go talk to the governor and the state legislature. There were also many people who wanted to have a big rally, with picket signs demanding lower drug costs either outside government offices or at the governor's mansion. "You can be sure he'll have good health insurance with drug coverage when he retires!" Mr. Delehanty commented.

I said that all of the ideas were good, and suggested that we start with me talking with staff members in the governor's office about their very real and poignant concerns about drug costs and what might be possible at the state level for making prescriptions more affordable, then making an appointment for a delegation to meet with them and let them see how real people are affected. Then, I suggested, we meet again and choose delegates who can represent the various plights they are forced to endure without limits on the cost of prescriptions for the elderly. I said I would help them express their concerns and feelings to the staff. "If all else fails," I said, "We can talk about a mass protest with picket signs and media attention." Mr. Yaeger was a little bit concerned that I, a woman, might not be taken as seriously as a tall man with a booming voice, but he agreed that the sequence of action made sense. Some of my clients who were in the room told him I could be quite persuasive, and I told him I was not a newbie and I didn't need to yell to make my meaning quite clear. This seemed okay with the rest of the people. I said I'd get back to them as soon as I'd had a meeting with the governor's staff.

During the meeting there was also some talk about my first statement that it's hard to be old, and that drug costs were not the only worries they had. Mrs. Hall said that many of them have so many feelings from over the years still all bottled up inside them and wondered if they could get together and talk about that. I saw a lot of nods, so I said I'd be glad to form small groups to do that if those who are interested just give me their names before they leave today. Later, more than twenty people gave me their names, and I formed three therapy groups to help people express and cope with painful feelings (Quadrant A).

In this illustration, the social worker organized the group's plans for action in accord with the principle of least contest. First, she would move from her starting point with the group in Quadrant A and her roles as conferee ands group worker to take the role of broker in Quadrant C, exploring possible opportunities and resources to help members with the escalating costs of prescription medication. Should her efforts not result in obtaining financial relief for them, she would take the role of mediator in Quadrant C to help a delegation from the group to talk to the governor's staff. If the governor is not moved to seek possible alternatives, then the social worker would move to Quadrant B and take the roles of advocate and community organizer in order to facilitate a mass protest in the presence of TV news cameras. This is her contract with the whole group to whom she will report her progress with the governor's staff.

The worker also agrees to work with small groups of those persons who wanted to explore and express their long-bottled-up feelings. In this enterprise, she will take the role of therapist in Quadrant A.

Notice, too, that the worker views the whole group so that every person realizes she is speaking and listening to her or him. This group worker task is elaborated in chapter 12. Requisite tasks and skills for performing all of the roles are described in that section.

THE PRINCIPLE OF HELPING THE CLIENT DECONSTRUCT OPPRESSIVE CULTURAL DISCOURSE AND REINTERPRET EXPERIENCE FROM ALTERNATIVE PERSPECTIVES

The principle of helping the client deconstruct oppressive cultural discourse (that is, analyze the politics or power relations involved in negative stereotypes and myths) and reinterpret experience from alternative perspectives requires the social worker to engage oppressed and violated persons in dialogue about the cultural ideology (that is, beliefs that circulate in the larger society) that recognizes (1) the disrespect and discrimination they are forced to endure, (2) the denial of wherewithal to meet the common human needs of themselves and their families, and/or (3) the violence directed against them. The principle further directs social workers to help people identify the particular social beliefs pertinent to their subjugation, identify which persons or groups of persons benefit from these beliefs and the actions they spawn, to undermine these beliefs, and to resist their messages that worm their way into persons' identity formation.

Cultural ideology is rife with false claims about various populations, beliefs that circulate to the detriment of their members:

Young black men are thieves.
Men are superior to women.

Lesbians and gay men do not deserve the rights accorded straight people.

Women who are battered deserve it.

There are enough jobs that pay a decent living wage, and poor people are just too lazy to work.

These are powerful social beliefs that are translated into laws and official acts that jeopardize people's sense of their own reality and insidiously infiltrate the identities they form.

When people understand who benefits from their oppression and how, the myths that keep subjugated populations believing what they keep hearing about themselves become dislodged, and it is then that the social worker can help them to examine past experience and see it without the filter of oppressive beliefs, thereby reaching different conclusions of who and how they are. These new perspectives open options that had not been available before, because the oppressed person's frame of reference, or life space, did not include the possibilities. Specifics related to this principle and the social worker's requisite tasks are detailed in chapter 10.

EXAMPLE OF HELPING THE CLIENT DECONSTRUCT OPPRESSIVE CULTURAL DISCOURSE AND REINTERPRET EXPERIENCE FROM ALTERNATIVE PERSPECTIVES

The social worker at an inner-city high school called sixteen-year-old Kanyesha and her girlfriend Chantelle to her office. She had heard from their teachers that they are smart, make excellent grades, and scored very high on the PSATs, yet they were thinking about dropping out of high school. When the girls arrived in her office, she told them what their teachers said and asked them what had led them to consider dropping out as opposed to graduating and going on to college.

At first they looked at each other and laughed. They seemed somewhat embarrassed. "School is so not for us in this lifetime," Chantelle said. "We got big families and there's lots of kids who need us. And they need whatever money we can bring in." "Yeah," Kanyesha added, "That's what girls like us do." "Where did you learn that girls like you should leave school to take care of your families?" I asked. "The oldest girl, she like the second mamma to all the little brothers and sisters. She gotta be there." Kanyesha said. "Why you don't know that? You an only child?" She asks me. I tell her *no*, that I have a big family, and my parents are real proud of me. But I also say that my big sister was like a mother to me. I say that I thought that was what she wanted, but that maybe that's not true. I say, "Maybe she felt like you do—that it was her responsibility." I ask, "Is that how you learned it? By watching other big sisters give up their own potential interests to take care of the little ones?"

"Well, in my family there's only Mamma to take care of everything. She works and all, but it doesn't cover the bills without my part-time salary put in. And she does second shift so she's there until I get home." Chantelle tells me. "And my younger sister, Viola, she leaves her baby while she works, and my aunt leaves her babies. Somebody got to feed them and bathe them and hug them and read to them." I say that in some black communities I've heard that called "daughters' work," that the oldest boy isn't expected to help with money or childcare; that he's not even expected to do his own laundry. There is silence for several moments. Then Kanyesha says, "It isn't fair, is it. But if you love your family—and I do—then you do what's expected. I don't want to stay in school and go to college for all those years and feel guilty about my family." "Maybe your older brother can step in for you. Does he have a job?" I ask. "He works on and off," she replies. "But he's a homeboy, and he'd get teased to death if he took care of the babies instead of hanging out with his posse."

"Sounds like "daughters' work" is a pretty strong belief in your family," I say. "Who benefits from your sacrifice?" There is a long silence. Finally Kanyesha says, "Well, for sure my older brothers do. And my mamma." Chantelle nods. "Do you girls benefit?" I ask. "I love taking care of the kids," Chantelle says. "I could have my own and take care of him along with the others, and that would be sweet," she adds. "Is that the way you *want* the rest of your life to be? If, say, you didn't feel such family pressure?" I asked. "Say you were free to choose school and college without risking your family's displeasure?" "I like school," Chantelle says. "If only my family could count on my brothers for some money and Viola or my aunt would help out." Kanyesha agrees, adding that her family, too, would have to get itself reorganized.

"If you do go to college," I ask, "what would you like to be or do?" "I wanna be a teacher—a kindergarten teacher," Kanyesha says without hesitation. "I wanna be a lawyer for poor folks," Chantelle blurts out. Again, they look at each other and laugh. "Remember what happened to Camille, though?" Kanyesha asks Chantelle. Chantelle nods, then turns to me and says, "Her mamma still won't speak to her, and it's been over two years." "*That can be so painful,*" I say. "Yeah," Chantelle says. "She writes to Kanyesha. She's doing good in college, but she says she's sad sometimes."

"Herbert, my boyfriend, doesn't want me to go to college, either. He says it'll change me and maybe I won't respect him anymore. Herbert's a great guy. He works steady, he's never been in trouble, he's fun to be with, he's cool and really cute, and he respects me," Kanyesha says. Chantelle pats Kanyesha's belly and laughs. "Herbert always says he wants his babies to come right out of there." "He is a wonderful man," Chantelle adds, "but I think he's afraid Kanyesha will get above him." "I don't want to lose Herbert," Kanyesha says wistfully.

"Where did you learn that men won't hang with girls who go to college?" I ask. "I've seen it. They just don't," Chantelle says. "I don't want to shame Herbert," Kanyesha says. "If the man isn't the top dog, he gets dissed by everyone—even the men in his family." "*So you learned that women are responsible for how men are treated; that women are not supposed to get more education than men, right?*" I say. "Well, I'm not gonna pretend I'm dumb!" Chantelle announces, "but I want a boyfriend." "Girls in college do have boyfriends, but not necessarily boys from the hood,"

I say. "Do you know there are good black men in college, too?" "Yeah," Kanyesha says, "but will I know how to be with them?" She looks scared. "*It can be scary to move on with your life and meet new people,*" I say. She nods. "In a way it can be exciting," Chantelle says, but shrugs her shoulders. "*You're scared, too, aren't you, Chantelle?*" I ask her. "In a way," she says.

"So, you learned from your families that you should be second mammas, and you learned from the boys that how they're treated on the streets is more important than what you want out of life," I say. Both girls seem more than a little bit shocked to hear it put that way.

In this exchange, the social worker engages the girls in a deconstruction of the "daughters' work" ideology (Dodson 1999) that enables many black families to limit the life options of their eldest daughters in order to use them as second mothers, babysitters for other family members, and sources of part-time income—while not requiring anything from their sons. She also helps them see who benefits from that part of patriarchal discourse that makes women responsible for what happens to men and teaches them to subjugate themselves and their own best interests to those of men. In this process, she *reaches for their feelings, reaches for information,* and *checks out an inference.*

In the excerpt below, the social worker helps Kanyesha and Chantelle understand their experiences from alternative perspectives.

"Did either one of you ever do something your families or boyfriends didn't like?" I ask. "I stay out later than I'm supposed to, and my mamma throws fits," Kanyesha offers. "Once we both stayed out all night," Chantelle says. "I remember that," Kanyesha says. "My mamma kept hitting on me, I didn't think she was ever gonna stop!" "I couldn't see my friends or talk on the phone for two weeks," Chantelle remembers "It was like I was locked up in jail." "Did you know you'd get in trouble before you did those things?" I ask. Both girls nod. "But you had the courage to do it anyhow, didn't you," I say. "I never looked at it that way before. I guess it did take guts, 'cause I knew I'd get it when I came home," Kanyesha said.

"What else have you done that upset your families," I asked. "Well," Chantelle began, "I never forget to feed the kids, but after that I sometimes try to study, or get on the phone, and before I know it, it's past time to bathe the kids and get them to bed." Kanyesha nodded. "Me, too; especially when it's Herbert on the phone." "Is that always by accident," I ask, "or do you know it just might keep you from those 'second mamma' chores?" They giggle. "Oh, it's always by accident," Chantelle laughs. "Is that what you tell your mamma?" I ask. "Yeah," Chantelle says. "Is it true?" I ask. "Of course not," she laughs again. "So," I say, "Sometimes you *refuse* to ignore your own needs. You don't *always* sacrifice yourself for the family. You do what high school girls have to do—and that takes courage, too. "I gotta have a life,"

Kanyesha says apologetically. I tell her there's no need for an honor student to apologize for studying, or for a teenager to feel bad about talking on the phone. I say it's natural and normal—but that it takes courage when families press you into servitude instead of encouraging you to be all that you can be. "They shouldn't make us slaves, should they, Mrs. Littlejohn," Kanyesha says almost inaudibly. "No, Kanyesha, nobody has that right," I tell her. "Families, especially large families, have every right to expect their children to do some chores to help out at home. Chores are important because they're necessary and being held to them builds character. But not if some or most of the children are not expected to do any, and one or two are burdened with all the work. Boys should be expected to do certain things every day, too. And younger sisters should be expected to share in the work that is appropriate for their age. Preschoolers can pick up their toys; young schoolchildren can set the breakfast or dinner table, clear the table, dry dishes, and empty garbage. As they get older, children—boys and girls—can shop for food, help prepare meals, help dress younger children, and read to them at bedtime. Everybody should be taught to and expected to pitch in. But that's not how it is at your homes. It takes great courage to say no to family expectations, whether you say the word itself or just hang on the phone to give them the message. Young women like yourselves should help out at home, but not be burdened with total mommahood when your responsibility to yourself should be education and a professional position after college and maybe graduate school. I realize I've been lecturing, so I apologize for it and just say I give you a lot of respect for the courage you've already shown." They tell me it's okay, that nobody tells them stuff like this, that it's good to hear it. Kanyesha tears up. "I can't let Herbert hold me back, either, can I?" She says rather than asks. I shake my head "no." Both girls ask me if they can come talk with me again. "'Cause I don't want to forget *me* with all that pressure out there," Kanyesha says. Chantelle asks if they can come back more than once, and I say they can come see me whenever they want to, and that if I don't hear from them, I'll call *them* back in. Each one of them hugs me on the way out.

In accord with the principle of helping the client deconstruct oppressive cultural discourse and reinterpret experience from alternative perspectives, in this example the social worker helps two black teenage girls identify the ideologies that sabotage their right to actualize their potential. She also begins to introduce them to alternative ways to interpret who and how they are and could be, that is, to the manifestations of multiple realities, different lenses through which to view themselves and their situations.

There are situations that sometimes trap people, however; for example, an elementary school student in a class with a particular teacher who sees him in a negative light and treats him as if he were of less worth than other students, who can neither get a transfer nor obtain a compromise through mediation. This makes it necessary to call upon the minimax principle for minimizing pain and maximizing positive outcomes and satisfaction.

THE MINIMAX PRINCIPLE

Sometimes, even though the demands of the client task have been fully and appropriately followed and every effort has been made to maximize supports in the client's environment, the needed resources are not forthcoming. It is at this point and in this situation that the minimax principle should be applied. It is not an intervention of choice. It is a last resort.

The minimax principle directs the social worker to identify, reinforce, and/ or increase the client's repertoire of strategic behaviors for minimizing pain and maximizing positive outcomes and satisfaction. This is not an effort to remediate, that is, to make up for deficits in the client. To the contrary, consistent with the orientation of structural social work practice, clients are seen as adequate people who can construe and interpret their political and interpersonal realities, and the behaviors of concern are for political and interpersonal struggles between self and withholding others, struggles that ought not to be necessary, but are. The social worker arms clients with strategic behaviors and provides them with opportunities to practice using them consciously and deliberately to maximize the probability of eliciting positive responses from an often unyielding social services community that may provide needed resources reluctantly or not at all.

It should be noted that the value society places on the myth of rugged individualism and self-sufficiency leads to a victim-blaming mentality even among persons who are themselves social or political victims. Therefore, to the extent that clients attribute their inability to obtain necessary resources to personal deficits, it is important to include deconstruction of oppressive cultural discourse. This challenges and exposes the fallacious attributions and recasts the client's plight as political rather than personal. To illustrate, in the practice example that follows, a social worker attempts to help a new member in a support group for adults molested as children to begin rejecting her self-blame based on the patriarchal discourse that holds little girls responsible for what their incestuous fathers do to them.

After sitting quietly and listening while two other members of the group told bits and pieces of the molestation horrors that ripped through their childhood, Maryann started to cry and said she never told her father no, that she should have and just didn't know it. "I should never have run around the house in those tight jeans," she said. "And my mother told me she'll never forgive me for luring my father out of *her* bed! She still hates me!" I said, "Maryann, your father deserves the blame, not you. You were a child and you deserved to be protected by both of your parents. Tight jeans is no excuse for a man to rape his little girl. And if your mother knew about it, she should have put a stop to it by reporting it to the police. You were the victim of criminal behavior, and you have a right to be very angry about what your father did to you! Your mother is horribly wrong to blame *you!*" Then I asked what other group members thought.

Lucy said she used to feel guilty and blame herself for wearing tight jeans and makeup, but she said all the kids wear tight jeans and makeup, and their fathers don't rape them. She said she's furious at her parents—at her father for doing it, and at her mother for holding onto her meal ticket instead of standing up for her when she needed her help. She said that she was only seven the first time. "It wasn't just once for me either," Maryanne said softly. Lucy leaned over and held Maryanne's hand. "If I'd been your mother," Wendy said, "I'd have held you in my arms. My own little girl is almost three, and I'll protect her with my life."

"There are lots of people who blame women when men rape them," I say. "They say, 'She was asking for it because she was out alone so late at night.' I've even heard people say, when a woman gets beat up, that she probably deserved it, she had a big mouth or something."

"Even women say it," Marilyn said. "I used to say it," she admitted softly. "We learn these beliefs from our culture," I said. "In a society where women are less powerful than men, stories that exonerate men and blame women circulate in neighborhoods, hospitals, schools, police departments, courts—everywhere. That's how we learn to blame ourselves even though we are not complicit. And we have to see that it is a function of power, a political issue we have to fight so it doesn't undermine us inside of ourselves."

All six principles and the processes through which the social worker uses them to guide direct practice are summarized in figure 4.1.

1. The worker must be accountable to the clients.	• Develop a service contract.
2. The worker must follow the demands of the client task.	• Look beyond the client to see if others are in the same plight. • Work in Quadrants A, B, and C, as needed. • Take all eight different roles and combinations of roles as needed. • Work with different numbers of people at different times.
3. The worker must maximize the potential supports in the client's environment.	• Bring to bear, modify, or create structures. • Do not occupy the central position in the helping process.
4. The worker must proceed from an assumption of least contest.	• Engage in C-type activity before B-type activity. • Take the role of broker before mediator, and mediator before advocate. • Escalate issues slowly up a bureaucratic hierarchy.
5. The worker must help the client deconstruct oppressive cultural discourse and reinterpret experiences from alternative perspectives.	• Involve clients in an analysis of the power relations in cultural myths that subjugate them. • Identify who benefits and how they benefit. • Introduce alternative lenses through which to view self and events.
6. The worker must identify, reinforce, and/or increase the client's repertoire of strategic behavior for minimizing pain and maximizing positive outcomes and satisfaction.	• Accept the client's construction of reality. • Identify and reinforce the client's repertoire of strategic behaviors and suggest others. • Provide practice opportunities.

FIGURE 4.1 Structural social work principles and processes

5

INTERVENTION PRINCIPLES AND PROCEDURES:

A PROCESS MODEL

THE WAY IN which structural social practice was described in the previous chapter can be thought of as an analytical paradigm, a conceptual framework or a model to provide social workers with an understanding of the internal workings of the practice. It identifies and explains the key elements (principles and procedures) and the interrelationships among them. But social work is not merely something one understands; it is something one does, one step at a time. Therefore, a second, complementary description is needed: a process model that guides what to do first and what to do next. This process model tells workers what to ask themselves every step of the way, and what to do contingent upon their answers.

This chapter provides workers with a process model of structural social work that translates the principles and procedures described in the previous chapter into sequential practice behaviors. Whereas the analytical framework was explicated in terms of *guiding principles*, the process model is organized in terms of *guiding questions*. The process model of structural social work has three phases: the contract phase, the task phase, and the termination/reentry phase.

THE CONTRACT PHASE

The contract phase involves worker and client in conversation about client need and tasks to relieve it. It culminates in an agreement between client and worker to proceed with the helping process. The contract phase begins with the social worker in Quadrant A (see figure 5.1). The worker takes the role of conferee and talks with clients about the pressures they are experiencing. Usually the worker asks an open-ended question such as, "What's happening?" then listens to the client's response. Perhaps a client in his late sixties will talk about how lonely he has been since his wife died two years earlier. After the client has spoken, and in this instance, after the worker has communicated empathy, she comes to the first key question, which can be seen in the diamond shape in figure 5.1: *Has the client described the pressures on him?* In this example, the client did describe the pressure he feels (loneliness), so the worker's answer to this first question she asked herself would be "yes." The answer to this question determines her next move. In other words, what the worker does next is contingent upon whether her answer to this key question is yes or no.

As indicated in figure 5.1, the move that is contingent on the worker following an affirmative response is to translate the pressure the client says he is experiencing into specific tasks that, when accomplished, will relieve that pressure. A task to alleviate loneliness in an aging widower might be formal involvement with other people on a regular basis. Such might include participating in a widower's support group or informal involvement in card games or chess, often offered on a drop-in basis by settlement houses, YMCAs, and Jewish community and senior citizen centers. There are also team sports as well as workout programs through which people get to know each other offered by such agencies.

Sometimes, however, unlike the man in the example, clients do not easily or readily describe the problems they are facing. At such times the worker's answer to the first key question is, "No, the client has not described the pressures on

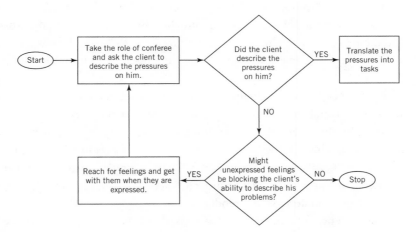

FIGURE 5.1 Phase 1. Contract: identifying the task

him." This signals that the worker should ask herself a second key question: *Might unexpressed feelings be blocking the client's ability to describe his problems?* If the answer to this question is yes (and, when clients are not initially responsive, it is ordinarily worthwhile to assume they are), then the worker must reach for the client's feelings. If feelings are expressed in response to her invitation, she should get with those feelings. Following her empathic questions and responsive comments, as indicated in figure 5.1, the social worker returns to her original request that the client describe his predicament. This time, however, the worker works slower and probes further, in an attempt to seek clues to the client's troublesome situation. If, despite the worker's best, prolonged efforts, the client still does not let on as to what is troubling him, the worker's answer to whether the client has described his troubles is no, and whether unexpressed feelings are the obstacle is also no. Hard though it is for social workers who care so much about people to admit, let alone act on, at this point, the worker's efforts to work with this client must stop. Perhaps the worker can suggest to the client that he come back later when he feels better prepared to discuss the struggles in his life, or that he bring with him someone authorized to speak on his behalf and communicate the situation for which he needs help.

Once the worker has heard the client's description of his difficulties and she has translated this into tasks for relieving it (which she did with her client, who is lonely), as shown in figure 5.2, she comes to the third key question she must ask herself: *Are the tasks she formulated agreeable to the client?* If her answer is yes, she must tell the client what she will do to help accomplish these tasks. For example, she may say she will contact local social service agencies to find out where there are afternoon card and chess games, as well as team sports and exercise programs. After checking with him to see if he can access and use the Internet to get information himself, if he can, the worker should not usurp his right to help himself by doing that part of the work. If he cannot, the worker may also offer to search the internet for local widower support groups.

If, however, the answer to the third question is no, meaning the client does not like or is not interested in the tasks the worker proposed, she must ask herself a fourth key question: *Does the client think the suggested tasks are not appropriate?* This is a question some social workers forget to ask when the client seems "negative" or "dissatisfied." Yet this question may be critical to increasing the probability that a satisfactory service contract can be developed and that appropriate service is rendered.

Clients tend to be the best consultants about their own pains and needs, and good social work includes maximizing opportunities to use clients as con-

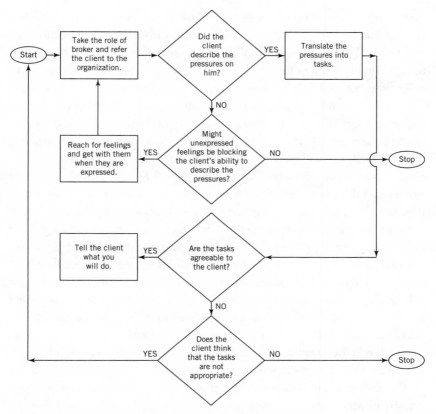

FIGURE 5.2 Phase 1. Contract: specifying worker's intended actions

sultants in their own behalf. For example, the client who is lonely may not be looking for ongoing contact with others through group discussion or recreational activities. His need may be more specific, such as the need of an elderly Polish man who has not spoken Polish to anyone since his wife died and longs to speak his native tongue again with another human being.

Sometimes, too, lonely people, despite their loneliness, are afraid of social contact. So if the answer to the last question is yes, indicating that the client does not see the proffered tasks as pertinent to his need, then the worker must begin again, asking the client for additional, more precise and/or more elaborated information about the pressures he is experiencing. For the lonely person frightened of face-to-face contact, Internet chat rooms may be a start—or even fully satisfactory. If, on the other hand, the client agrees that the suggested tasks are appropriate but does not wish to go ahead with them, no service contract can be developed at this time, and the worker/client relationship terminates. There are times when people do not want to change their situations, particularly when they believe that by doing so they will be exposed to other pressures that may be even harder for them to bear. For example, a client may not want the worker to confront his landlord about his persistently dripping faucet for fear of increased rent or eviction when his lease is up.

After the worker tells the client what she will do to help accomplish the tasks to which he has agreed, she reaches the fifth key question: *Are her proposed actions agreeable to the client?* If the answer to this question is yes, the worker and the client have developed a service contract, and the process of their work together can move ahead to the task phase. If the client does not agree to the worker's proposed actions, however, the worker must ask herself the sixth key question: *Does the client have ideas about how the worker could be equally or more helpful and preferable to him?* If the answer is yes, the client does have alternative acts in mind—and these alternative actions are acceptable to the worker (goal-oriented, legal, ethical, possible), a service contract has been developed and the process can move to the task phase. Should the client not have alternatives to suggest, or if the alternatives he suggests are not acceptable to the social worker, then no service contract can be developed at this time, and the worker/client relationship ends.

The entire social work process in the contract phase is shown in figure 5.3. To illustrate this flow in a practice situation, consider the following examples.

EXAMPLE: THE PROCESS IN THE CONTRACT PHASE WITH ONE CLIENT

The following transaction takes place between a school social worker and a new student at the regional middle school. As the worker prefers working with students in their normal context, he meets them in their classroom, rather than sit in his office.

I went into the ninth-grade math class, as I usually do on Wednesday, and sat next to the new boy. *I turned my chair so I was at a right angle to him.* I introduced myself as a social worker and asked, *"How's it going for you?"* He responded nervously, "Ahaight," and shrugged his shoulders. Then he asked me what does a social worker do here. *I told him we help people get what they need from the school.* "Is there anything

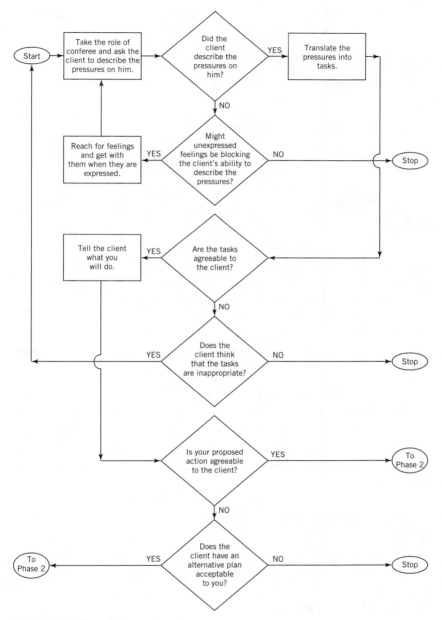

FIGURE 5.3 Phase 1. Contract

you need?" I asked him. He hesitated, almost spoke, but then just slumped in his seat. I also slumped and turned my chair again so we were both facing the front of the room. I waited. He seemed to be struggling but then hung his head and stared at the floor. I said, *"You look like you have something to say, but can't."* He sat up and said, "You help us get what, we need at school, right?" *"Right,"* I answered. *"You want me to help you?"* He nodded his head, meaning yes. I nodded also, saying, "Yeah." He said, "These kids, they make me crazy, y'know what I'm sayin.'" *"In this section?"* I asked. "No, they cool. It's the ones in my section." He said. *"You're not in this section?"* I asked. He said no, that he was just "kinda sittin' in." *I said I didn't know the school had a procedure like that.* He turned his head away and his body seemed to tense up. I said, "You *turned away from me."* There was some silence, so *I waited.* Then he explained that he had been in this class the preceding period, and since he liked the math teacher, he stayed, rather than going on with his regular section's schedule. He said he really didn't like his roster or any of the people in his section, and that he wanted his section changed to this one. I saw this as the pressure he was feeling (not liking his roster and the kids he had to put up with), and switching to this section, which he suggested, as an appropriate task. So we both agreed.

I then asked, *"Have you asked your counselor to change your section?"* He said he tried, but she was always too busy to see him when he stopped by. I said, *"That can get old real fast."* He shrugged. I asked, *"Do you want me to get your section changed?"* (My way of telling him what I could and would do and seeing if it was okay with him). He assured me he did want me to do that, so we had a workable service contract.

In the example above, the worker employed several different skills illustrated in chapter 4. Initially, he *positioned* himself. This was followed by alternatively *reaching for information, giving information,* and *reaching for information* again. He then *waited* as the student seemed to struggle, apparently drew an inference from the struggle he perceived, and appropriately *checked out his inference.* In response to the boy's question, he *gave information,* then *reached for* three different pieces of *information* himself.

When the student said that he was "sittin' in"—an unlikely, but not impossible, practice in middle schools—the worker did not challenge him, for doing so could well have destroyed the beginning rapport. The social worker was not there to uncover infractions. Priority was on helping the boy have a good beginning in his new school. Therefore, the worker gave information instead. He told the boy that he was not aware of the procedure—and even that seemed to generate tension and threaten the relationship. So the worker wisely reached for the feelings that seemed to be building, then waited.

When the boy began to talk about the problem that he was experiencing, the worker listened and accepted the boy's description of his need. He did not undermine the student's sense of reality, nor put him off with a, "Let's wait and see if you feel the same way next week." Further, he accepted the student's concept of the task that would alleviate the problem as the boy construed it. The worker then reached for consequential information, reached for the boy's feelings once again, and ultimately reached for the information that, when given by the student, resulted in the service contract between worker and client.

EXAMPLE: THE PROCESS IN THE CONTRACT PHASE WITH A GROUP OF CLIENTS

In the following practice example, the social worker develops a service contract with a group of older adults. The worker convened the group because she noticed that a lot of the older people sat around the lobby of the senior community center but did not interact with each other, and many always seemed to be sad. She begins by telling the group what she perceives to be some of their pressures and proposes weekly group meetings aimed at alleviating them.

I was introduced to the older adults during their weekly luncheon. I told them that I saw many of them come every week, but few of them talked with each other when they were here. I wondered if some people would be interested in a book club where members could read the same book and discuss it. I also wondered if some of them would be interested in a group for talking about their troubles. There were many nods. I said that anyone who is interested in a book club could meet me in room 110 right after lunch, and those interested in talking about troubles and helping each other think about different ways of coping could meet me at one o'clock in the same room.

After lunch eleven people came into the room. Mrs. Shutts and Mr. Curtis immediately put their chairs next to mine. Mrs. Kramer stood between Mr. Curtis and me. Mrs. Harding told her to go around to the other side of the table where there was more room. Mrs. Kramer told everyone in that row to move down. Nobody moved. Mrs. Shutts told me to tell Mrs. Kramer to go to the other side so the group could get started. *I said that where people sat was up to them and the group, not up to me,* and *suggested that if Mrs. Shutts wanted Mrs. Kramer to go elsewhere, she could tell her.* She did. Mrs. Kramer said she was all right where she was and sat down at the corner of the table between Mr. Curtis and me. Mr. Curtis, Mrs. Harding, and Mrs. Linton moved down, and Mrs. Kramer put her chair where Mr. Curtis's had been.

I began by asking them what book they would like to start with, and got a variety of suggestions. The group rank-ordered them, and I agreed to order copies of the one they chose first. They agreed to read the first three chapters once the book came in. Thus a service contract was formed.

At one o'clock, twenty-four people crowded into the room. Because of the number of people interested, I suggested we divide into two groups and asked them if it was okay if I did the dividing. They said that was fine. I said that they could meet together every week and my job would be to help them talk to each other and help each other. Again, there was agreement. I said I could meet with one group before lunch, and one group after lunch. They seemed fine with that, so a service contract was developed.

In this example, the social worker took the role of group worker and developed a service contract with the group. Note that she used two particular group work skills. When a group member told her to tell another member to move, the worker did not take over her responsibility for communicating her own desire. Rather, she suggested that the member herself tell that person what she wanted her to do. The group worker *redirected the message* to the person for whom it was intended. During the same interaction, she told the member (and the whole group) that "where people sat was up to them and the group," not to her. This skill is called *turning issues back to the group* which is part of an ongoing theme that the group is responsible for its own destiny. More group work skills are introduced and elaborated in chapter 12.

THE TASK PHASE

The task phase involves doing the work agreed upon in the service contract. Once the service contract has been developed, the social worker is responsible for practicing in accord with it, and the process of structural social work flows into phase two, the task phase. As in the contract phase, the worker's behaviors in the task phase are contingent on her answers to a series of key questions.

The first two questions are: Is there an existing organization that should alleviate the client's predicament? Are persons other than the client in the same plight? These two questions combine to tell the worker which of four possible actions she should take as the initial step in following the demands of the client task (agreed upon in the service contract), the second principle of structural social work practice.

As shown in figure 5.4, the origin of the four choices can be identified in a two-by-two table where the above questions form the two dimensions and the answers "yes" and "no" constitute the categories on each.

Is there an existing organization that
should alleviate the client's plight?

	YES	NO
YES	**Yes-Yes** Change the organizational structure.	**No-Yes** Create a self-help network.
NO	**Yes-No** Refer the client to the organization.	**No-No** Create a resource network.

Are there persons other than the
client in the same plight?

FIGURE 5.4 Phase 2. Task: activities contingent on the first two questions

THE YES-NO CONDITION

In the yes-no condition (lower left-hand cell), there *is* an organization charged with meeting the client's need, and *no other persons* seem to have this need. The social worker discovers that no other persons seem to have this need, when *she looks beyond the client to see if others are in the same plight,* in accord with the principle of following the demands of the client task. Finding that others are not in the same plight suggests either that other people are getting that need met through existing organizations, or that this is a unique situation. In either event, the worker should take the role of broker, move to Quadrant C, and refer the client to the existing organization for needed goods and services including therapy and case management. If a low-income or no-income client needs dentures, for example, and other low-income or no-income people have had free access to them through the Board of Health or Bureau of Vocational Rehabilitation, the worker should refer the client to that agency.

THE YES-YES CONDITION

In the yes-yes condition (upper left-hand cell), there *is* an organization presumably mandated to meet the client's need. Yet, when the worker looks beyond the client to see if others are in the same situation, she finds that *many others have the same unmet need*. In this instance, it is reasonable to assume that the policies and/or procedures of the organization responsible for meeting the need in question do not adequately recognize and/or respond to persons with that need. This tells the worker to direct her efforts toward structural change.

Guided by the principle of least contest, the worker starts by taking the role of broker in Quadrant C and tries to initiate joint problem-solving meetings with key staff members of the relevant organization. If the worker with the client who needed dentures looked beyond him and discovered many other people in poverty who needed dentures, she would have to approach staff at the Department of Health and the Bureau of Vocational Rehabilitation in order to learn what obstacles prevent these agencies from providing dentures. Perhaps deep financial cuts in health and social welfare resulted in a Board of Health decision to eliminate dentures from their category of basic needs. Perhaps the Bureau of Vocational Rehabilitation, in similar financial straits, now focuses entirely on basic job training and placement. If this were the situation with the Board of Health, the worker would take the role of advocate in Quadrant C. To build an arguable case that supports the need for dentures, she could present evidence that shows dentures prevent problems in the digestive system—problems that could prevent far more costly medical care in the future. With the Bureau of Vocational Rehabilitation, the worker would also take the role of advocate in Quadrant C. In this instance she would argue that a nice smile plays a major role in who gets hired and who does not. In any event, the worker would be trying to open or reopen minds, monies, and channels through which people needing dentures can get them. If her arguments in Quadrant C are not productive, however, and provision of the needed resource is not forthcoming, the worker may have to move to Quadrant B and add community organizer and group worker to her role as advocate.

THE NO-YES CONDITION

In the no-yes condition (upper right-hand corner), *many people have the same unmet need*, and there are *no organized arrangements* for service delivery to alleviate it. For example, mothers forced into minimum wage jobs by the demise of Aid to Families with Dependent Children (AFDC) and the strict lifetime limit of Temporary Assistance for Needy Families (TANF) cannot find decent, reliable childcare that they can afford in minimum-wage jobs. Some may even be at risk for having their children removed from their custody for neglect because they cannot afford daycare. Yet there is little free daycare available, and tens of thousands of mothers require it.

Given such a situation, the worker is directed to take the roles of broker and group worker in Quadrant A to create a self-help structure such as a child care cooperative in which mothers in poor neighborhoods who work different shifts can look after children during times they are not at their jobs, and perhaps fill in with retired persons known from church and high-school student volunteers needing community service to beef up their college applications. This is consistent with the principle of maximizing environmental supports.

THE NO-NO CONDITION

In the no-no condition (lower right-hand cell), there is *neither an agency* assigned to meet the need of a client *nor are there others* with a similar need. For example, one of the children of a single parent with a full time minimum wage job needs transportation to and from kidney dialysis three times every week. This suggests that the worker take the role of broker in Quadrant C and create a special resource, such as three neighbors who will share responsibility for taking the child to the assigned clinic for his medical service, then bringing him back to school on each of the three days it is required. This, too, is an instance of maximizing environmental supports.

THE FLOW OF INITIAL INTERVENTION IN THE TASK PHASE

Following performance of one of the four activities indicated by each of the four conditions shown conceptually in figure 5.4 and described in the preceding section, the flow of work in accord with key questions is illustrated in figure 5.5. The worker begins by looking beyond the client to see if there are other persons in the same plight. This enables her to answer the first key question: *Are there others in the same plight?* If the answer is no, she asks herself: *Is there an existing organization that should alleviate the client's plight?* If the answer is yes, she takes the role of broker in Quadrant C and refers the client to the organization for therapy, case management or other goods and services. If the answer is no, she takes the role of broker in Quadrant C and tries to create a resource network for the client. Then she asks: *Was it possible to create such a network/system?* If the answer is yes, it was possible to create a resource network, she proceeds to the termination/recontracting phase. If the answer is no, she takes the role of conferee, engages the client in the minimax process, then moves to phase three.

If, when the social worker began the work in the task phase and looked beyond the client to see if others were in a similar situation and found that there *were* others, she also asks herself: is an existing organization that should be alleviating this predicament? If the answer is no, there are no organized arrangements for meeting this need, the worker takes the roles of broker and group worker and tries to organize some of these persons into a self-help system, perhaps a support group. After working to create this structure, the worker must ask herself: *Was it possible to create such a system?* If the answer is yes, she proceeds

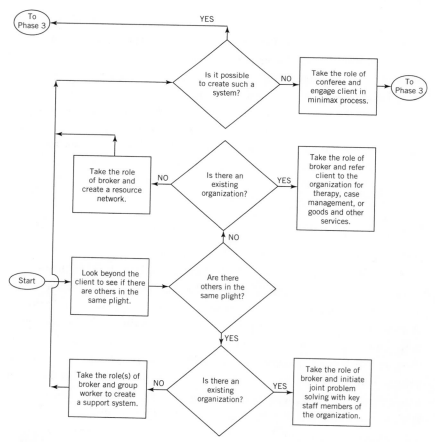

FIGURE 5.5 Phase 2. Task: flow of action contingent on the first two key questions in the task phase

to phase three. But if the answer is no, she engages the client in the minimax process, then goes to phase three. On the other hand, if the worker found that an organization to meet their need *does* exist, she takes the role of broker and tries to initiate joint problem solving with key staff of that organization.

Next, as shown in figure 5.6, the social worker must ask herself: *Was the task accomplished through brokerage? Is the client's need now being met?* If the answer is yes, the process immediately moves into the termination/recontracting phase. If the answer is no, however, if the unsuccessful effort was directed toward creating a self-help structure or a resource network (as shown in figure 5.5), the worker takes the role of conferee and moves into Quadrant A. As conferee in Quadrant A, she engages the client in the minimax process described in chapter 4. In all instances, after applying the minimax principle, the worker goes to the termination/recontracting phase.

If the task was not accomplished through referral (prescribed by the yes-no condition in figure 5.4), or through efforts at joint problem solving with the staff of an existing organization (described by the yes-yes condition in figure 5.4), then, in accord with the principle of least contest, the worker should take the role of mediator, as shown in figure 5.6. In the role of mediator, the social worker brings the client, with his need for service (Quadrant A), face-to-face with a representative of the agency with its need to deliver service (Quadrant C). She asks them to talk with each other, with her help, in order to work out a mutually beneficial resolution in which the agency provides service, as it should, and the client receives service, as he should. The role of mediator is a difficult, yet frequently necessary one. It is described and illustrated in chapter 8.

As shown in figure 5.6, after mediating, the worker must ask herself the fourth key question: *Was the task accomplished? Is the client's need now being met?* If the answer is yes, the worker moves directly to the termination/recontracting phase. If the answer is no, however, and the client's need is still unmet, the worker is required to take the role of conferee in Quadrant A in order to thoroughly discuss the possible consequences of advocacy for him. This process is essential for informed consent. Because the next step in the process is advocacy (in Quadrant C), it is incumbent upon the worker to be sure that the client is fully cognizant of the potential positive and especially the potential negative consequences that may ensue *before* he decides to agree to advocacy or refuse to involve himself with it. Advocacy can result in retaliatory action by the target person or agency, and the client must decide if the possible gain is worth the risk. Because it is the client who will bear the consequences, it is the client who has to make an informed choice.

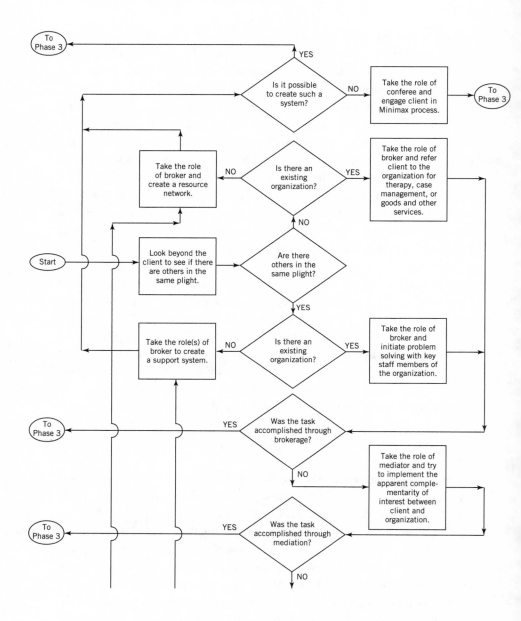

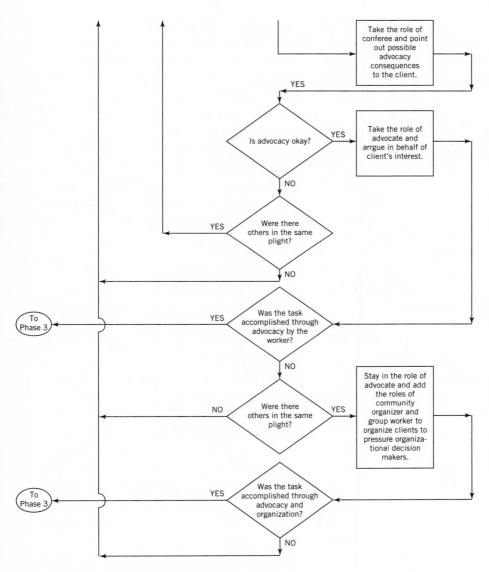

FIGURE 5.6 Phase 2. Flow of action in mediation and advocacy

If clients do not think the potential gain is worth the risks involved and choose to forgo advocacy, the worker must take the role of broker to try creating a structure—a self-help structure if others are in the same plight, or a special resource network if the client's plight seems to be unique. If the worker succeeds in creating such a structure in accord with the principle of maximizing environmental supports, and the client's need is now being met, the process moves to the termination/recontracting phase. If the worker is *not* able to create a satisfactory structure, she must engage the clients in the minimax process and then proceed to the third phase.

If, on the other hand, following thorough discussion of potential risks of advocacy, the client indicates that he wishes to proceed with it, then, consistent with the principle of least contest, the social worker takes the role of advocate in Quadrant C. In the role of advocate in Quadrant C, she argues her client's case for the goods or services he needs with the people representing the organization. After this, she asks herself: *Did arguing for the client accomplish the task? Is the client's need now being met?* If her argument did in fact accomplish the task, the process moves to phase three. If, however, the task is still not accomplished, and no others appear to be in the same predicament as the client, the social worker should proceed as if no agency existed. She should take the role of broker in Quadrant C and attempt to organize a special resource network of nonsufferers to help alleviate the client's pressures. If it is not possible to develop such a network, the worker is directed to engage the client in the minimax process, then move to phase three.

If arguing in behalf of the client did not produce the needed resources and there *are* persons other than the client in the same adverse situation, then the worker is advised to stay in the role of advocate and move into Quadrant B. In Quadrant B she should try to organize similarly situated others to join together in order to bring pressure to bear upon organizational decision makers and/or other key persons who might influence them. Specific tasks and skills for such grassroots organizing are delineated in chapter 13.

Once pressure has been brought to bear on decision makers, the social worker must ask herself: *Did organizing some of those in need and pressuring the decision makers result in task accomplishment? Is the client's need now being met?* If the answer is yes, the process moves to phase three. If the answer is no, however, the worker should take the role of broker, move to Quadrant A, and try to organize the persons in need into a self-help structure. If this effort is successful, the process can move to phase three. If the effort is unsuccessful, then the worker is obliged to engage the client in the minimax process before moving to the third phase.

EXAMPLE: THE PROCESS IN THE TASK PHASE

To illustrate the process of structural social work in the task phase, recall the service contract developed by the school social worker in which he was to help a new student change his section and his class schedule. Once that contract was developed, the worker recorded the following:

Under ordinary circumstances I would have taken the role of broker in Quadrant C and referred Jarrod to his guidance counselor. Since he already tried to see her several times on his own and she was too busy whenever he tried, I figured I should follow the principle of least contest and move up one notch and try to mediate the situation. To do this, I first took the role of conferee (in Quadrant A) and pointed out to Jarrod that I would try to get the counselor to sit down and talk with him, but that he would have to convince her to change his section and class schedule. I said that I would help him talk with her and help her talk with him. He said that was okay with him.

In the role of mediator, I then spoke with the counselor (in Quadrant C). She told me that Jarrod's records from his last school showed poor grades and sporadic attendance. She also said she had reservations about dealing with the situation because his records also indicate that he was a discipline problem, and she didn't trust his motives for wanting to change sections. In addition to that, she said the two sections he was interested in were already large classes. She said something else I tucked away for later: she was afraid that granting Jarrod's request would result in a deluge of requests to change sections. I decided that later I would check into student satisfaction with sections and class schedules. If many other students felt they were not where they thought was best for them, I would try to engage in joint problem solving with the counselors and the vice principal. For now, though, I had a contract with Jarrod, and it didn't look like his counselor would be willing to sit down and talk with him.

I was all set to be Jarrod's advocate (in Quadrant C), when I remembered that his counselor did have a stake in talking with him. She really hated to see any kids drop out of school, and lots of kids here drop out as soon as they can. So I pointed out her stake—that she doesn't want kids to drop out—and Jarrod was quite likely to, unless the school seemed to care about him and be responsive to him once in a while, like making some adjustments to meet his felt needs. She nodded and reluctantly agreed to talk with him while I mediated.

When they did meet, I helped them talk to each other and *hear* each other. Jarrod promised to improve his attendance and his grades if his section was changed, and the counselor agreed to recommend the change to the vice principal. I said that I would meet with Jarrod every two weeks to see how he was doing at school. Both Jarrod and the counselor agreed to that. Because I was afraid to let this get lost in the shuffle, I suggested that all three of us go see the vice principal right then and there, which we did. Both the counselor and I recommended the change, then the vice principal wanted to talk to Jarrod alone. When he came out about five minutes later, his section and his class schedule were changed.

The social worker followed up with Jarrod every two weeks, meetings, he reported, that Jarrod seemed to appreciate. Three months later, the counselor reported that Jarrod's attendance, attitude, and grades had all improved markedly over his performance at his last school.

The social worker also acted on what he discovered to be a widespread scheduling problem. In order to recommend realistic and effective changes in the process and outcome, he initiated discussions with teachers, administrators, and counselors to investigate the causes of the problem.

THE TERMINATION/RECONTRACTING PHASE

The third and final phase of the process model involves terminating the service contract on which worker and client had focused their attention, and, if the client so wishes, recontracting with him to alleviate other pressures. Therefore, as can be seen in figure 5.7, part of this third phase looks much like the contract phase (figures 5.1, 5.2, and 5.3).

The process begins with the social worker taking the role of conferee in Quadrant A. First, the worker engages the client in summarizing their work together and assessing the outcomes in terms of the task specified in the service contract. This brings the worker to the first key question in the termination/recontracting phase: *Was the task accomplished?* If the answer is yes, the work is done, and the worker/client relationship terminates. If, on the other hand, the task was *not* accomplished, the worker must ask herself the second key question: *Is there an alternative task? Can the pressures which the client originally described be relieved by accomplishing a different task?* If the answer is no, then the work is done, and despite lack of success, the engagement terminates. To continue beyond this point is to wander aimlessly, frustrating the worker and the client. When the social worker's best efforts fail to accomplish the task and there is no alternative task, it is time to stop.

If there is an alternate task to alleviate the pressures the client is experiencing, the worker should ask herself the third key question: *Is the alternative task agreeable to the client?* If it is not, the work stops and the relationship ends. If the client agrees that the alternative task valid and valuable, the worker indicates what she can and will do to help accomplish it, then asks herself the fourth key question: *Are the actions she has proposed agreeable to the client?* If the answer is yes, a new service contract has been developed and worker and client reenter the process at the beginning of phase two, the task phase (see figure 5.5) in order to work on the new task. If the client does not agree to the

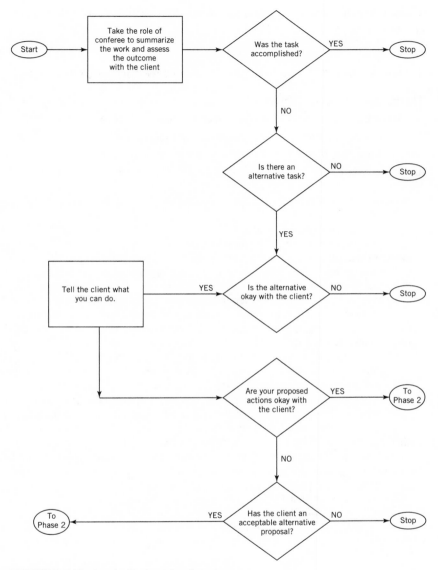

FIGURE 5.7 The termination/recontracting phase

actions the worker has proposed, however, the social worker asks herself the fifth and final key question: *Does the client have a proposal regarding possible worker activity, a proposal that is also agreeable to the worker?* If the answer is yes, there is a new service contract and the interventive system is reentered at the start of the task phase (figure 5.5). But if the client neither agrees to the worker's proposed actions nor offers an alternative acceptable to both, the process terminates.

EXAMPLE: PRACTICE IN THE TERMINATION/RECONTRACTING PHASE

The following process recording illustrates structural social work in the termination/recontracting phase. The social worker and her group of Latino parents have completed the contract and the task phases and are now entering the termination/recontracting phase. First the worker summarizes the work on the tasks and their outcomes in the original, and, at this point, the *only* service contract:

I took the role of conferee in Quadrant A and started summarizing where we had been and where we are now. (I'm not fluent in Spanish, but I try, and I'm not too bad. Group members don't seem to mind that I talk slowly sometimes and sometimes ask them to repeat what they say.) I said we started working together when some of them got upset that their children weren't learning much in school. I found out it was because everything was taught in English even though this is a primarily Latino neighborhood and the city has a large Latino population. We agreed, in the original service contract, that I should talk with the teachers and the principal to try to change the situation. But when I talked to the teachers they said they didn't want to learn Spanish. They said the children are going to have to learn English in order to get jobs later, so they should start learning it now. I asked if there was a class in English as a second language (ESL), and they said no.

Also in accord with the original service contract, I talked to the principal about getting some bi-lingual teachers, and he said it wouldn't be fair to get bilingual teachers and fire teachers who had been at that school for years and years. He also said they couldn't afford to add an ESL class. So we all went to the school board meeting, and during the public portion we tried to pressure them into sending at least some Spanish-speaking teachers, but all they said was that they'd look into it. So we didn't get anywhere. I said I was sad, and I knew they were. One of the men shook his head and said in Spanish that America isn't supposed to be like this, and lots of others nodded. I nodded, too.

Once the social worker summarized the tasks and outcomes of the original service contract, and she and her group are about to terminate their work together, a new idea occurs to the worker, and this idea leads to recontracting with the group instead of terminating. The recording that continues below shows the recontracting process.

After summarizing and preparing to terminate, I suddenly got another idea. I told the group about it to see if it was okay with them. I said that maybe we could get the school board to hire some bilingual aides who wouldn't be replacing any teachers, just helping the children understand what the teacher was saying. Or maybe they would accept some bilingual parent volunteers to do it. I also said that maybe I could get someone to teach the children English after school a few days a week. I told them I thought they and their children deserved better than this, but since we couldn't get bilingual teachers, would this be okay to try for? They were pretty enthusiastic about it, even though I wasn't, so I agreed to look into it and do what I could for them. This was a new service contract, so I reentered the system at the beginning of the task phase [figure 5.5].

WHY TWO TYPES OF PARADIGMS?

The analytical paradigm of structural social work, described and illustrated in chapter 4, sets the boundaries for practice. It tells the social worker the nature of the outcomes to pursue, the guidelines to use in their pursuit (principles), and the available roles and types of activity (Quadrants) in which to engage under various circumstances. The analytic model articulates and explains practice on a conceptual level. But it does not answer the social worker's important, on-going questions: *What should I do first? What should I do next?* For this, the process model provided in this chapter is necessary. The analytic model sets the stage for practice while the process model provides a basic script for the play that will unfold on that stage.

CONCLUSION

This chapter provided charts and a discussion of the three-phase process model that shows the flow of the principles and procedures of structural social work in practice. It also provided process records that demonstrate how the roles and the quadrants function in relation to each other and to the principles and procedures in the process of the practice.

The following section details the tasks and skills required by the roles the worker must take at various times. Each chapter in the section describes and illustrates one of these essential roles.

PART III

ROLES

6

THE CONFEREE

THE LABEL "conferee" distinguishes a set of tasks that structural social workers use at particular points in the direct practice process. The term stems from the notion of the "conference," that encounter where two or more persons consult together, compare opinions, deliberate, and devise actions to be taken after the conference. A basic assumption underlying this role is that all participants are equal and that each has an equal part in determining subsequent action. Key concepts inhering in this role, then, are partnership and mutuality. When the social worker assumes the role of conferee, the reciprocal role—for the client—is also that of conferee (Wood and Middleman 1989).

The social worker, with special knowledge and skill acquired through professional education and developed through experience, and the client, with special knowledge of her of his life situation and all that it takes to live her or his life, consult together to decide what ought to be done and what the worker will do to reduce the pressures which the client is experiencing. To insure the integrity of the conference, the worker must take the role of conferee through behaviors that clarify that the client is also a conferee. The worker must help the client understand and realize that she or he is not in a one-down position even if she or he expects to be and has had more experience with it. In other words, it is the responsibility of the social worker as conferee to initiate and maintain, through all that she says and does, that the client, too, is a conferee. It is the social worker who must set this role relationship in motion.

In every instance of structural social work practice, the worker begins with the client by taking the role of conferee in Quadrant A. Her goal is to establish a service contract with the client. Thus, she listens while the client describes his situation, the pressures he feels, and what, if any, help he may want. For the most part, a client does not ask the worker to "be my broker," or "be my advocate." Rather, he narrates what is going on in his life, talks about how he feels about what is going on in his life, how he feels about his life situation, and what he initially thinks might make a difference for him.

As Charmaz (2005) indicates in her description of interviewing in accord with constructionist grounded theory, in discussion with the client, the social worker listens and probes deeper for views, values, beliefs, ideologies, structures, and situation as well as for facts. Workers who understand these tacit meanings do not challenge clients' versions of reality; rather, they aim to clarify them.

Three tasks are required of the social worker in the role of conferee: translating pressures into tasks, facilitating decision making, and concluding the work. Within each task, we describe the skills needed to help accomplish it.

TRANSLATING PRESSURES INTO TASKS

Once the social worker as conferee has listened carefully to the client's narrative of his struggles, she and the client identify the tasks which, when accomplished, may relieve his struggles. For example, the worker translates the client's struggle to stay warm when he can no longer afford his gas and electric bill into the tasks of having his heat turned back on and obtaining money to provide him ongoing help with his utility bills. Two skills facilitate this work: (1) engagement with empathy and (2) identifying options.

ENGAGEMENT WITH EMPATHY Engagement with empathy refers to responding to the client's emotions, whether verbalized or not, as the client narrates a troublesome life situation. The engagement requires the social worker to *reach for information* and probe for specificity. It is only through identifying precise needs that she and the client can pinpoint outcomes that, when accomplished, will relieve the client's troubling situation. But as the client responds to the worker's questions by telling that story, the client may express or otherwise indicate the presence of emotions that the needs and struggles tend to precipitate. When the client does express emotion, the worker must *get with the client's feelings*. If the client does not express emotion, the worker has to *reach for the client's feelings*, because unexpressed emotion can result in gaps and distortions in information offered by the client. Reaching for information and feelings and getting with feelings are described in chapter 4.

IDENTIFYING OPTIONS Exploring with the client a range of alternative courses of action and their consequences refers to discussing possible ways to proceed and examining their potential. This begins with translating needs and pressures into tasks, formulated as outcomes, for alleviating them. Then, for each potential course of action, the conferee engages the client in a discussion of its potential consequences, both positive and negative. Use of this skill enhances the client's ability to make informed decisions.

EXAMPLE: TRANSLATING PRESSURES INTO TASKS

In the following process recording, a social worker in a hospital takes the role of conferee and engages a woman with empathy as she helps her explore options in order to identify tasks that may relieve some of her pain. Encountering a tearful Mrs. Coia in the corridor of the oncology wing, the worker *gets with her feelings* and *reaches for information* with an open-ended question in order to explore the situation. She suggests a place to talk, *positions* herself, and waits out the woman's feelings. When Mrs. Coia indicates that she is ready, the worker *reaches for feelings, reaches for information,* and *attends* while Mrs. Coia describes what is going on. When Mrs. Coia seems finished, the social worker *reaches for and gets with her feelings.*

When Mrs. Coia stepped out of her husband's room, I could see that she was crying. I walked over and touched her shoulder. *"You look upset,"* I said. *"What's happening?"* She shook her head. "Why don't we go down to the family room where it's a little more private," I suggested. She nodded wordlessly and we walked around the corner to the unit's family room. *I pulled two chairs to a ninety-degree angle to each other* and handed her a box of tissues. *We sat silently for a few minutes* while she cried and tried to compose herself a little bit. I said, "Please don't feel you need to stop crying." She said, "No, I really need to talk." *I said, "You seem terribly discouraged."* She wiped her eyes and said, "Well, I'm afraid the news isn't very good according to some tests that just came back." *I asked, "What's happening?"* She sighed and said, "All of his blood counts are very low, even though they've given him blood transfusions. The results from the biopsy also show that the cancer cells are now in his bone marrow. Dr. Willis said that he just doesn't have the strength to undergo any more treatment. The treatments themselves would make him feel worse and break his body down more quickly than the disease."

I said, "I'm so sorry. This must be such a blow since he seemed to be doing a little better last week." She said, "I know. He's really got the doctors confused. First he'll do real poorly, and then he'll perk up and his fever will go down and he'll eat again." *I said "That must be doubly hard on you."* She said, "Well, you know, it really is. I keep thinking maybe this time he really *will* pull through, and I get my hopes up and then the next day he gets worse."

As the record continues below, the social worker as conferee helps Mrs. Coia consider alternatives and consequences. In doing this, she reaches for two pieces of information, draws an inference from Mrs. Coia's responses, and checks out that inference. When Mrs. Coia acknowledges that the inference is accurate, the social worker provides relevant information about self-incurred consequences. She then waits out Mrs. Coia's feelings, draws and checks out two additional salient inferences, and continues to draw and check out inferences by way of speculating with Mrs. Coia about more of what may be going on. The worker then tries to create an empathic connection between Mrs. Coia and her husband, gets with Mrs. Coia's feelings, and gives her more relevant information.

"How much does Mr. Coia know about his condition now?" I asked. Mrs. Coia said, "I've been afraid to say anything to him—he wants to go home so badly. That's all he talks about." *"What about the rest of your family—your son and daughters?"* I asked. "I haven't told them anything, either," she responded. "I'm afraid to." It'll just destroy them." *I said, "It sounds to me like you're trying to protect them."* "I am," she said, Then I said, quietly, *"But that also means you have to keep all this painful knowledge to yourself. That can be an incredibly heavy burden."* She began to cry again and said, "I know, but I just can't bear to see all the people around me feeling so bad. It just tears me up inside." *I remained silent* for a moment or two, then I said, *"Do you think your husband and your family might suspect things may be getting worse—or not getting better?"* She said, "I think so. Sometimes he talks about how I ought to talk to the accountant to get some tax things straightened out for next year, as though he won't be there to take care of it. But he never asks the doctors how he is! I'm always the one to sneak away and talk to the doctor."

I said, *"I wonder if he might be trying to protect you from hurting too much."* "Maybe," she said. I said, *"Maybe you're both trying to protect each other by not talking about some very important things. It seems to hurt you very much not to be able to talk about it with him or anyone else. Do you think he might be feeling a little bit of that hurt also?"* She said, "I guess I haven't thought of it that way." I said, *"It's painful and frightening for both of you. Maybe both of you could reach a point where you could talk to each other about the fears and hurts you're each feeling. It won't make it go away, but it might make it a little easier to bear the burden if you share it."* "That sounds like a good idea," she said, "but I need to think about it." *"Of course you do,"* I said. *"You're the only one who knows what feels best to you, so you are the only one who can decide what to do."*

We talked about some other things, then I walked her back to her husband's room. She asked me if I'd be there tomorrow, and I said that I would be, and that I'd come see her in the afternoon.

FACILITATING DECISION MAKING

The role of conferee is all about decision making with clients. Initially the worker converses with the client to generate details about his troubles in order to decide with him what outcomes seem likely to ease them. Should advocacy become necessary, she first discusses potential consequences with him to determine if he is willing to risk it. Ultimately, she helps him decide when the work is done. Through all of this, the social worker as conferee encourages the client to make his own decisions thus guarding his right to decide his own destiny. Two skills are prominent in performing this task: (1) encouraging the client to decide and (2) confronting preconceptions.

ENCOURAGING THE CLIENT TO DECIDE In every instance of decision making, the conferee encourages the client to make his own decision rather than a decision that others may want him to make—the client's husband or wife, his parents, his friends. She encourages him to make decisions in light of his own feelings about what he can and cannot bear. She advises him to assess for himself what is and is not congenial to his cultural and individual values and lifestyle, and to choose the course of action that he considers best for himself. The social worker as conferee does not try to influence the client to choose the alternative that the worker thinks is best, nor does she judge the client from her own frame of reference. She does not evaluate the client's ability to make decisions based on how similar the client's decision is to the worker's own preferred course of action or personal values. Rather, the conferee recognizes that the decision belongs to the client and only the client, because the consequences are the client's and only the client's to bear.

CONFRONTING PRECONCEPTIONS Facilitating decision making requires activities aimed at identifying and bringing into the open possible preconceptions, born of cultural narratives and prior experiences. A client may have preconceptions about the profession of social work or the social worker's race, gender, or age. These preconceptions could be obstacles to a client's disclosure of full and honest detail about her situations and needs. When a client is initially standoffish, seems reluctant to make eye contact, or shows other signs of discomfort, the worker has to *reach for feelings* of discomfort. If feelings are not forthcoming, and the signs of discomfort do not abate, it is incumbent upon the worker to draw and *check out inferences* about preconceptions.

EXAMPLE: FACILITATING DECISION MAKING

The following recorded exchange between a social worker at the county probation office is particularly illustrative of the need to confront preconceptions. The worker checks out a powerful inference that precipitates talk that might otherwise remain unacknowledged and serve as an obstacle to the work.

A man came into the office saying the secretary told him to talk to Mr. McAvoy or Mr. Carlson. Because both of these workers were busy with other clients and I do the same work they do, I walked over to him and introduced myself. The client, whom I recognized as Mr. Jackson, looked a bit startled. I asked him to have a seat, and I proceeded to get out his file. Mr. Jackson sat down rather rigidly and did not take his coat off. A look of disgust came over his face, and he began to stare straight ahead, avoiding all eye contact.

 "You look uncomfortable," I said, *reaching for his feelings.* "Umph," he mumbled. *"It can be upsetting to talk to a different worker when you are used to seeing someone else,"* I offered, again reaching for his feelings. No response. *I waited.* Still no response. *Then I said, "Does it bother you that I'm a woman?"* Mr. Jackson did a double take and immediately looked at me. "Yeah," he responded. "I'm used to reporting down here, but I'm not used to speaking with a lady other than the secretary."

Sometimes this kind to conversation is necessary for worker and client to clear the air so they can talk with each other about the real things that are happening in the client's life. Because such obstacles can block the work with any client, the worker should always be aware of this. But it is especially important in work with nonvoluntary clients and when meeting with clients in their homes. Since facilitating decision making is a prime element in social work practice, the conferee must consciously and deliberately seek to minimize the power of preconceptions by verbalizing them so they are not a persistent, silent threat to the integrity of the work.

Because decision making is never a purely rational process, it must be understood that feelings and attitudes will arise to distort or otherwise modify people's beliefs as they consider alternative courses of action and their potential consequences, and, with the conferee's encouragement, to make choices by themselves, for themselves. Thus the social worker as conferee must be prepared to engage her own attitudes and feelings and to help others do the same.

More specifically, the worker must raise the positive and negative feelings that the client may be experiencing, but not expressing. The worker may need to help the client realize that it is all right to have feelings, and that facing these, whatever they are, will be necessary in deciding upon action, hard as this is sometimes. And if the client expresses only one side of his feelings, the social worker should raise the less known ones that might also be there, for these become part of the information on which the client can ultimately base his decision. All decisions are heavily influenced by a combination of attitudes, cultural beliefs, experiences, and emotions.

CONCLUDING THE WORK

The role of conferee is also prominent in the termination/reentry phase of the work (see chapter 5). Therefore, the third task for the conferee is determination of when the work is over and the service contract concluded. Much as the worker and client begin their work together by mutual consent through the conference process, so do they end their work together by mutual consent through the conference process. The ending is apparent when the tasks are accomplished, and/or when the worker and client agree that the work should be concluded.

As the client is central in defining the pressures on him at the outset, so is he central in determining the need to conclude or to reenter the process to work on additional needs or problems. If the client wishes to work on other struggles, the conferee engages him in developing a new service contract. Two skills are required for concluding the work: (1) preparing the client and (2) fostering independence.

PREPARING THE CLIENT Preparing the client refers to helping him come to terms with the impending termination of the helping relationship and his subsequent need to cope without the social worker. Social workers are privy to intimate revelations, especially when clients describe their problems and struggles, with all the accompanying emotion. Workers are also empathic and supportive of clients throughout the helping process. Thus, through their work together, close relationships develop, and the client may come to rely on the presence of the worker in his life. Under these circumstances it is not surprising that clients may experience ending as a loss. Termination, therefore, should not be sudden. The ending should be discussed throughout the working process, so that even if it is emotionally difficult, clients are somewhat prepared for it.

Two or three sessions before the ending, the worker should deliberately raise the idea that the work is almost finished and their time together is drawing to a close. When the ending session arrives, the worker should summarize their work together, including the emotional moments they shared, assess the outcome with the client, and engage the client in conversation about his strength and coping skills. Ultimately, she should acknowledge that she will miss the client. This frees the client to express thoughts and feelings as well. Then worker and client go their separate ways.

FOSTERING INDEPENDENCE Fostering independence refers to helping the client identify his strengths and abilities, so he can rely on these to move on with his life without the social worker's help. From the beginning of the worker/client relationship, the worker sees the client as an adequate person beset by problems that limit his functioning. Through their work together, the worker and the client try to reduce those limitations so that the client has access to more resources in his life. Especially as they end their work together, the worker tries to bolster the client's confidence in himself and his use of his new resources as he negotiates the systems of demand and relationship in his world on his own.

In some instances, the social worker may see many more needs and problems that could be worked on and may think that the client should contract with her again for further service. Once the worker tells the client the specifics of her perception, if his view is different or he is unwilling to continue, the worker accepts his construction of reality and proceeds with summarizing their work together and concluding the service contract. In her summary she supports the client's strength to cope and recognizes aloud her faith in his competence to make decisions about his own life. The conferee does not force her reality onto the client or use her relationship with him to substitute parts of her reality, subtly, for parts of his. Nor does she undermine his reality and his confidence in it. He *will* survive without her, and she must *let go*.

ILLUSTRATION OF THE TASK OF CONCLUDING THE WORK

In the following process recording, the conferees, worker and client, meet to conclude their work together. The situation is unique in that the client, a stroke victim, is still suffering from aphasia, limiting her ability to convey her thoughts in words that can be understood. She is leaving the rehabilitation center to live with her sister, so she will not be seeing this worker again.

Mrs. Walsh motioned for me to come sit by her, which I did. *"I know you'll be leaving tomorrow,"* I said. She just looked at me and nodded. I said, *"You've made a lot of progress in the four months you've been here."* She nodded again, then she reached for my hand, pressed it, and started to cry. *I held her hand.* She had a difficult time getting the words out for her next thought, so she just said, "Oh, Lordy," and looked at me. *I said, "We became pretty close during our work together."* She nodded. I said, *"I've seen you really improve, and I'll miss you very much."* She cried again, and *I got teary, too.* She said she was going to her sister's for a while, but that as soon as she could walk the stairs a little better, she wanted to go home. She showed me how well she could walk with just a cane. I said, *"That's fantastic! You're a strong woman,"* and she joked that she sure could lift fifteen pounds now (she lifts a hand weight as part of her therapy). We talked a little more, then I had to leave for an appointment. She cried a little when we hugged goodbye, but then she smiled and said, I'm on my way." *I agreed that she did a lot of hard work and that it really paid off.*

The worker as conferee began concluding the work by *giving information*, then *getting with feelings* nonverbally. She *summarized* both acts and feelings, and again *got with feelings* nonverbally. Later, when there was more talk, the social worker *got with feelings* verbally. Ultimately, she gave the client some final positive feedback and took her leave.

CONCLUSION

This chapter described the role of the conferee in terms of three major tasks. The initial task, translating pressures into tasks, takes place primarily during the contract phase and is once again prominent in the termination/reentry phase. Translating pressures into tasks was shown to be supported by two skills: (1) engagement with empathy and (2) identifying options.

The second task, facilitating decision making, is salient throughout the work. It requires two skills: encouraging the client to decide and confronting preconceptions. The third task, concluding the work, is primarily performed during the termination/reentry phase of the process and involves two skills: (1) preparing the client and (2) fostering independence.

The social worker always begins her work with the client in the role of conferee in Quadrant A. She also always ends her work with the client in the conferee role. In other words, it is with the social worker as conferee that the client has his first and last experience with the helping process. Thus competence and compassion are mandatory, for the conferee holds the client's first and last impression of social work help in her hands.

7

THE BROKER

IN SOCIAL WORK, the aim of the broker is to link clients with community resources. Brokerage presupposes complementarity of interest between the client in need and the agency that provides the needed service. Ideally, the broker uncovers and clears access routes between clients with their needs and resource distributors whose purpose it is to meet various needs. The broker functions at the level of least contest, for presumably service providers must have populations in need, just as clients must have some place to turn for particular services that the broader community has determined to disperse. This chapter describes the broker role. It identifies and illustrates the tasks of the broker and details the skills associated with each.

The role of broker is perhaps the oldest and best-known social work role, dating back to the friendly visitors and settlement-house workers of the late nineteenth and early twentieth centuries. These workers were expert in finding, alerting people to, interpreting, and creating resources for the poor and new immigrants. Imbued with the spirit of social reform, settlement-house workers brought immigrants to English classes, alerted young adults of the ghettos to upcoming civil-service tests, described the advantages of day nurseries and credit unions to the poor, and provided vacations in the country at the "milk farms," with lots of food, rest and clean air, for the mothers and children of the tenements. These early social workers also found "angels" to sponsor an aspiring young talent, told the ladies' auxiliaries where to distribute the holiday dinners, and worked with politicians to get garbage removed, streets lighted, and clinics established (Levine and Levine 1970; Wald 1915). Today, with the exception of hospital-discharge planning, brokerage has become so mundane that it is barely discussed in the professional literature as the complex and extremely important role it is. Now, policy and research articles dominate journals, and when direct service articles do appear, they tend to focus on forms of people-changing activity. Yet, the needs of people for goods and services have been and continue to be the primary concern in social work. Millions of children are hungry, the homeless population is growing, enormous numbers of people do not have health insurance, alcohol and drug addiction is rampant, elderly people living on social security cannot afford their prescription drugs, and all over the country jobs that pay a living wage are scarce. Brokerage is essential to their survival.

If resources were available in abundance, well known to all segments of the community, accessible without question and offered without stigmatization, the role of broker would be relatively easy. The practitioner would merely tell the resource seeker where the distributor is located. Since current social arrangements do not meet these conditions, however, the complexities of the broker role are enormous.

The supposed complementarity of interest between client need and agency service often has broken down, or perhaps it has never existed in today's world, where economic arrangements are based on scarcity. Thus brokerage demands more than merely linking needs with resources. Within the reality of current social arrangements for service delivery, two tasks are essential for the social worker in the broker role: learning the community and using the community.

THE TASKS OF THE BROKER

Competent brokerage is predicated on knowing the community, which involves continuous learning, and using one's knowledge of the community to identify providers of various resources. It also involves using knowledge of resources to link clients in need with the particular organizations that meet their needs. Each of these tasks is described below, and the requisite skills that enable the social worker to take the role of broker and perform the tasks are elaborated.

LEARNING THE COMMUNITY

Learning the community refers to acquiring knowledge of the organizational arrangements for service delivery, as well as the unofficial service system of informal outlets for people in need. Furthermore, it involves making and maintaining contact with individual workers within each of the formal and informal resources, as well as ongoing relationships with persons who have access to individuals who can be called upon in some instances of need. To this end, two skills are useful: (1) knowing the resources and (2) cultivating them.

KNOWING THE RESOURCES Knowing the resources is more complex than it may initially appear. Involved here is knowing what services are offered, how and to whom they are available, what demands are made upon the seeker, and other formal aspects of the service-delivery pattern. In addition, the social worker in the broker role has to have an informal reading of these delivery systems. The broker has to know what actually happens when people try to avail themselves of any particular resource. Moreover, it is not enough to know the range of resources available within the network of social service agencies. If brokers are to be effective, they must be familiar with resources offered under political auspices, by religious institutions, self-help organizations, schools, through health delivery systems, and all other enterprises in both the public and private sectors of the community. In short, brokers should be able to feel the pulse of the service community and have access to the formal and the informal resource networks at their fingertips. Further, they should constantly revise their inventory of resources and distributors in accord with information learned in day-to-day contacts.

Keeping one's own updated community resource database is essential. Knowledge about the diverse access routes to each resource is especially important, as is the name of a key individual within each agency. Such detailed information cannot be obtained from a directory of services. Entailed here is firsthand knowledge amassed from actual contact with the distributing agents and their resources. This means that one priority for the broker is that of becoming personally acquainted with related service centers and their personnel so that they know exactly what they are talking about when they suggest various resources to clients.

CULTIVATING THE RESOURCES In addition to having up-to-date knowledge of community resources, the broker must attend to and cultivate them in the long-term interest of clients. Brokers should maintain contact with workers in agencies. For example, lunch dates are excellent opportunities to maintain good relationships. The broker confronted with a critical need for a particular resource can tap these previously established channels rather than begin, at the point of crisis, the time-consuming search for, and the effort to open up, a connection for the first time.

USING THE COMMUNITY

Using the community involves referring people to existing resources, and inventing resources for them where none exists. This goes hand in hand with the principle of maximizing environmental supports, and it requires two skills: (1) making referrals and (2) creating resources.

MAKING REFERRALS Making referrals involves linking clients to resources. To make a referral, the social worker communicates with a particular resource distributor. Ideally, she contacts agency personnel with whom she has developed a good relationship. This is done to pave the way for the client's arrival. Later, she follows up to be sure the client received the required service. In addition, the worker tries to engage her contact at the agency in developing and maintaining a direct channel to that resource for those who need it. When this is successful, people in need of the service could access it directly—self-referred, with no unnecessary runaround.

The use of informal resources, while welcomed when formal ones are not forthcoming, often requires the broker to check them out carefully and thoroughly before making linkages. This prescreening avoids making referrals that may not be in the best interests of the client. In the following case record, the social worker attempts to do a thorough prescreening by going to a potential parolee's proposed home placement to see if the person there really wants the man to live with her. The worker wants to see if the situation seems likely to help the man stay out of jail. The person offering a home is the man's wife of eighteen months. The couple met through a local biker organization prior to his first incarceration. When he was paroled, she offered him a home placement, and they were married immediately after he moved in. He was returned to prison only two weeks after his marriage, charged with a new offense.

After some introductory remarks, *I told Mrs. Austring that her husband listed her as his home sponsor and her home as his placement.* She said, "Yeah, Johnny lived here before and everything went okay." "*No, it didn't,*" I said, "*he ended up going right back to prison, and according to the records, part of the reason was that he didn't stay here during his curfew when he was supposed to.*" "Well, yeah; you're right," she said, "but I mean Johnny and I got along all right. You see, I know Johnny, and he's got a bad drinking problem," she continued. *I nodded that I knew.* She said that Johnny would never do well until he gets help and that he had already been through D & A (a local drug and alcohol rehabilitation program), and AA before she ever met him. "So I don't know what to do to help him," she said. I said, "*It sounds real frustrating.*" "Yeah," she said. "What are we supposed to do if Johnny's got a problem but there ain't no place that can help him?" *I told her I would talk to him and if he wanted treatment for the drinking problem I'd try and find a program for him.* She said she goes to see him all the time and she knows he wants treatment.

We then went through a question-and-answer period where she wanted to know about curfew time, travel restrictions, etc. She asked a couple of questions about whether Johnny had to stay at her home if, once out, he could change his home placement. After she raised that several times, I said, *"Mrs. Austring, the way you keep asking me about him moving out … You're trying to tell me something, right?"* "Well," she said, "I think after he's out he's gonna want to move." *I asked her what made her think that,* and she said, "Ya see, he can stay here and all, this is his legit home placement, it's just that he already told me he wants a divorce. He's got this girl that comes to see him at prison, and that's who he was going to see when he missed all them curfew checks." *"Whew,"* I said, *"that hurts."* Then she started to cry.

The social worker began the interview with the informal resource provider by giving information. She then confronted Mrs. Austring's misrepresentation of what had occurred. The worker listened as Mrs. Austring spoke about her inability to help her husband with his drinking problem, then *reached for her feelings* of frustration. As the women continued to talk, the worker inferred that Mrs. Austring was trying and trying not to tell her something, so the worker gently *checked out her inference.* Then Mrs. Austring's whole story came tumbling out. At this point the worker wisely decided that Mrs. Austring's home was not an appropriate placement for her client.

Although Mrs. Austring was not the worker's client, she responded to Mrs. Austring's pain and was able to refer her to a community mental health center for counseling and grief work. It should be noted that because so much of brokerage takes place with the persons who most closely affect and are affected by the broker's clients, it behooves the broker to be available to them in at least a limited way. In social work, good brokerage involves respectful concern for all members of the client's resource network.

CREATING RESOURCES In accord with the principle of maximizing environmental supports, creating resources, the second skill for using the community, involves the broker in developing resources where none exist. Since brokers stand at the interface between client need and community resources, they must do whatever needs to be done to induce the forces within the environment to produce resources. In other words, if there are no resources to serve the client, then part of the broker role must include the creation of a resource. Details of resource creation are provided in the next section.

THE BROKER IN QUADRANTS A, B, AND C

The broker ordinarily operates in Quadrant C, but when creating resources can also operate in Quadrants A and B. The following discussion of resource creation in each quadrant is organized by frequency of use.

CREATING RESOURCES IN QUADRANT C: NEEDS AND NETWORKS

Most resource creation takes place in Quadrant C. It begins with an idea about need and how it might be met. Once a reasonable idea occurs to the worker, she must consider who else might be interested in it, and how those who are interested can be engaged as co-implementers, allies, or both. Sometimes the worker can organize others in the community to provide a particular resource systematically. In other instances, the worker can interpret the need to their own colleagues, organized groups in the community, legislators, or other funding sources in the interest of providing resources to meet client needs. The following process record illustrates the broker's use of the community to create a needed resource that would be able to exist independent of the worker who developed it. The work began in Quadrant A, as all direct practice does, with the worker taking the role of conferee. Note the sensitivity the worker demonstrates as she reaches for and gets with the angry and deeply painful feelings that the interaction generates in the client.

I got to Mrs. Cruz's about nine a.m. and knocked on the door. There was no response. I knocked louder, then waited. After several minutes Roberto, age seven, peeked his head through the door and said, "Hi," kind of sheepishly. I walked in and Roberto ran back to the couch, beside his five-year-old brother Esteban, who was watching TV. Mrs. Cruz was in bed. (I could see her bed from where I was standing).

While I waited for Mrs. Cruz to get out of bed, I asked Roberto if he was sick today (because he was not in school). He shook his head, no. At this point, Mrs. Cruz came into the room with a scowl on her face. She walked over to where Roberto and Esteban were sitting, passing me very abruptly. She stood between the TV and the children and raised her arm as if she were going to hit them, but didn't. Instead, she began to shout at Roberto, "You little S.O.B., I told you never to turn on this TV before you go to school in the morning! Why aren't you in school? You're going to get me in all kinds of trouble."

Roberto cringed and placed his arm over his head as if to ward off any blow that his mother might deliver. His face looked frightened. Then Mrs. Cruz turned to me and said, "He makes me so damn mad! He knows he's supposed to be in school. But there he sits, in front of that damned TV." Drawing closer to her and the children, I looked at her and said, "*It is frustrating when children don't do what you tell them to do.*" Then *I angled my body into the couch and sat down.* Mrs. Cruz sat down in a nearby chair. *I asked her if this happens often*, and she said yes, that these little brats know that they're supposed to be in school, but sometimes they just won't go. *I asked if they had trouble getting up in the mornings*, and she said no, that she puts them to bed early, so they get up early enough and they do dress to go, but then they sit here and watch TV instead. Then *I asked if she was able to get up with the boys in the morning*. She said she didn't see why she should be expected to get up when she's tired from taking care of the girls (ages eighteen months and three years) all day and all night, too, because neither of them sleeps through the night. I said, "*Two little ones who don't let you sleep plus attending to the boys can really keep you hopping!*" "They do," she said, "I'm always tired."

The worker, still in Quadrant A as conferee, began by *getting with the powerful feelings* Mrs. Cruz had expressed. She then *positioned* herself and began to *reach for information*. When her third question seemed to trigger more strong affect, she temporarily abandoned her quest for information and *reached for the client's feelings*.

As the interaction continues, worker attention to client feelings continues. When her *checking out of an inference* prompts Mrs. Cruz to verbalize some painful childhood memories, the worker listens, then reaches for that pain. After the client acknowledges the hurt she still feels, her nonverbal behavior suggests the need for a "time out," a subtle cue that does not escape the worker's notice. In response, the worker *waits silently* until Mrs. Cruz indicates that she is ready to move on.

After a brief silence, *I said it seemed like the boys needed some help getting out in the morning*. Immediately, Mrs. Cruz said, "I didn't have anybody to help me when I was little and I did the things I was supposed to do. If I didn't, I got the shit beat out of me." She grabbed her cigarettes. Her body got rigid and her facial expression was taut. "*Just remembering that can make you feel hurt and angry*," I said. "Yeah," she said, "and I'll never forgive them for it either." There was a long silence while she stared off in space. I waited.

When she turned her head back to me, *I said that since caring for the little girls even during the night was so exhausting, maybe we could get a morning helper to come in for an hour each school morning and see the boys off*. She looked kind of wary and asked me what I meant. *I said maybe I could get an early riser who's retired from work to volunteer*. Her look changed from wary to surprised. When I *called attention to that*, she laughed and said all her other workers figure she's just lazy and threaten to take the boys away from her. *I told her she didn't seem lazy to me, that it seems to me that she has an exhausting schedule and could use some help with it*. Then *I asked her if she wanted me to see if I could get someone* and she said that would be awesome. I said, "*No guarantees, but I'll do what I can and get back to you as soon as possible*. She asked me if I'd like some coffee before I left.

> When Mrs. Cruz seemed ready to move on, the social worker suggested a task to relieve some of the pressure on her—a morning helper. This surprised Mrs. Cruz. Still very attentive to feelings, the worker reached for that surprise and gave the client perhaps the most important kind of opinion-type information that social workers can give, the kind that can begin to restore some dignity where too many self-righteous feet have trampled it almost to death. And it is only after this that Mrs. Cruz tentatively reached out.

In the afternoon, the social worker, having made a contract with Mrs. Cruz, proceeded to the follow the demands of the client task. First, in Quadrant A, she looked beyond Mrs. Cruz to see if others in her caseload could also benefit from morning help, and found two other families which, when called, were pleased and relieved to think such help could be in the offing. She then took the role of broker in Quadrant C and called a worker whom she had cultivated at the local senior citizen center. She said that she was seeking at least one volunteer, but hoped to find three. The worker at the senior citizen center said that several people were looking for volunteer work that would be helpful to other people, and that some of the women might find this an ideal situation for them. The broker then asked if they could jointly meet with interested people, and they arranged a date and time. Six women came to the meeting, one who was prepared to help Mrs. Cruz starting the following morning, two others who could start with the broker's other two families starting the following week, and three hoping to "be assigned" to families they could help. The broker suggested that they form a Family Helpers group since, for example, many families could use after-school childcare. And, consistent with the principle of maximizing environmental supports, the broker enlisted the worker at the senior citizens' center to meet with the Family Helpers volunteers monthly, recruit additional helpers, and coordinate the volunteer project. The broker obtained morning help for her client, Mrs. Cruz, *and had created a resource* that could function without her from which other families could get help.

Too many social workers (and many other people, including politicians) see personal struggles like Mrs. Cruz's as a function of inadequate character traits or individual irresponsibility. They work, usually in vain, to change the people, as if Mrs. Cruz could be awake day and night if she only attended parenting classes or responded positively to threats to remove her sons who are clean, well-fed, appropriately clothed, and loved. Much of the taxpaying population has been led to *blame the victim* instead of providing the often small bits of help and support to end their victimhood. When individuals are blamed for universal gaps in the socioeconomic system, government is freed from responsibility to respond with money and programs to stem the flood of *predictable* need. Children should not go to bed hungry in America. Nor should adults. Parents who love their children should not lose them to the state because their personal resources are inadequate to provide for their basic needs. Rather, help to meet the missing basic needs should be provided, including housing, food and clothing. And not spottily, by charities.

CREATING RESOURCES IN QUADRANT A: SELF-HELP SYSTEMS AND TRADE UNITS

Whether by choice or by default, whether preferred by clients over alternative service systems or necessitated by the lack of alternatives, there are times when the needs of clients can be served through self-help structures. At these times the social worker brings the requisite resource systems into existence, and because of this the worker's activity can be properly be called brokerage.

While most brokerage and resource creation takes place in Quadrant C, as in the preceding example, when creating self-help systems and trade units, the broker engages clients in their own behalf, thus she is working in Quadrant A. The following example shows the social worker as broker in Quadrant A, where she creates a self-help system. The context is a high-rise retirement community complex. The social worker is from the senior citizens' program of the local community ministries. As in all instances of direct practice, the worker initially takes the role of conferee in Quadrant A.

I went to see Mrs. Carter to tell her about the place I found that will give her a free eye examination, and while I was there, she told me about another problem—not being able to go to the park anymore. Her legs had gotten worse so that now she has to use crutches. She said she used to enjoy sitting in the park with her neighbors and watching children play. I asked her what other people in the building with canes or walkers, or even wheelchairs, do about getting out for some air and socializing in the park. She said she thought maybe relatives sometimes came and took them out.

I asked her if she knew other residents who wanted to go out but were similarly hampered. She knew of several and told me about them. She also said there were some in wheelchairs, perfectly able to take care of themselves except they weren't strong enough to wheel themselves to the park. And then there were the people who just weren't steady enough on their feet.

I asked her if, instead of using crutches, she could hold onto and push a wheelchair. She said she certainly could, that her arms were strong. So I said maybe we could get her and some others like her together with some people in wheelchairs, and they could take each other to the park. She seemed delighted with the idea. She gave me a list of the people who might be interested, and I started knocking on doors that evening.

In three days we had a meeting in the community room with more than fifteen enthusiastic people. When one of the "walking people" sadly noted that they out-numbered the "wheelchair people," one of the wheelchair people said she didn't mind going to the park twice. In fact, she said she'd like to go to the park in both the morning and the afternoon anyway. Most of the wheelchair people agreed that two trips was no problem at all.

They decided to meet in the community room Monday morning and pair off for the first trip. I said I'd go with them the first few times if they wanted me to, and they said they didn't need me, that they would do just fine by themselves.

A few weeks later, when I was there helping some new residents fill out social security forms, Mr. Taggart, one of the "wheelchair people," told me they were doing just fine with their trips to the park, and were now even getting together and having dinner parties on Saturday nights. He also said he hasn't felt this good about life in a long time. He patted my hand. I said I was real glad for all of them.

A special form of brokerage in Quadrant A involves the creation of trade units—informal bartering structures of two or more people through which participants meet each other's needs. The creation of such structures is predi-cated on the social worker's recognition that every client is not only a person in need; every client is also a person with resources. It is further predicated on the assumption that social workers make it a matter of course to know what resources their clients have to offer, thereby making it possible to identify potential trade units. For example, if the worker knows that a disabled client who is a great cook needs some general repairs around his house, she tries to identify someone capable of general household repairs who would enjoy some home-cooked meals. With both of their approval, she makes a match to create a mutually beneficial trade unit, in accord with the principle of maximizing environmental supports.

Trade units need not be limited to pairs of persons. One structure a social worker created involved Mrs. Mervine who needed three things: transporta-tion to medical appointments, access to less expensive food than she could get at the local grocery, and a source of clothing alteration so that her younger children could wear outfits outgrown by her older children. The worker knew that this woman enjoyed children and was good at childcare. The worker also knew of three women (Mrs. Felton, Mrs. Clark, and Mrs. Washington) who worked outside the home and needed after-school childcare. Each of these women could meet one of the three things Mrs. Mervine needed. Mrs. Felton was good with a sewing machine and altered clothing for her own children.

Mrs. Clark could offer transportation to medical appointments, and Mrs. Washington, who did her own weekly shopping at a warehouse outlet market on the other side of town could easily take Mrs. Mervine with her. With their permission, the worker introduced the women to each other, and they all felt relieved. Thus, a trade unit comprising three bartering pairs with one person belonging to all three structures was created, and the pressing needs of four persons were able to be met.

CREATING RESOURCES IN QUADRANT B: COOPERATIVES

In Quadrant B, the structures the broker creates are resource cooperatives intended to benefit both those involved in creating and maintaining them *and* those who have similar needs. A classic example of this is the food co-op, an enterprise in cutting food costs through bulk purchasing from wholesale distributors. Ordinarily, the broker works with a small cadre of families to develop and run a food co-op, making the goods available to the larger neighborhood. If the families that did the work involved in establishing the system were the only ones to benefit from it, the creation would more properly be called a Quadrant A self-help structure. When the intended beneficiaries extend beyond those persons with whom the broker is directly engaged, however, the project is a resource cooperative and the broker's activity is rightly placed in Quadrant B.

Resource cooperatives can be developed for many different goods and services and can provide for small and large geographic areas. Depending on the nature of the goods or services and the size of the area to be served, the social worker may have to take both the broker and the community organizer roles. In the following example, a social worker helps some of the residents in a subsidized housing project develop and run a "block watch" for the protection of everyone who lives there.

Somebody stole Mr. Collier's TV set and he was really upset. He told me he'd been robbed three other times that month, but this time it was the worst because he relied on that TV to keep him company as well as entertainment. I told him I'd keep an eye out for someone who is buying a new TV and may be willing to give up their old one, and he said he'd be real grateful for that.

I asked him if he knew what a "Neighborhood Watch" program was. He didn't, so I described it to him and he thought it was a good idea. Then I asked him if he thought some of the people who live in the neighborhood would volunteer to become part of it, and he said not him because he's too old. He told me to talk to the young ones. I asked him to give me some names and addresses, but he said he didn't want to get involved.

On the way out I saw some little kids playing, so I asked them where they lived and I went to the door one of the little boys pointed to. I told the woman who I was, and she said she had seen me around there before and asked what I wanted with her. Without using his name, I told her about Mr. Collier and what "Neighborhood Watch" was all about. I told her it involved watching other people's houses and notifying neighbors and the police of suspicious activities. I said that people with police scanners could be particularly helpful, because they could notify neighbors of reported criminal activity. Those with scanners would call a couple of others who would each alert still others, and so on. I asked if she or her husband and any others she knew might be interested in participating. She said she didn't have a husband, but her brother lived around the corner and he had a police scanner.

By the time I found her brother, Mr. Williams, and told him everything, too, it was beginning to get dark and I wanted to leave and come another day. Mr. Williams wanted me to tell some other men he knew about the neighborhood watch idea, though, so he told me he'd walk me to my car later and see that I got off all right. I agreed to stay, and he phoned up some friends and invited them over.

Not everyone he called could come, but three men did come, and two of them had wives and children they wanted to be sure were safe. All four men were interested, and they talked about some other people they might be able to get, some of whom had scanners. I asked them when they thought they could get all the people together, and since they weren't sure, I gave them my number so they could call me to come organize it. About a week later, they called me to set it up, which I did.

By the time the meeting was over, they were all organized, a telephone tree had been created, and they were ready to keep tabs on a six-square-block area. I agreed to talk to residents outside that area about getting together and doing the same thing.

CONCLUSION

The broker has two major tasks: learning the community and using the community. The primary skills involved in learning the community are knowing the resources and cultivating them. Using the community requires the broker to make referrals and create resources where none currently exist. Resources are usually created in Quadrant C, but there are times when human needs can be met only through resources created in Quadrant A. Less frequent, but broader in scope and potential, are resources the broker creates in Quadrant B.

8

THE MEDIATOR

MEDIATING REFERS TO "intervention in disputes between parties to help them reconcile differences, find compromises, or reach mutually satisfactory agreements" (Barker 1999:295). This chapter describes the tasks and skills that constitute the role.

Mediating is based on the concept of mutual aid and presumes that a common bond exists between persons in conflict. The common bond may be a *complementary* one, as the bond between clients with their need for a particular service and an agency organized to provide that service to persons who need it. Or the common bond may be an *identical* one, as that among all members of a support group who need each other for comfort and help in coping with their loss of a child. Whether the common bond is complementary or identical, when conflict arises between or among the persons involved, it is presumed that those in conflict have lost sight of their need for each other. When this is the case, the social worker takes the role of mediator.

THE TASKS OF THE MEDIATOR

When conflict arises and common ground is obscured, the conflicting persons cannot meet each other's needs. It is the aim of the mediator to help those in conflict to rediscover their common ground, which is the basis of their need for each other. Doing so frees them to contribute to each other's welfare. To achieve this aim, the mediator must perform two salient tasks: (1) identifying common ground and (2) helping each person reach out to the other.

IDENTIFYING COMMON GROUND

Common ground is a point of reference belonging to more than one person. It is an area of overlap between the self-interest of one person and the self-interest of another person. Where it can be recognized, it constitutes the basis of people's need for each other and their motive for cooperative action.

Unfortunately, common ground may become obscured by the complexities of everyday life. Conflicting interests can blur long-range mutual interest. When the social worker takes the role of mediator in order to implement the complementarity or identity of interest between persons in conflict, she must begin by recognizing the point at which their apparently different self-interests converge. Identifying the common ground requires the mediator to use three skills: (1) tapping into motives for cooperating, (2) introducing motives, and (3) confronting obstacles.

TAPPING INTO MOTIVES FOR COOPERATING Tapping into motives for cooperating refers to analyzing potentially generative values and interests of each of the persons involved in the conflict and choosing those that relate to the situation at hand. For example, a social worker in the role of broker refers her client to a service provider. Because of volume, the client waits three hours to see a worker at the agency to which he was referred. When it is finally his turn, out of sheer frustration, the client yells at the worker, who retaliates by refusing to process the application forms for his disability insurance. When the broker calls the client the next day to see if service was provided, he tells her what happened and asks her to help him. She then takes the role of mediator.

In her role as mediator, the social worker meets with the angry worker at the disability office and points out to her that, having taken a job to help disabled people, she must care very much about their well-being, that and she is clearly a compassionate person. She then invites her to think about her reasons for such compassion. Might someone close to her be disabled? Could this be the reason she involves herself so deeply in disabled people's needs, or is there another reason? The worker tells the mediator she went to school with two disabled children and has always wanted to help people. The mediator then says that surely, feeling the way she does, she will at least meet with the man so that the mediator can help him talk to her about what happened from his perspective as well as help her tell him what she wants to. The worker agrees to the meeting. Tapping into motives for cooperating tends to bring out the best in people, and is thus an extremely important skill for the social worker to master in order to bring the parties to the table.

INTRODUCING MOTIVES Introducing motives refers to informing each party to the other party's motivation for agreeing to the conversation they are about to have. Motives for cooperating with others constitute common ground; thus, when the mediator engages both persons involved, she introduces each person's motives for coming together to deal with the conflict. That is to say, she clarifies each person's stake in the engagement. She also clarifies her role, indicating that she will help them do what they came together to do, and that her interest is in their encounter rather than in any particular outcome. She tells them that she sides with neither one person nor the other, but stands between them, equally concerned about both, and believing that their need to help each other is strong enough to triumph over the obstacles that have been blocking that from happening. For example, when the disability worker and the client sit down together, the mediator tells the client that the worker agreed to the meeting because she cares deeply about the welfare of people with disabilities. Then she tells the worker that the client agreed to meet because he desperately needs disability insurance.

CONFRONTING OBSTACLES Confronting obstacles refers to verbalizing whatever seems to be blocking progress toward a mutually agreed upon outcome. As two persons work to effect cooperative action, many obstacles can arise to block valid communication. Variables such as culturally based ethics, norms, and personal needs, for example, can intervene to obscure the common ground further. Norms against comparing salaries can prevent employees from discovering and substantiating the existence of inequities, thereby hindering united action to rectify them. Likewise, norms that prohibit the open communication of emotion prevent essential information from being exchanged and can render a potentially meaningful relationship sterile. Problems of authority may also become obstacles to valid communication and reciprocal help when they operate just beneath the surface. Manifest efforts to cooperate both hide and serve as a medium through which a counterproductive game of who's-on-top is played.

A highly pervasive obstacle to arriving at mutually satisfying resolutions to conflicts involves reputational concerns—primarily loss of face. People can go to great lengths in order to save face, even when the costs to them are very high. If someone is reputed to be a person who never backs down or maintains zero tolerance, for example, and if that person places a high value on this reputation, motivation to save face may well outweigh motivation to cooperate, if cooperation is construed as backing down.

When obstacles such as these subvert authentic efforts to cooperate, the mediator should verbalize the obstacle and challenge both people to deal with it openly and honestly. She should point to the common ground and ask each if his need for the other is sufficiently strong to motivate him to find a way around or through the obstacle. In other words, the mediator forces underlying issues to the surface where they can be tackled with purpose and affect.

EXAMPLE: THE TASK OF IDENTIFYING COMMON GROUND

The following process record illustrates the task of identifying common ground. A social worker in a prison takes the role of mediator to help an inmate and a volunteer who teaches hairdressing rediscover their complementary need for each other and arrive at a mutually beneficial resolution to their conflict.

The social worker opens the conversation by *reaching for information* with an open-ended question, then *gets with the feelings* the client expresses. To explore what happened, the social worker again asks an open-ended question. After the client describes the situation, the worker gives her some relevant information, asks a close-ended question to obtain an important detail, then gives information again, this time outlining what it is that she can do to help.

Chris came in and sat down. "Hi," I said, "*What's up?*" "Things are all coming down on me," she said. I said, "*That's terrible.*" "Yeah," she said, "I messed up but good." "*How?*" I asked. "I went off on Mrs. Geery and she threw me out of the hairdressing program. I really *need* to finish hair school to make parole. And I only have a month and a half to go before I qualify to take the test this year. Can you get me back in? I really *need* it. I said, "*It's up to Mrs. Geery, not me; so I can't get you back in it.*" She started to cry. "So what am I gonna do?" "*I asked her if she had talked to Mrs. Geery since the explosion,* and she said, "How could I? I am *so* out of her life after the names I laid on her. I'm hoping you can talk to her."

I told Chris that what I can do, if she wants me to, is ask Mrs. Geery to sit down and talk with her about what happened and how bad you want to get back in the program. "Then," I said, "*if you're both willing, I can set up a meeting between the two of you and try to help you talk to each other.*" "I'll do anything to get back in," she said.

Next, the worker speaks with Mrs. Geery. In the following interaction, the worker starts by giving relevant information, then listens supportively. Although initially averse to it, Mrs. Geery agrees when the worker reminds her of her stake in the encounter, her motivation for agreeing to talk with Chris, and challenges her to act on it.

I went to see Mrs. Geery and told her about Chris coming to see me and what I said to her. "Look," Mrs. Geery said, "I come here without getting paid, and I work hard to help these girls learn a vocation they can count on when they get out. I even get most of them licensed. But I don't put up with abuse. The girls know I don't. And let me tell you, Chris was totally abusive when I kicked her out. Did she tell you the language she used and the names she called me?" *Not exactly,"* I said, *"but she told me she called you names."* "She did, huh," Mrs. Geery said with her eyebrows raised in a surprised look, "She's got quite a mouth on her!" *"Yeah,"* I agreed, *"and you've worked with a lot of the angry women we've had here over the years."* "That's right," she said, "I have." *"And you turned a lot of them around as I hear it,"* I said. "That's right, too," she said, then, "Oh, I see what you're getting at. Well it won't work."

"You mean your pride in turning around angry women and sending them out with a vocation isn't strong enough to get you to just sit down with Chris and talk about what happened and how it happened and what you were feeling and what she was feeling?" I asked with a smile. She smiled, too, and said she'd talk with Chris, but that I shouldn't expect her to take Chris back. I assured her that was entirely up to her, that my concern was that they talk together, not what they decided.

Following these individual meetings, the social worker arranged a joint meeting. The excerpt below shows the process of that meeting and the way in which the worker mediated the engagement. Note the way in which the social worker as mediator connects the two persons on a feeling level. More will be said about this later.

The mediator starts the session by *summarizing the reason each participant agreed to meet with the other (their need for each other, which is their common ground) and asks if these reasons are accurate.* When talk between Chris and Mrs. Geery begins, the worker listens and *redirects* what they say to her, instead of to each other, to the person for whom the message is actually intended. She does not help them avoid each other by becoming their conduit. At an appropriate moment, the worker *reaches for Mrs. Geery's feelings* and *redirects* her affective expression to Chris. She then tries to *create an empathic connection* from Chris to Mrs. Geery, and *redirects* Chris's acknowledgment. Chris and Mrs. Geery do the rest.

I set up a meeting, and when all three of us got together, *I looked at Chris and said, "You're here because you want a chance to talk with Mrs. Geery about the blow-up: what you were thinking and feeling and some of your thoughts and feelings since then. Is that right?"* She nodded. *Then I turned to Mrs. Geery and said, "And you agreed to come and listen to what Chris has to say, mainly because you've turned around a lot of angry women since you've been here and you're proud of that; it means a lot to you."* "It certainly does," she said. "And this is the first time any of my women called me vile names, and in my own classroom, in front of everybody there!" She was looking at me when she spoke, so *I asked her to tell that to Chris.* She turned to Chris and said, "I don't take abuse from anybody!" Chris looked down and said in a small voice, "But you yelled at me first." "Yes, I did," Mrs. Geery said, "because you were making the same mistake with that hair color that you made all last week—after I spent so much time going over it again and again with you. I had to get your attention. But I never called you names and I never cussed you." Then there was silence.

Chris broke the silence. She looked at me and asked, "What am I going to do? That's my future down the drain." *I told her to tell that to Mrs. Geery.* She turned to Mrs. Geery and said that the hair school was all she had. Mrs. Geery told her she should have thought about that before she sounded off, cussing and calling names. I looked at Mrs. Geery and said, "*Being called names can really hurt.*" "It did hurt," she said to me. "I felt this big," she said, holding her thumb and forefinger about an inch apart. "*Tell Chris,*" *I said, nodding.* Turning to Chris she said, "You cut me down to nothing." *I asked Chris if she ever felt like Mrs. Geery did, chopped down to nothing.* She looked at me and nodded. *I motioned her to tell Mrs. Geery,* and she did. She told her that her husband used to cut her down bad and smack her around, right in front of her parents and her children. Instantly, Mrs. Geery looked at Chris and said, "Don't you ever let him or anybody else do that to you again!" Chris looked a little startled. "Nobody has a right to humiliate you," Mrs. Geery continued, "and that's what it is, being humiliated. Chris got a little teary and nodded. There was another silence.

This time, Mrs. Geery broke the silence. She said, in a kind of sarcastic tone, "So now you expect me to take you back in the program." "I hope you will," Chris said softly. "Well I'm not going to do that. I've got my pride, and I don't want anybody to get the idea that they can treat me the way you did. The only way I'll take you back is for you to spend the next month washing heads and sweeping up only. If you're willing to do that, and you do it well, when the month is up I'll take you back in the program and work with you on color again." Chris nodded and said, "I'll do it; thanks—and I really am sorry."

HELPING EACH PERSON REACH OUT TO THE OTHER

Once common ground has been established and reinforced for both persons during a joint meeting, the mediator is then required to facilitate the flow of conversation. Often this entails giving information relevant to the situation which one or neither person may have, and performing a sequence of acts to bring about mutual compassion. These are the two skills essential to helping each person reach out to the other for mutual self-fulfillment: (1) giving information and (2) developing mutual compassion.

GIVING INFORMATION Giving information refers to sharing all material that is relevant with both parties and asking them to do likewise. The extent to which people can make decisions about what to do depends largely upon the amount and kind of information (ideas, feelings, opinions) they have regarding the situation in which they are involved. In other words, information is a resource and, like any other resource, when it is differentially distributed, it produces power differentials.

When one of two persons in conflict possesses relevant information that the other does not, the social worker, in the role of mediator, should help establish parity. This is done either by asking one person to share additional information with the other, or by the worker's providing it to the other person. If the worker has access to relevant information that neither of the persons have, she should provide both with the information so they will be neither dependent upon her every step of the way nor forced to make decisions without taking into account all possible considerations.

When the mediator provides ideas, feelings, suggestions and opinions, it is important that she present these as her own, rather than as "truth," and she should only provide information that has direct bearing on the issue at hand. Opinions presented as "facts" serve to distort and manipulate, and information that is not relevant, if it is heard at all, can divert the attention of the people from the particular piece of work they came together with the mediator to do. If information is presently honestly and in a suitable manner, it can increase the power of people to exercise some measure of control over their relatedness to others and the outcome of this relatedness to their individual lives.

DEVELOPING MUTUAL COMPASSION Developing mutual compassion refers to connecting persons on a feeling level. Many of the mutually satisfying outcomes of mediating, such as in the example at the prison-based hair school, seems to flow from the social worker's use of all or a part of a particular sequence of acts through which mutual compassion is developed. This sequential pattern consists of (1) reaching for feelings, (2) redirecting them, (3) trying to create an empathic connection, and (4) redirecting the response. Mutual compassion develops through these. The sequence is used after the worker has reiterated the common ground and gotten agreement to it from the persons in conflict, and after they have done some talking with each other.

Usually the sequence begins with the worker reaching for the feelings of one of the people. Since the worker is the one who invited that person to express feelings, the person would understandably address her feeling response to the worker. At this point the worker would not get with the person's feelings as she would do if she were meeting with the person individually. Instead, she asks the person to express the feelings to the other person. Once she has done this, the social worker immediately tries to create an empathic connection from the other person to the person who has just expressed her feelings. The worker as mediator does this by asking the other person a question such as, "When have you felt a little bit like Amanda did at that moment?" When the other person starts to talk about an instance in which she had feelings similar to Amanda's, she tends to tell it to the worker, again, because the worker is the one who asked her the question. So now the worker asks her to tell her story to Amanda.

This sequential pattern of reaching for feelings, redirecting them, creating an empathic connection, then redirecting it, is then repeated with regard to the other person's feelings. People seem to be more responsive to and have more compassion for each other when their own feelings are attended to with genuine concern and their capacity for empathy with each other is tapped.

EXAMPLE: HELPING EACH PERSON REACH OUT TO THE OTHER

In the following recording, the social worker as mediator calls upon the sequence for developing mutual compassion, described above, as she tries to help an AIDS victim and his estranged parents talk to each other about their pain. Initially, the worker takes the role of conferee in Quadrant A and makes a service contract with the AIDS victim. The task is to call his parents. Note that, as mediator, following her phone encounter with his parents, she gives him all the information about her interaction with them.

Nick's parents haven't spoken to him since he told them he was gay about nine years ago. Now he's dying, and he thinks that maybe if they know that, they'll come to the hospice to say goodbye. When I asked him if he had tried to call them over the years he said yes, but when they heard his voice, they hung up. He says that once he tried from the hospital, but they hung up before he could tell them he was in the hospital. I asked if he had written to them, and he said that he tried that, too, several times, but the letters were returned, unopened. He asked me if I would call them and tell them, and I said I would.

When I called and told his parents, his mother burst out crying and his father told me not to call and upset Mrs. Wayne again. Then he hung up. I didn't even get to leave my phone number. Apparently they have caller ID, though, because about forty minutes later, his mother called me back and said they'd come on Sunday.

I told Nick the whole thing: the call I made, his parents' responses, and his mother's call back. He seemed excited, but scared, too. I commented on that, and he agreed. He asked me if I would be there with him when they come, and I said I would. I told him that I would try to help him and his parents talk to each other about what they're thinking and feeling. I didn't have to ask the elder Waynes if it was okay for me to be there because Mrs. Wayne already told me on the phone that they'd like me to be there if I could.

The worker accepts Mrs. Wayne's request that she be present as her service contract with the Waynes, but she neither told them what her role would be nor explicitly checked any of it out with Mr. Wayne. As seen in the following interaction, this latter omission becomes problematic as soon as the transaction begins.

I met the Waynes in the lobby and showed them to Nick's room. They both seemed a bit nervous. Just outside the door, they hesitated. "*A first meeting after nine years of silence can be frightening,*" I said, quietly. Mrs. Wayne nodded, swallowed hard, and pushed the door open. I held the door for Mr. Wayne and followed him in. For a few moments there was dead silence, then Nick said, "Hi." They looked at him but said nothing. I motioned them over to the three chairs I had put in a semicircle to Nick's bed. Mrs. Wayne sat down. When I motioned Mr. Wayne over a second time, he said, "No, this is *her* visit. I'll just stand back here." "Dad," Nick said to him. Mr. Wayne looked down at the floor and didn't respond. I made a quick decision to let that be for now and dragged one of the chairs over to the door so Mr. Wayne could sit. Then I sat down next to Mrs. Wayne. "You're thin," Mrs. Wayne said to Nick. "Yeah," Nick replied. Silence. Mrs. Wayne turned to me and said, "I don't know what to say to him." "Tell him that," I replied. She gave an embarrassed smile, then told Nick she didn't know what to say to him. He told her she doesn't have to say anything, that just being here is enough. He extended his hand. "Is it okay to touch him?" she asked me. "Yes," I said, you won't get AIDS from holding his hand." "I wouldn't ask you to do anything that would hurt you, Mom," Nick said to her. "The hell you wouldn't!" Mr. Wayne shouted from his spot near the door. He was standing up now. "Bud ... "Mrs. Wayne began. "No," Mr. Wayne interrupted. Then there was a long, loud silence while Mr. Wayne and Nick stared at each other.

The worker reached for the Waynes' feelings as they hesitated outside their son's door, and once inside she moved to position everyone for the interaction to come. But her oversight during the contract phase came home to roost. She could not hold Mr. Wayne to any prior agreement since she did not have a service contract with him. She couldn't say, for example, "Mr. Wayne, you said you wanted to see your son one more time and say your final goodbye. Is your commitment to that strong enough to motivate you to work around the obstacle your anger is creating right now?" Apparently recognizing she could not challenge his commitment because she hadn't obtained it in advance, she quickly assessed the potential consequences of her remaining choices and decided to allow Mr. Wayne to be present, yet physically distant. And at least up to this point she had chosen not to engage him. The worker restricted her attention to Mrs. Wayne and Nick, helping Mrs. Wayne speak directly to Nick by redirecting her message and providing information.

When Mr. Wayne sat down again, Nick turned to his mother and asked her how she had been doing. She said she had been well, even doing some yoga and water aerobics. This was followed by some talk about Nick's condition and what the various physicians said. Then Mrs. Wayne said, "There's no cure, is there. That's why you're here, isn't it." Nick nodded his head, yes. Her eyes filled with tears. *"You're crying,"* I said to her. "Yes," she said, "I don't want him to die." *"Tell Nick that,"* I said softly. "Oh, Nicky," she sobbed, tightening her grip in his hand, "I don't want you to die." Nick patted her hand. Then there was more silence.

Nick broke the silence. "I was afraid you wouldn't come, Mom," he said. "I was afraid you stopped loving me." She looked at him. "You can't imagine what you did to us. We thought we knew you. We had such dreams." Her voice broke a little. *"Shattered dreams can be so painful,"* I said. She nodded. *"Nick,"* I said, *"When have you felt a little bit like your mother has—pain when a dream falls apart?"* Nick nodded. *"Tell her about it,"* I said. "Mom, remember, I was first in my class in med school?" he began. "How could I forget?" she said. "Well," he continued, "I didn't get the residency at the Mayo Clinic. Even Massachusetts General turned me down. I felt betrayed, Mom. I still do. The pain hasn't gone away." She looked at him sadly. "I'm sorry, Nicky. You wanted that so much … and my pain, it never goes away, either."

At that moment, Mr. Wayne started to walk out of the room. "Dad," Nick said, "Please don't leave." Mr. Wayne pushed the door open and turned to go. I asked him to wait a minute. *"Nick,"* I said, *"Tell your father how his walking out makes you feel."* "I feel like he can't … " Nick began. *"Tell him,"* I interrupted. "I feel like you can't stand me, like you wish I was never born, and it hurts like hell." Nick told him. *"Mr. Wayne, how does what Nick just said make you feel?"* I asked. "There's nothing he can say that matters to me," Mr. Wayne said. *"But you're here!"* I said to him. "Only to bring my wife," he replied. *"You could have waited in the lobby,"* I said, *"or just outside this door. But you chose to be in this room."* "I'm here for my wife, he said; that's all." "Dad," Nick said, I think you came to see me too, and I'm glad you did. I want you to know I love you." "You don't know what love is!" Mr. Wayne responded, and left the room.

In the preceding sequence, the mediator reached for Mrs. Wayne's feelings, and when she responded, the worker redirected her message to Nick. Shortly thereafter, the mediator again reached for Mrs. Wayne's feelings, but this time, after Mrs. Wayne responded the worker tried to create an empathic connection from Nick to Mrs. Wayne, and redirected his message to her. A moment later, Mr. Wayne started to leave; Nick spoke to him, but Mr. Wayne did not respond. The worker then reached for affective information from Nick, and in the same statement, redirected Nick's message to his father. She followed this by reaching for affective information from the father, confronting his distortion, and confronting it a second time when he continued to deny his feelings.

The social worker reaches for Nick's feelings, then redirects his message to his mother.

As soon as the door closed, Mrs. Wayne said, "You have to forgive him, Nicky. He's still so hurt and angry." "I know he is, Mom," said Nick; "how about you?" "I guess I am, too," she said. *"What about you, Nick?"* I said. *"Being rejected by parents can hurt a lot—and make you very angry."* "I used to feel that way," he said. "Tell your mother," I said. "Mom," Nick said, I don't have time to be angry." She kissed his hand and cried. He lay back, exhausted.

Nick died five days later. Both of his parents were in the room.

THE MEDIATOR IN QUADRANTS A AND C

When the social worker is mediating between conflicting members of a client group, she is working in Quadrant A. Since all of the group members are clients, and only those people are the ultimate intended beneficiaries of her interventions, Quadrant A is where she is doing her work. Similarly, when a client and a nonclient are in conflict, while meeting with the client to listen and understand the client's perspective on the situation and help him decide whether he wants to talk with the nonclient with whom he has a conflict, and whether he wants the worker to mediate that conversation, the worker is in Quadrant A.

If the client does want to try to work out a mutually satisfactory resolution with the nonclient and does want the worker to mediate that conversation, then the worker has to approach the nonclient about whether that person will meet with his client. When the worker does meet with the nonclient, she in working as a mediator in Quadrant C, where work with others for the benefit of specific clients is appropriately housed.

When actually mediating the conversation between client and nonclient, however, the social worker is standing on the line (horizontal dimension) between Quadrant A and Quadrant C. Her concern is with the interaction between the two parties; thus she has a foot in each of the two quadrants.

CONCLUSION

This chapter has defined mediating as helping people resolve their disputes with each other and discussed the tasks of the mediator as being twofold: identifying common ground, and helping people reach out to each other. The three skills necessary for identifying common ground were specified as (1) tapping into motives for cooperating, (2) introducing motives, and (3) confronting obstacles. To help people reach out to each other, two skills were described: (1) giving information and (2) developing mutual compassion. For this latter skill, we suggested a repetitive four-act sequence.

We saw that the role of the mediator was located in Quadrant A when disputes were among members of a client group, and primarily on the line between Quadrants A and C when the disputes were between a client and a nonclient. That is to say, the worker had one foot in Quadrant A and one foot in Quadrant C.

Mediating requires considerable skill, and, because human beings can never be neutral, it demands an ability to be multibiased, to care about both parties to the enterprise while focusing on the interaction as opposed to the outcome.

9

THE ADVOCATE

ADVOCACY HAS BEEN defined as providing active, verbal support for a specific position or cause, and advocates as being those who speak in favor of a cause or position or those who intercede or act on behalf of another. Thus, advocacy and social work have always been linked. From the earliest efforts of social reformers such as Dorothea Dix, Lillian Wald, Jane Addams, and Jacob Riis, who were committed to the social justice movement of the late 1800s and early 1900s, to those social workers who staff today's centers for battered women, homeless shelters, and other organizations dedicated to providing services to vulnerable populations, social workers have always been concerned with obtaining and protecting the rights of people. Over time, advocacy has developed into an elaborate set of social work behaviors that continue to be some of the most important to the social justice mission of the social work profession. While opportunities for visible advocacy ebb and flow with shifts between liberal and conservative philosophies, the role is always vital to ensuring the protection of human rights. It is therefore always a critical part of social work practice in general and of structural social work in particular.

This chapter argues that without advocacy, the profession of social work would be like a deodorized skunk—never really able to make a stink about individual victims or classes of victims who are unable to obtain access to basic human needs and human rights. Further, the chapter elaborates a set of expected behaviors for social workers to participate in advocacy activities. The tasks of advocacy are detailed in each of the four quadrants and presuppose attention to other structural concerns as they arise.

WHAT ADVOCACY IS

From the charity organization societies (COS) and settlement house movement of the latter part of the 1800s and early part of the 1900s, advocacy has played a role in social work. While performing the role seems to decrease with an increasing emphasis on highly conservative perspectives in the prevailing philosophy of an era, advocacy has never been totally ignored. The 1930s and the Great Depression provided ample opportunities for advocacy, but World War II and the relatively conservative 1950s saw a decrease in these occasions. After the Cold War era, the heightened political consciousness of the 1960s and early 1970s gave rise to increased advocacy efforts. These efforts then tended to be eclipsed by the increasingly conservative views of the 1980s, 1990s, and early 2000s, when enormous budget cuts, welfare "reform," and gradual economic downturn made the role of advocate even more necessary yet less likely to be played. It is against this backdrop that advocacy now exists—exceedingly necessary, yet often ignored in favor of what some view as more benign social work roles.

Though seen as a glamorous role when there is a liberal social, economic, and political climate of genuine concern for alleviating social problems, there are reasons why advocacy may be eschewed by practitioners in a conservative, even repressive era. First and probably foremost, in most social work agencies social workers are not paid to be advocates, and visible advocacy during working hours is rarely tolerated. Workers are encouraged to do their jobs and counseled not rock the boat. Second, schools of social work these days rarely teach students how to be advocates. Students are encouraged to learn required curricular content and not rock the school's or the field placement's boats. Third, once students become practitioners, they tend to forget their professional responsibilities and become agency-oriented and somewhat minimalistic about their job responsibilities—doing enough to get the job done, but not willing to do much more, least of all rock the boat. Advocacy often requires some boat-rocking and extra effort to make things better—better for one client or one worker or for a group of clients or workers.

Whether a particular form of advocacy entails rocking the boat, it always requires a belief that things can be better and, that by using advocacy and social action, it is possible for social workers to make things better. Given recent history, such idealism may seem hard to retain. Yet many social workers do remain dedicated to social change and committed to a profound belief in the profession's values of social justice. They know that in a repressive social environment, the need for social work in general and advocacy in particular is more necessary than in times when liberalism is dominant. Thus, social workers who are dedicated to advocacy and social change focus on what is possible as opposed to what is not possible. This can-do approach is at the heart of the structural approach (Wood and Middleman 1991). Advocacy is crucial to social work and social change, inasmuch as it creates the foundation for social justice and seeks to protect human rights.

WHO IS INVOLVED

The structural approach entails helping clients connect with existing resources, assisting them in traversing knotty situations, and creating change in social settings where change is possible and such change would alleviate human suffering. Advocacy has a major role in this mission and can involve individuals and groups of clients, workers, supervisors, agency heads, or any one else who can effect changes necessary to assist clients (Wood and Middleman 1991). The basis for advocacy in social work is protection of clients' rights, and advocates act with and for sufferers and groups of those who are suffering to ensure their rights are protected and their basic needs met. In practice, that means making social service systems (public welfare organizations, hospitals, schools) more responsive to clients and their needs, as well as intervening with unresponsive slumlords, harried schoolteachers, overprotective mothers, or angry grocers. Acting on behalf of another can be as simple as involving only the social worker and the client or as complex as involving the social worker, the client, all others who are struggling and similarly situated, and all those who can alleviate the suffering. Hence, advocacy can occur in all four quadrants.

WHO BENEFITS

Since the basis for advocacy is the protection of the rights of clients, the ultimate intended beneficiary of advocacy efforts is not only the client but also all future clients who may face the same situation. From a structural perspective, the aim of advocacy is always universal, as opposed to individual. The idea is to pave the way for cooperative action intended to modify or create structures by which all present and future clients can obtain entitlements without needing an advocate. This is driven by and consistent with the principle of maximizing supports in the client's environment.

Beyond the client, advocacy efforts benefit both the social worker and the agency. Once organizational norms are stretched (see chapter 15) to include the changes created by advocacy efforts, the worker is better able to meet a client's needs in relation to previously targeted issues and the agency is better able to serve its clients. For example, a terminally ill AIDS client had been excluded from a nursing home facility because of her condition. Following advocacy activities by the nursing home's social workers, the ban on AIDS patients was lifted and the nursing home evolved into an excellent service provider for those with terminal illnesses, including HIV/AIDS.

Another beneficiary of advocacy and social action is society itself. Were it not for social activists such as Jane Addams, Dorothea Dix, Julia Lathrop, Susan B. Anthony, Barbara Jordan, Martin Luther King Jr., Paulo Freiere, and hundreds more, problems such as acculturation issues of immigrants, mental illness, child labor, women's rights, or civil rights would never have become the targets of advocacy and social change to redress these issues would not have happened.

While advocacy can take many forms, it is always predicated on the assumption of a potentially conflictual situation. But force generates counterforce, and this makes it necessary for advocates to follow the principle of least contest by initially treading lightly, by trying to win over or co-opt the target. For if the target of the advocacy efforts accepts the reciprocal role, that of an adversary, the goal of the advocate's efforts may not be realized. If, for example, the owner of the nursing home who denied AIDS patients retaliated against an organizational protest sponsored by agency social workers that identified him as a bigot, that owner may have linked his position to religious beliefs from which he could not budge despite the best efforts of his social workers. Thus, the goal of accepting AIDS patients would never have been realized. In such warring encounters, it is the client who gets lost, because neither side can bear to lose the contest. Even when done properly, there are times when advocacy efforts do not produce any beneficiaries. Nonetheless, if the role is not taken when situations require it, it is guaranteed that nothing will change for the better.

THE TASKS OF ADVOCACY

There are five tasks associated with the role of advocacy: (1) identifying those affected by a problem, (2) identifying the issue, (3) deconstructing the issue, (4) advising those involved and gaining their consent to intervene, and (5) undertaking the intervention process itself. Embedded within these five tasks are related skills.

IDENTIFYING THOSE AFFECTED BY A PROBLEM

Advocacy involves looking at the world through the eyes of the client, hearing what issues are of importance to the client, and identifying when and under what circumstances advocacy is an appropriate strategy of intervention. This involves two skills: (1) listening to the client's story and (2) looking beyond the client.

LISTENING TO THE CLIENT'S STORY Listening to the client's story utilizes the tasks and skills described in chapter 6, but a key difference is that as an advocate, one is listening for circumstances when advocacy should be employed; not all situations require advocacy, and advocacy should be used only when other social work roles (broker, mediator) have failed to produce the desired outcome. But some situations do.

Mrs. Parsons, a client, constantly complains that her nine-year-old son Dashiel hates school and comes home from school each day crying and saying that he is being picked on by other students. Mrs. Parsons is at her wit's end. The social worker suggests that he meet with Dashiel to try to determine what is going on.

When the worker meets with Dashiel, the boy confides that it is not he alone who is being picked on; all the children who live in the homeless shelter and attend Elm Street Elementary School are targets for verbal abuse. Dashiel says that he told his teacher about the problem but the teacher was unwilling to intervene because she knows Dashiel would not be in school long and it would not be worth the trouble. Armed with this new information, and with Mrs. Parsons's permission, the social worker, as broker, visits the teacher and teacher's aide, who both confirm their unwillingness to deal with the "problems of transient kids who smell bad and steal lunches." Further, both refuse any attempt to engage in a dialogue with the homeless parents in hopes of coming to terms with the situation, saying it would merely be "wasting time."

This problem now requires advocacy, and this is the appropriate role for the worker to assume at this time. To do so, and to determine if the problem is a structural one or an individual one, requires looking beyond the client to determine who else may be affected by this particular problem.

LOOKING BEYOND THE CLIENT Looking beyond the client involves working with the client to determine who else is potentially affected by the same or a similar problem, if there are others talking with all of the others who are similarly situated to get a fuller understanding of the issue. Here the worker as advocate must do some detective work. Dashiel gave the worker a starting point when he noted that all the homeless children attending Elm Street Elementary School were targets of verbal abuse. If he is correct, the problem is a structural one. Thus, the worker must devise a way to identify other homeless children at Elm Street School and, more important, their parents. Since homeless children seemed to be victims, the worker visited the local women's homeless shelter. During that visit, a total of twelve mothers were identified as having seventeen children in various grades at Elm Street, and each mother indicated having behavior problems with her children when it was time to go to school. None had considered the role the school may have played in generating their children's problematic behavior, thinking it was just a phase all children go through. And given their busy lives trying to find work, food, and shelter, they had little time to dwell on it. Each mother did agree to meet with the worker and the other mothers as a group to discuss the behavior problems in terms of something other than merely a childhood phase. That meeting would provide an opportunity for the worker and client or clients to identify more specifically potential underlying issues related to problems seeming to emanate from Elm Street Elementary School.

IDENTIFYING THE ISSUE

Identifying an issue has two components: (1) looking for patterns and then (2) defining the problem.

LOOKING FOR PATTERNS Looking for patterns means examining the information obtained from the client and others in the same situation and identifying themes that run through the material. In addition to a lack of protection from verbal abuse at school, the worker may find that homeless children are also subjected to emotional abuse from teachers, lack of appropriate access to remedial help, and faculty apathy regarding students' language differences. In the group meeting with homeless mothers of children attending a specific elementary school, it may be that some of the children are simply having difficulties for reasons unrelated to being harassed by school bullies. If that is the case, and no other common patterns are found, the problem is not a structural one, and the worker will have to help each mother and child solve the unique problems they are experiencing. But if the meeting yields data to support a pattern of behavior related to a number of children, as in the preceding example, then a structural problem exists and advocacy is appropriate.

Perhaps the worker's analysis shows that several times a week a gang of sixth-grade boys chases the homeless children away from the playground where they are supposed to wait for their mothers to pick them up. This bullying behavior scares the younger children, and the older ones who stay and fight often get beaten up. The teacher's aide who is on daily playground duty seems to ignore the bullying, chasing, and fighting saying to the girls who complain, "Forget it, kids will be kids."

Once certain patterns are discovered, the work of defining the problem begins. This, too, should be done in conversation with those affected by it.

DEFINING THE PROBLEM Defining the problem can be as simple as having the client identify a problematic situation or as complicated as having several persons involved with a complex issue that looks like one thing until you dig beneath the surface and discover that the real issue is something quite different from what was originally perceived. Such complexity is the case with our struggling students at Elm Street Elementary. On the surface, each student at Elm Street was seen by her or his mother as simply going through a childhood phase. It was not until the social worker, with the help of Dashiel, met with a group of homeless mothers that other potential reasons for acting-out behaviors became known. It was not until the worker had shared the experience of having failed to convince the teacher and teacher's aide that bullying and fighting were deleterious to Dashiel and had indicated that both the teacher and the teacher's aide had made bigoted remarks about homeless children, that the real issue — *discrimination* — came into focus. This underlying issue is the root cause of the continued acceptance of bullying behavior by those in charge, and it is far more insidious than Dashiel's daily crying, which may have been seen as the precipitating problem. Now that the problem has been clearly defined, the work of deconstruction can begin.

DECONSTRUCTING THE ISSUE

Deconstructing the issue is next step in the advocacy process. It involves two skills: (1) identifying deleterious discourses and (2) identifying who benefits and how they benefit.

IDENTIFYING DELETERIOUS DISCOURSES The advocate, like the therapist, must identify deleterious discourses that constitute or contribute to the problem. This is a cognitive skill. The process involves ferreting out community and cultural myths that circulate in society and enjoy the status of "truths."

Using the problem of discrimination faced by the homeless students at Elm Street Elementary, the worker must ask two questions: (1) "Where did the school's teachers and administrators learn that it was acceptable to devalue, disrespect, and deny protection from taunting to homeless children?" (2) "Who else in the school system believes that this is okay?"

There exists within our culture a belief that homelessness and the poverty that accompanies it are avoidable, and that all one has to do is pull oneself up by one's bootstraps to ensure a decent income. Therefore, anyone who is homeless must be somehow inferior, and those who are inferior and their "offspring"—the stigma extends to the children—deserve to be chided and abused for their shortcomings. There is also a belief that boys who bully are merely doing what comes naturally and should be excused for it. With these beliefs prevalent, it is no surprise that the teacher and teacher's aide took no action. Identifying these deleterious discourses is only part of the task—the worker must then explore who benefits from these beliefs and how they benefit, for it is only through these avenues that change strategies can be constructed.

IDENTIFYING WHO BENEFITS AND HOW The advocate asks herself, "Who benefits from discriminating against these homeless children and how do they benefit?" Transient children appear, disappear, or reappear across a school year. For the principal and her staff the transient nature of homeless children causes administrative nightmares. Processing enrollments, obtaining prior school records, and forwarding records when the children move on creates pounds of extra paperwork—especially in schools where there are large numbers of homeless children. Thus, it could be to the school's administrative benefit to keep transient children from enrolling. For the teachers, integrating homeless children into already existing cohesive classroom groups can be hard, even nearly futile, and they, too, can benefit from not having homeless children constantly disrupting their classroom settings. Thus having a school that has a reputation for not welcoming homeless children might benefit a number of Elm Street employees.

But there are even more possible beneficiaries who are associated with the school. Sometimes children benefit from having others to pick on, taunt, and bully—making them feel macho in a domineering role that increases their group cohesion and sense of self-worth. Another potential beneficiary might be the parents of nontransient students who are concerned about the potential for having their children get head lice or ringworm from children who live on the street.

These are the possible beneficiaries of concern to the social worker. Once deleterious discourses and beneficiaries have been identified, the advocate must take the next steps. The first of these is to explore the other side of advocacy.

ADVISE AND CONSENT: THE OTHER SIDE OF ADVOCACY

In general, the clients of the social work advocate are relatively powerless. That is, their resources (money, political influence, and the like) are not equal to those of the parties that control opportunities and resources. In fact, clients are frequently dependent on resources doled out by the more powerful. Thus, while the consequences of not receiving withheld benefits may be deleterious to the social welfare of the clients, the consequences of opposing the powerful system on which clients are dependent may be even harder for them to bear. Advising clients and checking to see if they consent to a proposed intervention involves three steps: (1) defining possible change strategies, (2) exploring potential positive and negative outcomes with clients, and (3) checking to see if there is consent.

DEFINING POSSIBLE CHANGE STRATEGIES Defining possible change strategies means meeting with those affected by the problem and examining various options related to change strategies. While the advocate may have some thoughts about the best way to create change, it is vital that all those who are suffering in a similar situation have input. One way to ensure that all voices are heard is a brainstorming session where the social worker and client meet and both participate in generating as many possible ideas as they can to create what they see as necessary changes. While some of the ideas may be fanciful or unrealistic, all thoughts should be explored. Once all the dreams and ideas are on the table, realistic options can be jointly evaluated and choices can be made. In the case of the students at Elm Street Elementary, when the social worker met with the mothers of the children who were being shunned and bullied, the mothers and the social worker aired their thoughts about possible changes that needed to be made. While Mrs. Nossel wanted to make signs and picket the school, Mr. Ma'awiya wanted to contact the television station and call the mayor, and Mrs. Kim, fearing such action would worsen the situation, wanted nothing done. Ms. Burman, Mrs. Parsons, and Mr. Holsman thought it would be better to have the social worker meet with the school's personnel on behalf of the parents. The trio and others eventually agreed that the social worker should present their concerns (cessation of all discriminatory behaviors toward the homeless children) and if change was not forthcoming they would meet again to discuss more public displays (contacting the media). Once possible change strategies have been brainstormed and evaluated and actual possibilities have been defined, the social worker in concert with the clients explores possible consequences related to each strategy.

EXPLORING POTENTIAL POSITIVE AND NEGATIVE OUTCOMES WITH CLIENTS

Since the social worker can never promise a successful outcome or an outcome without repercussions, the client is often faced with what amounts to a Hobson's choice—that is, a choice that is not really a choice for either. There is really only one option, or all options are equally noxious. This can cause ambivalence on the part of the client in response to the social worker's offer of advocacy. Because it is the client who must bear the consequences, it is the client who must decide whether to oppose the powerful other and bear whatever problems their actions may incur. It is therefore incumbent upon the social worker to raise the other side of advocacy—the pros and cons of alternative actions. The parents of the Elm Street students had identified a variety of possible change strategies and now needed to understand the consequences related to each. Mrs. Kim's suggestion to do nothing appealed to some because it was nonconfrontational and easy, and it would not create still more problems at the school. Other members of the group said that her solution did not really address the problem and overruled it in favor of "doing something." Mrs. Nossel's suggestion of making signs and picketing the school and Mr. Ma'awiya's wish to call the media and mayor were thought to be too "public"—many did not want it known that they were homeless and feared their identities would become known. But many did agree that a public display might force the school to cease the discrimination because of bad press. The ultimate decision to allow the social worker to act as their advocate in a discussion with school personnel seemed to be a middle-of-the-road approach though which their concerns could be presented.

All possible positive and negative outcomes the social worker can foresee must be shared with clients for their benefit and to fulfill the social worker's ethical responsibility for full disclosure. If, for example, the social worker has worked previously with the administrator's and faculty members of Elm Street and had a positive experience, this could be a plus. But, if the social worker has battled unsuccessfully with those at Elm Street, this might be a negative. This means that the advocate must disclose her prior dealings, if any, with the target of change. The advocate's actions with other schools and the positive or negative results that ensued must also be made known, for this is vital information for clients to consider before they are able to give truly informed consent.

CHECKING TO SEE IF THERE IS CONSENT Once possible change strategies have been defined and the positive and negative consequences of each action have been explored, the social worker must check to see if the clients consent to advocacy. If, after engaging the clients in a full discussion they decide advocacy is not appropriate, that is their choice. The social worker will not proceed with advocacy. Hearing the clients say no may be the hardest part of for the enthusiastic and idealistic social worker, but it speaks to the heart of client self-determination and a genuine respect for the rights of people to decide their own destiny.

But, often the answer is yes. In that case, the social worker must ensure that informed consent has been given (see chapter 3). With the homeless parents of Elm Street's students, informed consent was unanimously given at the meeting. Thus prepared, the social worker set out to begin the agreed-upon interventions.

INTERVENING

Intervening as an advocate means launching the plan of action the social worker and client determined to remedy the problem entity best at a particular time. Intervening is done only after all the other previous steps related to advocacy have been completed. As an advocate, there are five ways to intervene: (1) consciousness-raising, (2) balancing power, (3) bargaining, (4) persuading and lobbying, and (5) arguing.

CONSCIOUSNESS-RAISING Consciousness-raising refers to increasing people's awareness of a particular issue or problem with the hope that once understood the problem could be addressed and overcome. The key question the worker asks herself is, "Are your clients aware that their interests are in conflict with the interests of those who control opportunities and resources?" If the answer is no, then consciousness-raising is appropriate. Consciousness-raising requires the social worker as advocate to have a thorough understanding of the problem at the political and personal levels, of its social genesis, and of its impact on clients. In the case of the Elm Street students who were facing various forms of discrimination based on their homelessness, consciousness-raising could be used by the social work advocate who would try to raise the consciousness of offending faculty members and administrators by describing, with clear examples, the effect the discrimination was having on the children's behavior both at home and at school. If the consciousness-raising is effective, the discrimination will stop. Since it is the least contentious form of advocacy, consciousness-raising is always a good place for the advocate to start, but it is not always the most effective means of creating change. Therefore, if this approach does not work, the advocate, in discussions with clients, should devise another approach.

BALANCING POWER Balancing power refers to ensuring that the client group for which one is advocating has power that is relatively equal to the power of the target group from which something is needed. The question that the advocate asks herself is, "In relation to the problem faced, is the client's group power approximately equivalent to the opposing group's power?" If the answer is, "Yes, both sides have relatively equal power," then the advocate can begin to bargain for the necessary changes.

Often though, clients are not in positions of power and do not possess the necessary economic, social, or political clout to have their advocate enter into negotiations with those who oppress them. In effect, clients have few chips to cash in, making bargaining difficult. Thus, the power base of the client group needs to be increased and the power of the opposing group needs to be decreased. The question the worker will ask herself is, "Can the power be balanced by increasing the client group's power base or by decreasing the powerful other's power base?" Since the aim of advocacy is to obtain benefits to which clients are entitled, it is the task of the advocate to determine how the opposing factions can be placed on a more level playing field. Because the power base of one group over another is based on the dependency of the other group on it (Emerson 1972a, 1972b), figuring out what it is that the client group has to offer that the opposing group values is vital.

For example, the Elm Street parents are aware that the school has an upcoming accreditation site visit, and picketing the school during that visit could be damaging to the principal. Therefore, the client group has something the principal might value—no picketing during the site visit. This can balance the power sufficiently for bargaining negotiations to take place. Thus, if consciousness-raising does not work, the social work advocate can relay, with the clients' permission, the group's "no picketing" offer in exchange for no discrimination.

BARGAINING Bargaining refers to negotiations between parties in order to reach agreement. The social worker as advocate should use bargaining if consciousness-raising has not achieved the desired result, but power has been balanced. There is an implicit assumption that both parties involved in bargaining are more or less on equal footing: that is, that one party is not all-powerful and therefore is not interested in striking a bargain. With bargaining, each party has something to offer the other that the other would find appealing to have. In an effort to gain some reciprocally agreed-upon resolution between parties, bargaining may be done explicitly or implicitly. This involves exchanging resources, rewards, and accommodations. Generally, bargaining initially involves asking for more than one's side is willing to accept in order to leave room for reducing one's request in response to the other side's increasing their offer. Concessions are made back and forth until both sides reach an agreement that is mutually acceptable (Parsons and Holloway 1978; Walton and McKersie 1965).

Relative to the Elm Street School situation, the advocate sits down at the table with the principal and indicates that the parents of the homeless children want the classroom teachers to stop ignoring their children and the teachers on the playground to keep other children from chasing and harassing their children. The principal, in turn, indicates to the advocate that he will try to arrange for both if the parents agree to become involved with the PTA. The parents were agreeable with the principal's requests for PTA involvement, and a bargain was struck.

Many bargaining situations will be far more complex than this, and the advocate needs to remember that often there are many trips back and forth to the bargaining table between concessions before both sides agree to a solution acceptable to each. Some of the skills necessary to effective bargaining include persuading, and special kinds of persuading—lobbying and arguing.

PERSUADING AND LOBBYING Persuading and lobbying (a special type of persuading) are two skills that enhance the advocate's ability to ensure success. Persuading is thought of as one person successfully urging another (or a group) to do something—to perform a particular task as a result of one's coaxing, cajoling, pleading, or reasoning. Persuasion may require the worker to stir the emotions of the other person, connect with the other person's values, appeal to the other's higher principles and sense of justice and fair play, or create cognitive dissonance in the other. Persuading, like arguing, requires the advocate to have an excellent understanding of both sides of an issue, compelling anecdotes, and well-thought-out reasons for why the advocate's side should prevail. And, again like the art of argument, advocates who persuade from informed and compelling positions often triumph.

If bargaining had not resulted in a mutual agreement, the advocate, with the consent of the Elm Street parents, might try to persuade the principal to cease the discrimination against the homeless children with sound reasoning, by presenting federal and state law, city policy, and the like as sound reasons why discrimination must not be tolerated. Or, if that failed, the advocate might present compelling stories of the homeless children's plight to stir the principal's emotions and appeal to his moral and justice-oriented sensibilities, as if to say, "How could anyone be allowed to hurt little children who are already hurting so bad?"

Lobbying can be conceptualized as a special kind of persuasion, inasmuch as it attempts to urge others to do something but is done in or on behalf of groups (such as the welfare reform lobby or the nursing home administrators' lobby). Lobbying is generally seen in a political context where specific groups like, for example, members of the National Association of Social Workers (NASW) lobby congressional bodies in favor of (or against) specific policies that relate to a specific constituency. While direct practice does not include lobbying (see chapter 1) the direct practitioner knows what hurts, whom it hurts, and how it hurts. As such, the direct practitioner is required to collect data from anecdotes and give them to macro social workers who lobby in Quadrant D. It is the macro workers who will try to persuade political bodies such as congress to vote for policies that will alleviate identified social problems.

ARGUING Arguing, like lobbying, is a distinctive form of persuasion. It is a specialized skill that many social workers dislike. It is seen to be unpleasant, causing conflict, damaging, negative, and not at all constructive. But because advocacy is based on the premise of conflicting views, for the advocate, arguing is an important and vitally necessary skill. Arguing has probably attained a bad rap because, for most of us, it is inexorably linked with anger. When people are angry, they argue, get red in the face, stamp their feet, even curse. With such a reputation, it is no wonder that many social workers shy away from arguments. However, if done without histrionics and armed with relevant data, arguing for one's position becomes an important tool necessary for social work practice.

In social work advocacy, arguing refers to presenting well-reasoned positions and data designed to have others support your position. These arguments should not be angry confrontations filled with vitriol, but rather strong, well-thought-out, forcefully delivered reasons for why one's position is superior to another's. Arguments may be presented in either oral or written form, but there is nothing stronger than a thoughtful argument from an impassioned advocate—recall Martin Luther King's "I Have a Dream" speech. In order to have well-reasoned views on one side of an issue, it is imperative to know and understand the other side. By analyzing both sides, the advocate comes to the argument armed with logical ammunition to deflect the deftest opponent.

Assume that the Elm Street principal was determined not to intervene on behalf of the welfare of children in her school regardless of the law. Faced with such, the advocate would have to argue with the principal.

Arguing needs to be done dispassionately, regardless of possibly escalating anger on the part of the other person. The advocate/arguer must also maintain an ability to separate the argument from the self so as to prevent oneself from retaliating in response to stinging comments from the other person. So, when the principal says that the advocate is "nothing but a bleeding-heart liberal," the advocate must counter with something like, "I can see why you think that, but federal law still requires that all children—even those without homes— receive public education." Rather than saying, "Yes, I am, but it is far better than being a bigot," the high ground must be maintained in order to change the principal's mind or at least to allow for more conversation another day.

THE ADVOCATE IN QUADRANTS A, B, C, AND D

Advocacy can and does occur in all four quadrants—but more frequently in some than others and not always by direct practitioners. In Quadrant A, an often overlooked form of advocacy, that of giving of information to clients, empowers them when the information is consequential and has not been well publicized. The more information people have that is immediately relevant to their situations, the better they are to make informed decisions and exercise a measure of control over what happens to them. It is in this sense that the provision of information empowers clients. For example, much consequential information that is not widely known pertains to agency policies and procedures. Advocates can empower teenage clients by telling them what can and cannot be kept confidential before significant conversations begin, and they can empower clients who are in the early stages of seeking to regain custody of their children what assessment criteria are used to make such determinations.

In Quadrant B, advocacy requires social workers to organize clients to protest en masse against the withholding of particular needed resources from them and others similarly situated. Together, with the help of the worker, clients can challenge policies that exclude them and others like them by pressuring local, state, and regional officials for increased options and opportunities as well as vote in blocs to influence the platforms of those running for office. Because this form of advocacy is done by groups of clients, it has a tendency to minimize the risks to any one client.

Quadrant B–style advocacy might be appropriate for a group living in Section Eight housing directly under the approach to an international airport. The social worker as advocate may encourage those impacted by the nightly noise of the cargo airplanes to mobilize and create a group of concerned citizens. Once formed, the worker can help the group advocate for what they call "sleeping silence" (no planes would fly directly over their homes between the hours of 11:00 p.m. and 7 a.m.).

In Quadrant C, advocacy involves speaking on the client's behalf after determining what the client wants or needs, and much of what has been covered in this chapter refers to this kind of advocacy. It is probably the most popular form and the most easily recognized. Advocacy in Quadrant D ordinarily is not within the purview of the direct practitioner. The direct practitioner's role is to gather informal and personal stories that the macro social worker can use to lobby for change at the political level.

CONCLUSION

Social workers are committed to social justice, and advocacy is important for meeting that end. This chapter has explored what it means to be an advocate, the five tasks associated with advocacy, and the skills related to these tasks.

10

THE THERAPIST

SOCIAL WORKERS have always provided therapeutic assistance to some clients. But since healthcare policies that created managed care reduced the amount of money available for mental health treatment provided by psychiatrists and psychologists in public agencies, clinics, and provider networks, increasing numbers of social workers are engaging in therapy. Social workers are now meeting with increasing numbers of clients who are beset with and oppressed by personal and interpersonal problems. Thus, the role of therapist has emerged as an especially salient one for social workers in direct practice.

While all social workers in direct practice are required to use their professional repertoire of interpersonal skills at all times, the tasks and skills of the accomplished therapist extend far beyond these general expectations. This chapter elaborates a set of expectations for worker behavior that form a postmodern, social-constructionist, narrative methodology for conducting respectful therapeutic conversations with clients. The tasks of the therapist presuppose prior and contemporaneous attention to structural concerns.

THE TASKS OF THE THERAPIST

Narrative collaboration, the therapeutic practice detailed here, is primarily based on the creative work of Michael White (White 1991, 1995, 2000, 2004), and the further elaboration of it by Jill Freedman and Gene Combs (1996). For narrative collaboration, the role of therapist comprises five expectations for behavior: (1) radical listening, (2) externalizing, (3) deconstructing oppressive discourse, (4) seeking counteracts, and (5) anchoring in history. While listed in chronological order here, these tasks are neither discrete nor always sequential. For example, the therapist externalizes while she helps the client to explore his situation, and she engages in radical listening whenever he speaks. Counteracts—that is, prior instances of the client's refusal to be oppressed—often arise while therapist and client are still exploring the problem. Further, the social worker in the role of therapist identifies and engages with the client in structural work when needed at various times in the process of the therapeutic work.

RADICAL LISTENING

Radical listening (Weingarten 1995) refers to inviting and attending to all aspects of clients' stories in order to understand the meanings they have made of their life experiences. Of particular concern is encouraging voice, gently persisting in the quest for detail of those aspects of life experience that run contrary to prevailing cultural beliefs, areas of concern that clients may be initially reluctant to reveal.

It is one thing to listen carefully and compassionately; while hard learned, it is essential to listen without the filters of diagnostic category schemes, personal ideologies, or religious, class, and gender beliefs. It is even more difficult to learn and risk bringing oneself fully to the relationship, yet it is mandatory for radical listening. Radical listening involves three skills: (1) listening through social consciousness, (2) attending, and (3) immersion.

LISTENING THROUGH SOCIAL CONSCIOUSNESS

Listening through social consciousness refers to feeling and demonstrating genuine interest in, seeking to understand, and being responsive to the complexities of the client's experiences in the context of the client's life. It is not helpful to simplify the complexities of the experiences by stripping them of context, as diagnostic taxonomies do, or to stigmatize the client by listening to the client's story through a filter of white, middle-class cultural beliefs.

ATTENDING

Attending refers to focusing entirely on what the client is saying. It requires the therapist to inquire into and appreciate clients' subjective experiences of themselves in their worlds of people and events. It also requires the therapist to listen for what is *not* said, for the unspoken speaks volumes. It is often important for the therapist to say, for example, "You haven't talked about what you think your son thinks about your not telling him things in order to protect him?" Or, "What are you trying to protect your son from by refusing to speak with him about what's going on?"

IMMERSION

Immersion refers to entering a mental zone in which no one else exists but you and your client, and nothing exists but what the client is telling you. This is what it means to bring yourself fully to the worker/client relationship: you are thoroughly involved in the client and the client's story. This is a segment in time so intense and immediate that the worker's concentration cannot be shaken by doubt or diluted by judgments. Rather, the worker visualizes the client's narration as one watching a fascinating movie, asking questions only to fill in gaps in the actions, emotions, or interactions among the players in the scenes the client describes.

To encourage the client to continue telling her or his story, the worker should lean forward slightly, as interested persons are wont to do, nod occasionally to indicate "I am listening and I want to hear more," and maintain good eye contact without staring. This is extremely difficult to accomplish across the expanse of a desk and the barrier it implies. With the client sitting at the side of the desk, however, the worker can turn her own chair so there is a corner-to-corner arrangement. This is far more conducive to intimate conversation, but avoiding the desk entirely is preferable if the office can accommodate such positioning.

Once the therapist has brought herself fully to the relationship and listened in depth, with great interest and care to what is said; once she has sought the unsaid; once she has listened to the client's story without the filters of cultural, generational, and sociopolitical-economic differences and checked out her understanding of the plight of her client, then she externalizes the problem.

EXTERNALIZING THE PROBLEM

In accord with White's (1988) now-axiomatic statement, "The person is not the problem. The problem is the problem," externalizing the problem refers to separating the client from the difficulty she or he is facing, by constituting it as a separate entity—something at least temporarily seen as outside of the client. This eliminates the blame associated with needing help and keeps away both the sense of shame that blame often generates and the defensiveness that arises in its wake—defensiveness that could serve to prolong the life of the problem.

Externalizing the problem requires the therapist to use three special skills: (1) initiating a linguistic shift, (2) standing with the client, (3) and exploring the problem using externalizing language. The process begins with the worker's initiating a linguistic shift.

INITIATING A LINGUISTIC SHIFT

The therapist initiates a linguistic shift by making statements and asking questions using the objective case, as opposed to the ordinarily used subjective case. The client's statement, "I have a problem," when spoken by the therapist, becomes, *"There is a problem in your life."* "My problem" becomes "The problem." "I got angry when the para (teacher's aide) got in my face" becomes *"The anger got into your head when the para dissed you."* This linguistic shift constitutes the problem as a separate, external entity, and the very important use of active verbs—"The anger got into your head"—implies that the problem entity itself is capable of doing things.

A sample dialogue may provide additional clarity. For example, the client says, "I cry at the slightest thing, and I'm not a crier. The last time I cried was when my father died. But now I'm really depressed.... Sometimes I cry at nothing." The therapist externalizes the depression and further constitutes it as an entity separate from the client when she uses active verbs as she asks, "When did *the depression* first *creep* into your life?" The client may or may not notice the linguistic shift at first.

"I started feeling down about three weeks ago," he says. "The therapist continues to externalize as she explores the way in which the problem entity, the depression, snuck up on him and gradually consumed more and more of his life, as she asks, "What had been happening just before *the depression wiggled its way* in?" After a few moments, the young man answers. "Well, my girlfriend told me I'm a great guy, and a lot of fun and all, but I'm not a keeper." The therapist further externalizes as she checks out an inference. "So *the loss*, and *the hurt* and *the sadness* that hang out with it, *opened the door* just wide enough for *the depression to slither in* and gradually *take over* more and more of your life—is that about right?" she asks. He nods. "Now *the depression is keeping* you from enjoying ordinary things?" she asks. "Absolutely," he says, "*the depression* has gotten in the way of everything."

When it is difficult for a client to separate self from problem, the therapist can introduce an empty chair, ask the client to imagine the problem—in this instance the depression in that empty chair—and ask, "How big is it?" "What color is it?" "What does it want you to do?" If the client has trouble responding, the worker can offer possibilities. "Maybe it's so big it can hardly fit in the chair." "Does it look like a cauldron of boiling oil?" "Does it look like a big, black blob that sucks in everything around it?" "Does it want to keep you sad and scared?"

If the empty-chair work seems productive, the worker can then ask the client to change seats and imagine that he is the depression personified. Then the therapist can ask, "Depression, what are you trying to do to Jimmy?" and encourage the client, acting as the depression, to respond. Perhaps the depression will say, "I want to make him so tired that he can't go to work." Jimmy can then go back to his own chair and ask the depression other questions. One of these might be, "Why do you want to do that to me?" Then he can sit in the depression chair and try to answer, perhaps saying, "So you won't earn money and you'll have to move back in with your mom." As Jimmy again, he may protest, "I don't want to move back home with her!" "But your mother wants you to," the depression might respond, "and you always do what your mother wants you to." This dialogue deepens the therapeutic experience and makes the externalization extremely vivid.

STANDING WITH THE CLIENT

Externalizing also enables the therapist and client to stand together and fight the problem entity together. Standing together further verifies the separateness of the client from the problem and adds strength to the client's otherwise singular struggle against whatever is oppressing him (racial or sexual epithets, depression, unbound anger). Once the problem has been externalized, worker and client together can explore the externalized problem's nature, intensity, scope, history, and impact.

Standing with the client directs the therapist to take sides, to side with the client against the externalized and active problem entity. From her side-by-side position with the client, she joins forces with Jimmy to figure out ways to try to defeat the depression, to outwit it.

If the problem entity cannot be eliminated, for example, a chronic gastrointestinal disorder, the therapist stands with the client helping him to negotiate a more livable arrangement with it (giving the problem entity less time to control him, refusing its efforts to isolate him from his friends). When the social worker as therapist initiates a linguistic shift, and stands with the client, the client is neither to blame for the problem, nor is the client alone with it.

EXPLORING THE PROBLEM

To explore the problem with the client, the therapist asks for details about the problem entity's origin. When did it first come into his life, when did he first notice it was troublesome to him, what happened after that realization, what happened next? She asks who else sees the problem as a problem and who does not. She asks about the problem entity's effect on his work or school grades and how it affects them. She asks for details about its effect on his interpersonal relationships. How has the relationship between him and his wife changed since the problem entered his life? How has it affected his interactions with his mother and father? With his children? His supervisor at work and/or his teacher at school? How has it affected his wife's relationship with their children, and his parents' relationship with one another?

The therapist particularly inquires into ways that the problem has affected his sense of who he is, his self-image, his confidence in himself; how it has affected his view of the world and the way he interprets events. To clarify each of his answers, she asks him for examples, especially examples of how life was before compared to how it is now.

DECONSTRUCTING OPPRESSIVE DISCOURSE

In therapy, deconstruction refers to the process of ferreting out and debunking cultural, community, and family discourses that have taught the client to subjugate herself or himself to their dictates. Often the demands for socially acceptable behavior embedded in these patriarchal discourses run counter to the client's own best interests.

An example of oppressive social discourse is the male sexuality belief that sends a message to many women and girls that they should not report rape. According to this discourse, which circulates in our society, once a man is sexually aroused, he is powerless to control himself. Women know that many police officers, judges, and members of juries believe this. So when women are raped, despite saying "No," if there was prior grinding on the dance floor or kissing in the car, they do not report the crime because they know that these prior activities may go against them in a court of law. They know that when a man disregards a woman's act of saying "No," it is supposed to be legally sufficient to constitute the crime of rape. They also know that in the mind of the court, any implication of women's prior activity that can be construed as seductive may well take precedence over the law. Courts, like the society they reflect, often hold women responsible for what men do to them. Thus, women do not report the rapes. They well understand how highly unlikely it is that their rapists will be convicted—and so, of course, do the men.

Another example of deleterious social discourse could play a role in Jimmy's struggle with the depression. There is a belief embedded in our culture that when a father dies, it is the duty of children to look out for their mother. Combined with children's learning to accede to their parents wishes from babyhood, is the idea that children who take care of their mothers are appropriately devoted sons and daughters. This belief is taught if not explicitly by the parents, then implicitly, with positive comments and smiles about those adult children who do. Those who do not tend to be considered ungrateful, selfish, and self-centered. The guilt that adult children often feel when they ignore their parents' wishes attests to the potency of this societal message.

Although societal beliefs are socially constructed and some do change over time, change comes about slowly, if at all. Thus, many people are locked in stigmatized categories which they, themselves, are led to believe accurately represent them. For years the *Diagnostic and Statistical Manual* (DSM) portrayed lesbians and gay men as mentally ill, while many churches taught (and still teach) that these persons are abominations before God. After a major political fight, the American Psychiatric Association finally dropped homosexuality from its list of mental disorders when the third edition of the DSM appeared in 1973.

Stereotypes still abound. Many people still believe that women who are battered deserve to be, that poor people are poor because they are too lazy to get jobs, and that black people are inherently inferior to white and Asian people. None of these oppressive ideas is accurate, but they are powerful. They can and do powerfully affect identity formation, thereby severely limiting these persons' access to opportunities and resources. Comedian Chris Rock emphasizes this point and elicits knowing laughter when he voices the ordinary experience of too many young African American men. He tells a story about being stopped by police while driving and accused of stealing his own car. They shouted at him and told him he stole it so many times, he says, even he started to believe it. He was terrified. "Oh my God," he said to himself, "I stole a car!"

People who come to or are sent for therapy generally have internalized some oppressive beliefs and characterizations about themselves and their life situations. Whether these result from broad societal/cultural discourse (ageism, sexism, homophobia), institutional discourse (school labels, church teachings, psychiatric labels), or family discourse (expectations and putdowns, verbal abuse and disrespect), the therapist is required to help clients break from these deleterious narratives. To facilitate this process of extricating and defusing negative beliefs that were foisted onto clients and later internalized by them, the therapist uses two critical skills to deconstruct oppressive discourse: (1) identifying deleterious discourses and (2) introducing multiple perspectives.

IDENTIFYING DELETERIOUS DISCOURSES

Identifying deleterious discourses that are wreaking havoc with the client's life requires the therapist to ask two key questions, expressed in externalized form, about each belief that arose during exploration of the problem. The first of these is "Where did you learn that?" Where did you learn that a woman is stupid and worthless if she doesn't have dinner on the table and the children quiet by the time her husband gets home? How did you come to believe you should drop out of school to take care of your brothers and sisters? Who says that depression is a sign of personal weakness? Who else in your family believes that?

The second major question is "Who benefits?" Who benefits from your trying harder and harder to quiet the children and have dinner ready by 6:30? How does your husband, Oliver, benefit? Do you benefit? Who benefits from your dropping out to take care of your mama's little ones? How does your mother benefit? Do you benefit? Who benefits from your believing that depression is a personal weakness? How do your parents benefit? Do you benefit?

While the first two situations above are relatively straightforward, the last is arcane. When a child learns from his parents that depression is a personal weakness, it is often difficult for him to identify, let alone want to identify, who benefits from his believing this. It is hard for a child to realize, for example, that parents, even very loving parents, can be loath to expose themselves to the still-existing social stigma and felt blame of having a child beset by depression. If they can convince their child that she or he is really fine, or just needs to straighten up, they benefit by avoiding the pain they might otherwise feel. Thus, denial is often their first response. Such denial certainly does not benefit the struggling son or daughter who needs parental acceptance and therapy. Rather, it adds to the teen's sense of self-doubt and unworthiness. When the origin or beneficiary of an oppressive belief is subtle or intensely emotional, far more dialogue is necessary to reveal the operational dynamics of the discourse.

Once clients understand where they learned the negative stories about themselves and they know that some persons other than themselves benefit from the grip these beliefs have on them, the therapist can start to loosen the clients' attachment to the debilitating discourses by introducing them to multiple realities.

INTRODUCING MULTIPLE PERSPECTIVES

Introducing multiple perspectives refers to helping the client to look at life experiences in different ways. The therapist gets at this by asking perspectival questions, that is, questions seeking alternative versions of reality—questions that elicit many different ways in which experience can be interpreted, different frames of reference from which to understand feelings and events. How would your little girl describe the way Oliver treats you? What would your grandmother say about your dropping out of school to help your mother? How would Miss Farmer (high school history teacher) view a person who is trying to cope with depression? Questions such as these tend to generate a variety of ways to understand and explain one's experience, new interpretations to counter the subjugating discourses that compel people to behave in manners contrary to their own best interests. Identifying discourses that oppress clients, unmasking the beneficiaries of these discourses, and introducing clients to multiple realities for interpreting experience constitute the process of deconstruction.

In therapy, deconstruction can be understood as a political process aimed at a therapeutic experience of undermining negative interpretations of self. It is political in that it exposes the hidden power holders at the cultural, community, and interpersonal levels of interaction. That is to say, the persons or categories of persons who benefit from the discourses are revealed, whether the discourses are codified in laws (the defense of marriage act that prohibits same-sex marriage) and/or official acts (profiling travelers at airport security checkpoints). Further, deconstruction explores how the exercise of this power interferes with clients' efforts to make decisions that are in their own best interests. In doing so, it opens therapeutic space for clients to develop more positive self-representations as they begin to seek counteracts.

SEEKING COUNTERACTS

Counteracts can be defined as thoughts, speech, or actions that fight oppression. These include all forms of defiance in the face of persecution of self and those one loves, all instances of resistance to subjugation, and/or every maneuver that blocked an effort to discount or erase one's knowledge of one's personal qualities, abilities, and skills.

Oppressed people *do* fight back. Some actively resist coercive restraints and bear the painful consequences of their actions. Others say nothing but refuse to believe the negative characterizations they hear about themselves. Still others fantasize aspects of life without subjugation. These are all acts of resistance, acts that counter oppression, acts that are the foundation of new ways of representing selves.

From childhood through old age, all people have lived experiences of fighting oppression, though they did not necessarily label these as such or regard them as significant at the time. Seeking counteracts ferrets out these acts of resistance, inquires into these events, and endows them with the salience they deserve.

All personal acts that counter oppression are the beginnings of stories about clients' lives as brave and strong people—stories left out of their personal histories, overlooked, or disregarded amidst the noise of negative discourses drowning them out. Recollecting these stories empowers persons to discover and value the positive aspects of themselves hidden in the counteracts. Using these newly discovered aspects of themselves, they can start to reinterpret who and how they are. Recollected stories and the positive aspects of self discovered in the counteracts provides the raw material from which to weave positive, alternative self-representations. To seek counteracts, the social worker as therapist uses two skills: (1) digging for defiant moments and (2) elaborating moments into lives.

DIGGING FOR DEFIANT MOMENTS

To begin seeking counteracts with clients, the therapist questions them about times when they did things that surprised them, things they ordinarily would not do when they were scared or being pushed around. Maybe they experienced an unfamiliar moment of hatred for someone who hurt their feelings. Maybe they tried to protect a younger child from a sexually abusive grandfather. Such inquiry digs for defiant moments, and might include, for example, "Did you ever not do *everything* exactly like Oliver told you to do it? Have you ever imagined yourself yelling back at him when he yells at you?"

"Did you ever so much as dream about staying in school instead of dropping out to take care of your younger brothers and sisters? Did any of your friends drop out because their families expected them to? What was the outcome for Chantelle?"

"Did you ever disagree with something your parents told you they believe? Have you ever thought they could be wrong about something? Even part of something?"

ELABORATING MOMENTS INTO LIVES

Once some counteracts have been identified, the therapist asks for as much detail about each individual counteract and the situation in which that counteract is embedded as it is possible to generate. The idea is re-create the whole event as the client experienced it, from inception through fruition to afterthoughts, including current reflections on it. In other words, the effort is to develop a full-blown story that fleshes out each counteract:

"Tell me more about that time you left the dishes to dry by themselves and spent time playing with your little daughter instead of drying them. How did you come to that decision? What did you tell yourself? Were you scared? Did you almost change your mind and dry the dishes instead? Were you afraid Oliver might notice? How did you feel later, when it was over and you were putting the dishes away?"

"What was it like for you when you filled out that college application form? What led up to your taking that bold step? Did you think about it for a long time, or was it a spur of the moment sort of thing? Tell me more about it. Where were you when you filled it out? Were you alone or was somebody else with you?"

"Say some more about thinking it may be okay to date a girl who isn't Italian even though your parents say it's wrong. What led you to question their belief about that? Had you been working on it in your mind for a while or have you doubted their idea from the first? Did you talk to anyone about your different viewpoint? A close friend or a relative? What did you learn about interethnic dating from your Internet search?"

Elaborating one's moments of resistance both marks and constitutes the genesis of new and liberating self-narratives.

ANCHORING IN HISTORY

Once some counteracts have been unearthed and endowed with the salience they deserve, they must be grounded in what can be understood as a long history of resisting and defying oppression. In addition to deepening the emergent perspective of the client as a fighter, this process also validates the expectation that habits of human behavior do not spring wholly new, but develop gradually over time. Further, the meaning of these counteracts must be analyzed, and all of the bits and pieces of the developing plot of the story line must be organized into a coherent whole.

To facilitate this, the therapist calls upon three skills: (1) seeking antecedent roots of counteracts, (2) inferring client attributes and skills, and (3) chronologizing the storyline.

SEEKING ANTECEDENT ROOTS OF COUNTERACTS

Seeking antecedent roots of counteracts involves a quest for stories from specific times in the client's life (childhood, adolescence, adulthood), that can be interpreted as containing acts of resistance to oppression. The idea is to demonstrate that the client has always fought oppression, beginning with the client's early childhood and continuing through adolescence and adulthood. For example, the child who ran out of the classroom when he could not cope with the demands of an oral arithmetic drill could have been defying the system that places children in academic competition with each other. The adolescent who shifted herself and her siblings to different beds in different rooms every night was foiling her incestuous father's otherwise easy access to her and her sisters. The young drag queen who, while speeding through a residential neighborhood, refused to comply with police who tried to pull him over. Instead, he drove to the safety of his home and called a lawyer. He was not running just because he was afraid. He was also defying the unfair police practice of throwing drag queens into male lockups where they were invariably brutalized.

Stories may not emerge along a neat timeline. A story from the client's teen years may trigger one from his remote past, which may suggest one from last week or last year. Rather than interrupt the client's stream of recollection in order to insert each story in its place along a temporal continuum, the therapist continues to ask for more details and more stories. Chronologizing is a task for later, after antecedent roots are recollected and attributes embedded in them are identified.

To begin seeking counteracts from the distant and recent past, the social worker as therapist can ask questions such as these: "When you were a little girl, did you ever think that something at home or at school was unfair? Tell me more about that. What did you believe that lead you to consider it unfair? Did you talk to anyone about it or do anything about it? How was it for you when you told the teacher that Alice screamed out during arithmetic only because

Billy threatened to cut off a piece of her hair? Later were you afraid Billy would hurt you for telling on him? Was there another time back then that you believed something was unfair? How about when you were middle-school age?"

Sometimes mention of the two-year-old developmental stage, when the powerful word "No!" was uttered, can jog a client's memory of defying a parent, grandparent, or babysitter. Likewise, the topic of "bullying" often reminds people of their efforts to avoid humiliation at the hands and mouths of other children. Such common topics can evoke still other memories of efforts to defy oppression.

INFERRING CLIENT ATTRIBUTES AND SKILLS

In addition to remembering and valuing acts of resistance from the distant and recent past, anchoring in history also involves extracting the meaning of each act for one's self-representation, one's identity. As the client interprets the meaning of each counteract, particularly the strengths, skills, and the abilities they reveal, the story is fleshed out and enriched. To begin this process of drawing collaborative inferences, the therapist can ask questions such as these: "What does it say about you that you risked Oliver's wrath in order to enjoy some playtime with your daughter? What skills and abilities did it take to make that choice and act on it?"

"What does it say about you that even though you love your mother and your little brothers and sisters, and even though you're afraid they would all think you're a cold and selfish bitch if you don't quit school to care for the little ones, you still think about staying in school, even filling out an application for college? What abilities have you developed that make it possible for you to cope with so much family pressure and still keep your need for education in mind?"

"When you accidentally tore your arithmetic paper while you were erasing and your first-grade teacher said you were the sloppiest child in the class, you didn't believe her. How did you manage to stick to your own belief? Was it a struggle? What does it say about you that you were able to hold onto your own self-assessment even though you were so young and she was an adult? What kind of person does that show you to be?"

CHRONOLOGIZING THE STORYLINE

Chronologizing the storyline refers to helping the client organize into temporal order the discrete events that support the client's lifelong display of courage and resistance to oppression and the attributes, skills, and abilities these events reveal. This ordering of events across time can be seen to form a wholly new narrative. The new story of who the client is replaces the story that was formerly, event by event, overlooked, dismissed, discounted, and/or erased. This new story represents the client today, her self-representation, with all the struggles and strengths owned and honored, from which she can think about and act in the present. This new self-representation serves as the potential springboard from which the client can plan and move toward the future.

Initially, the worker helps the client put all of this together by suggesting that the client tell the story from the beginning. The social worker as therapist joins to help the client remember the earliest event they developed and elaborated, then the next, and so forth. It helps for worker and client to note these events in their order for later, when the client will tell and retell her entire alternative story. Once the chronology is up to date, the worker shifts to questions regarding the way in which the client's construction of current events and relationships are relevant to her life.

Questions about possibilities for the future that the new story may have for the client are now appropriate—the next month, six months from now, hopes and dreams for still later. The client's constructions of the present world of people and events and speculations about the future also become part of a new narrative. Then the whole new story of self, including the client's ideas about the present and future, is further deepened by telling and retelling.

Tellings and retellings of one's own storied experience and the meanings one makes of it are narrations of identity. In a conversation with the worker, the client begins to tell a newly chronologized self-story. During this telling and those to come, the therapist can prompt the client as needed and draw inferences from what the client says. More than one telling is necessary not only because the client may want to include aspects of the therapists inferences, but also because stories evolve in the telling, becoming ever richer in the process.

CONCLUSION

The six tasks of the social worker as therapist are carried out by using fourteen skills elaborated in this chapter. These tasks and skills enable transformational events in the lives of many clients.

11

THE CASE MANAGER

CASE MANAGEMENT has been described as both a concept and a process. As a concept, it is the system of relationships among clients, service providers, and administrators. As a process, it is the provision of services that facilitates a client's functioning at as normal a level as possible (Weil and Karls 1985). Case management has also been called both a problem-solving process and the system that includes this process—all the needed administrative supports, systemic arrangements, and formal and informal community resources (O'Connor 1988).

While these double-barreled definitions seem to be indicative of case management's uncertain status in the late 1980s, today case management can be understood as a role that social workers assume when the client requires it. As such, the role has flourished and is now widely accepted as a salient one. This chapter describes the role of the case manager and the tasks that comprise it. Social workers provide case management in all three direct-practice quadrants (A, B, and C), and the process guide to case management (figures 11.1–11.4) assists the social worker in determining when and how to use the four primary roles that have been elaborated in other chapters (conferee, broker, mediator, advocate) to perform the complex role of case management.

THE EVOLUTION OF CASE MANAGEMENT

The need for coordination among service providers is as old as social work itself. The Charity Organization Societies (COS), birthplace of social casework, emerged in the 1870s partially in response to the lack of coordination of social services. In subsequent years, the impact of urban industrialization, with its accompanying demographic shifts plus uncertain economic and social policies, affected vulnerable populations and required a more complex emphasis for social work. In the 1950s, case conferences became one means of coordinating services for clients, and the 1960s and 1970s saw an even greater emphasis on activities related to case management and the coordination of services. It was also during this era that there was a shift away from the medical model and a move toward a legal perspective that emphasized client rights. This move toward acceptance of the rights of clients heralded a shift in the balance of power between workers and clients. Social workers were no longer seen as "the experts," and clients were considered equal participants in the helping relationship.

In the 1980s there was a systemic shift from centralized programs and services to social services that were decentralized and presumably more accessible to clients. This brought with it more local responsibility and funding for human services and reduced federal spending ushered in the concept of "cost containment." For service providers, this meant cutbacks in management and services. In response to the cutbacks, over time, an entrepreneurial, competitive social-service delivery system developed. Research on this changed position in federal funding cited privatization of the most profitable services (selecting clientele on their ability to pay) and the medicalization of social services (as when, for instance, aging becomes a medical problem) as the primary reasons for the shift from the formal delivery system to services provided by home and family (Wood and Estes 1988).

As service providers became more and more decentralized and clients were constantly moving from agency to agency, there was a need to coordinate which agencies were providing which services to which clients. At the programmatic level, case management was developed to organize and coordinate service delivery that had been seen as fragmented and frequently ineffective. At the direct practice level, case management emphasized the quickest, most effective and cost-efficient means to enable the client to live in the community with as much independence as possible. Case management should achieve needed linkages between people needing services and service resources that are *available*, and it also should ensure that there is *continuity* of services for each client. This aim of case management in the 1980s remains basically the same today—to keep clients from falling through the cracks of the social welfare system.

Spurred by the fragmentation of service delivery systems, severe deficits in available resources, lack of the development of adequate services, the impact of managed care in health settings, continued funding cutbacks, and the need to coordinate clients in service systems, the number of social workers taking the role of case management has burgeoned since the 1980s (Rose and Moore 1995). There is now a professional organization dedicated to case management (Case Management Society of America), journals devoted to its practice, and licensure and certification for full-time case manager positions. With emphasis on providing a safety net for clients, the role of case manager continues to enable each client to be linked with appropriate, decentralized services in a coordinated manner.

TASKS FOR WORKING AS A CASE MANAGER

Case managers are required to link clients with services, develop individualized contracts with them, and monitor the process. To do so entails use of four tasks: (1) assessment, (2) planning, (3) linking, and (4) monitoring. Embedded within each of these are relevant skills for performing that task.

ASSESSMENT

Assessment aims at appraising the client's current and potential strengths, challenges, needs, and interests. The case manager must know the client's situation, level of functioning, strength of supports, resources, attitude toward services, and all the additional information she can glean that will help link the client with appropriate resource providers. All of this information helps determine the direction of action for their work together, that is, goals and particular activities that may lead to attaining them. There are five skills germane to the task of case management: (1) reaching for the client's feelings; (2) waiting out the client's feelings; (3) getting with the client's feelings; (4) defining current needs/problems; and (5) translating each need/problem into a desired service outcome. Chapter 4 (especially the section related to the principle of accountability) explains the first three. The last two are described here.

DEFINING THE CURRENT NEED/PROBLEM Defining the current need/problem refers to conversations between the client and the social worker in which the client describes the current situation in terms of the disconnect between what she or he needs to ensure basic human needs and rights and what is currently available. Often clients have many problematic situations with which they need help. When problems and needs are multiple or require coordination of a variety of services, the social worker should take the role of case manager as opposed to other social work roles. Initially, the client may not spell out or even be aware of underlying needs/problems that sustain the ones the client presents. Often worker and client discover these as they discuss the pressures the client does report. Some clients, though, immediately articulate a list of needs. In either event, case management is the requisite role. The following example shows how the defining the need or problem clarifies the need for the case manager role.

Juanita Jimenez and her six-month-old baby recently moved from New York City to Tucson, Arizona, to stay with her sister. Juanita is recovering from a work-related injury and receives a small disability check from her previous employer. Because she was new to the city and needed food and medical care for herself and her baby, her sister told her to go and apply for public assistance. Juanita went to a multiservice center, where she was told that because of her income she would not be eligible for financial assistance; but when she elaborated her needs/problems as not having adequate money for food or medical care, she learned she would qualify for case manager services until she could return to work.

TRANSLATING NEEDS/PROBLEMS INTO SERVICE OUTCOMES Translating defined needs/problems into specific service outcomes involves identifying what resources are required to meet the defined needs/problems and discussing available options with the client. In the preceding example, once the worker and Juanita agreed that case management services were appropriate, the worker took the role of case manager. In this role, she and Juanita determined that there were two appropriate service outcomes. The first was getting food, the second getting medical care for Juanita and her baby. Each need/problem was connected with a specific, measurable service outcome.

THE PROCESS GUIDE IN THE ASSESSMENT PHASE The process guide to case management in the assessment phase (figure 11.1) delineates the way the case manager works. She begins by asking the client to describe current needs or problems. As shown in figure 11.1, if the client expresses feelings about her current plight, the worker *gets with the client's feelings* and again asks the client to describe her unique situation in terms of needs/problems. Should the client express neither needs and problems nor feelings, unexpressed feelings may be blocking the process. Thus, the worker should *reach for those unexpressed feelings*. If the client then expresses them, the worker should *get with*

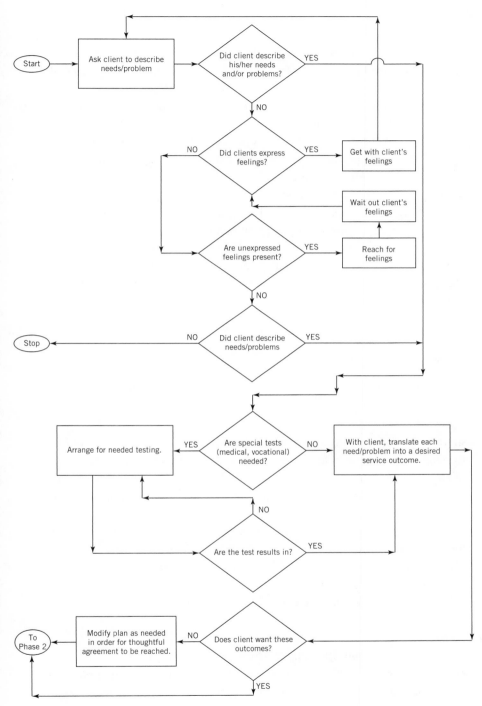

FIGURE 11.1 Process guide to case management in the assessment phase: Phase 1

the now expressed feelings and get back to requesting some form of description of the client's situation and problems. If the client does not express feeling that may have been preventing her from supplying some indication of needs, and *still* does not provide this basic information, the work must stop until it is possible for the client (or a guardian) to do so.

Once the client does describe needs/problems, the case manager explores whether there are specialized tests (medical or vocational, for instance) that are needed in order to facilitate the provision of appropriate services. If there are, the case manager arranges for needed testing and waits for the results. Once the results are in (or if no tests were needed) the case manager and client translate each need/problem into a desired service outcome. Together they explore whether the client wants the specified outcome. If acceptable, the work moves to phase 2. However, if the client does not want the identified services, then the service contract is modified to reflect what outcomes are acceptable to the client, and then the case manager moves to phase 2.

PLANNING

Planning refers to the case management phase that follows assessment. A service contract developed with the client and perhaps including interdisciplinary team members as well, lists such things as presumably needed services, short- and long-term provision objectives, actions to take to reach these objectives, agencies to contact for services, time frames for activities, and the identification of potential barriers to service delivery. This service contract is in many ways similar to the contracts developed between any client and social worker (see chapter 4).

The process guide to case management in the planning phase illustrates the flow of activity through which the task of planning is activated. Planning calls for the use of six skills: (1) identifying formal resource providers; (2) contacting service providers; (3) advocating; (4) identifying informal resource providers; (5) creating resources; and (6) defining service referral/implementation dates.

IDENTIFYING FORMAL RESOURCE PROVIDERS Identifying formal resource providers refers to the thoughtful process of consciously connecting possibly existing formal resources in the community with the client's specified need. This occurs after the client and case manager have defined specific needs and problems as well as specific service outcomes. In Juanita's case, the case manager first addressed the need for food. To assist Juanita with food immediately, she identified the Great Harvest food bank. She then identified a local food co-op where Juanita might be able to, for minimal volunteering, get food for herself and her baby regularly. For additional ongoing help with food, the case manager also helped Juanita apply for food stamps. To assist with necessary health care, the case manager identified a maternal and well baby clinic run by the Sisters of Loreto. All three of these services existed and seemed appropriate for Juanita's needs.

CONTACTING SERVICE PROVIDERS Once the client and case manager have assessed the client's service needs and have created a service plan, the client must be linked with the requisite services. This is accomplished by having the case manager contact the service provider to determine whether the client is appropriate for services and whether the service provider will be able to help the client. This is usually done by having the case manager telephone the agency on behalf of the client. Often a case manager knows various staff members who work at community welfare organizations and uses these connections to assist the client. If, however, a case manager does not know any agency personnel, she should get the name of whichever person she has contacted. That way, the next time the case manager has to call the agency, she will have a contact on the inside.

Needing case management in some areas of life should not be construed as lacking competence to make decisions and negotiate other aspects of one's life. Thus, clients who wish to contact the agency on their own behalf should be able to do so. In such instances, the case manager should provide the contact information request that the client inform her when the connection has been made. In such an instance, to ensure that the client's needs are met, the case manager should provide whatever assistance the client needs to make the connection.

The kind of information the case manager wants to gather from prospective agencies relates to what the client can expect when working with the service provider. Will the agency be able to meet the identified service needs? When can the client be seen for an initial intake assessment? Are there fees associated with services? Where is the agency located? Are transit tokens given to clients? How long will the client need to schedule for agency visits?

If the client makes the initial connection with the agency, the case manager should provide as much information about the agency to the client as is known. If the case manager does not know anything about the prospective agency, she should ask if the client would like her to ferret out what information is available before the client makes the original contact.

Traci Olsen, a thirty-four-year-old unmarried mother of three preschool daughters, was eligible for case management services. She stated that her daughters were keeping her from finding employment and she needed to find adequate daycare for them. She also needed help with training for and getting a decent job so that she could pay the daycare fee and still make ends meet. The case manager identified two possible daycare providers, contacted both and provided Traci with detailed information about both service providers. With that information, Traci made an informed decision opting to go with the Teddy Bear Toddlers. The case manager again contacted the agency and found that Traci's needs could be met there. A referral was made and the initial date of service delivery set.

With respect to Traci's need for training and at least a temporary job while preparing for a better one, the case manager made several contacts. She called Creative Employment Services about available jobs, and she spoke with admissions officers at local technical schools to find out what courses were offered and whether Traci might be eligible for financial aid. The case manager then met with Traci and discussed what she had learned. Traci agreed to meet with counselors at Creative Employment Services and, because she was only somewhat enthusiastic about becoming a paralegal, she said she would think about applying to school. The case manager made a referral to Creative Employment Services, a service delivery date was set, and the worker made another appointment with Traci to discuss school.

ADVOCATING Advocacy is explicated in chapter 9 and is also discussed in depth here. Briefly, it means that the case manager, as advocate, intercedes on behalf of the client when agencies are not responsive to client need. Obviously, not all clients will need advocacy services, but some will. In the case of newly arrived Juanita, the case manager would have had to act as advocate if Juanita had an emergency need for food, but the formal resources had an eligibility requirement that enabled only established residents of Tucson to get emergency provisions.

IDENTIFYING INFORMAL RESOURCE PROVIDERS Identifying informal resources providers refers to finding resources outside the formal network of service delivery systems. Often these include friends, relatives, churches, or other neighborhood services. Had Juanita been found not eligible to get food immediately from an existing formal resource (the food bank), the case manager would have had to determine if there were resources available in the informal network that could provide her with food. One possible source would have been her sister with whom she was living; another might have been the neighborhood grocer or local pastor. Identifying these informal resources and determining who should contact them is done in conversations between the client and the case manager.

CREATING RESOURCES Creating resources refers to the bringing into being a resource when none exists. Occasionally, in order to ensure that clients receive needed services, case managers may have to be creative. While services from existing formal welfare agencies may not be available, clients still have needs that must be met. It may become the job of the case manager to create informal services where there are no formal welfare organizations. Clients, too, can become part of developing informal services, for they may know better than the case manager what possibilities exist. The following example describes such a situation.

Cindy Stephenson lives in an extremely remote part of Montana where there are few formal resources and even fewer people. Because of a fire that left her homeless and without the bare necessities, she is eligible for case management services from an agency in Anaconda, about fifty miles west of her home, but formal resources in her immediate area are nonexistent. In order to assist Cindy and her family, the case manager and Cindy talked with Cindy's pastor and asked her to help locate blankets, food, and temporary shelter. When church members heard what happened to Cindy's family, they realized Cindy's plight could be their own. They willingly donated clothing and household goods, a neighboring rancher provided shelter in his bunkhouse, and many families pitched in to help Cindy and her family rebuild.

DEFINING REFERRAL AND IMPLEMENTATION DATES Defining referral and implementation dates refers to the case manager's, the client's, and the specific service provider's determining the specific date and time of the client's first appointment. For example, Steve, who was receiving case management services for multiple needs, required AIDS testing. He had been engaging in risky sexual behaviors and wanted a referral to the AIDS clinic as soon as possible. His case manager and he agreed that Steve needed to be tested quickly, so she called her contact at the AIDS clinic to arrange for testing the following morning. In this instance, the referral and implementation dates were identical and immediate, but often there is lag time between the referral and the date services start. For example, there may be a delay of several weeks or even months between when a person is referred to Meals on Wheels and when their first meal is actually delivered.

PROCESS GUIDE IN THE PLANNING PHASE Once the assessment phase is complete, it is time to begin the planning process (figure 11.2). In the planning phase the client and case manager must first identify all the desired *formal* resource providers that could meet the client's various needs. If there is more than one that can deliver the required service, the case manager discusses each with the client. Together, they consider the agency's location, eligibility requirements, staff attitudes toward consumers, possible fees, and other information that could help the client make an informed decision among the various agencies. Once the client has all the necessary information, the case manager and the client rank order the agencies according to the client's preferences. Having decided on a specific agency the case manager contacts the agency and asks whether the agency will accommodate the client. If the answer is yes, then the case manager, service provider and client, identify a target date for the services to begin and the case manager refers the client to the agency. At that point, phase 3 of case management commences.

If there are not multiple agencies that provide similar services, but only one, the case manager tells the client about the agency and then, if the client wishes to be referred, the case manager (or client) contacts the agency and asks if it can accommodate the client. If it can, all identify the date for service to begin and the case manager makes a referral. At this point, the planning phase of case management is complete, and the linking phase begins.

If any formal service provider is not willing to accommodate a client, then the case manager must ask herself whether the refusal is legitimate. If the refusal for services was not legitimate, the case manager advocates for the needed service on behalf of her client. If she was successful and the needed services were obtained, a target date for implementation of service is established and the client is referred to the agency. If her advocacy was not successful, the needed service was not obtained, and other formal resources *do* exist, the case manager contacts the provider she and the client ranked second. She asks if that agency will accommodate the client. If the answer is yes, a target date for service implementation is established, the client is referred to the agency, and the case manager moves to phase 3.

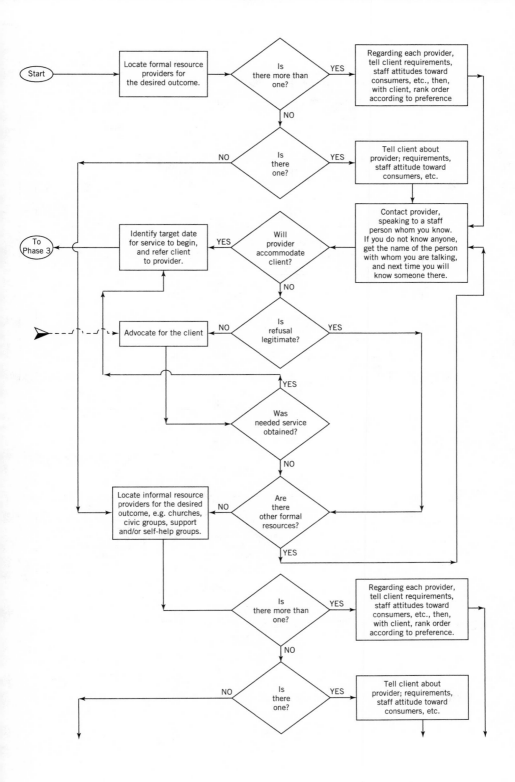

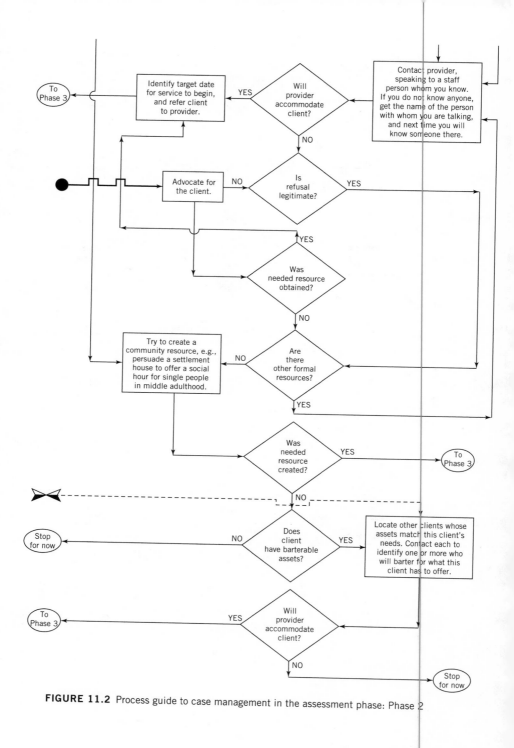

FIGURE 11.2 Process guide to case management in the assessment phase: Phase 2

If there is only one formal resource and that resource either legitimately cannot provide the service (no beds available in the women's shelter) or the refusal of service was not legitimate but advocacy was not successful, the case manager must scour the community for *informal* resources (such as churches, neighbors, or the family) to meet the desired outcomes.

If there is more than one informal resource, as with the formal resources, the case manager explains each to the client and they jointly can rank order preferences. Once the client and case manager have identified an acceptable informal resource, as with the formal resources, the case manager contacts the informal service provider and asks whether they can accommodate the client. If the answer is yes, a target implementation date is set, the client is referred for services, and the work moves to phase 3.

If there was only one informal source of service provision, the case manager tells the client about it, and, with the client's permission, contacts the provider to ask whether the provider is able to accommodate the client. If the answer is yes, the case manager identifies a target date for services to begin, refers the client to the provider, and moves to phase 3.

If the informal service providers are not able to accommodate the client, the case manager asks herself whether the refusal is legitimate. If it is not, then the case manager advocates on behalf of the client. If the needed resource is obtained, a date for services to begin is identified, the client is referred for the service, and the case manager moves to phase 3. If needed service is not forthcoming as a result of failed advocacy or if the refusal for services is legitimate, the case manager tries to create a community resource to meet the client's needs. If the case manager is successful in creating a resource to meet the need (as happened in Anaconda, Montana), the case manager moves to phase 3.

If, however, the case manager could not create a resource, she explores whether the client has any assets that could be used to gain needed services. If the answer is yes, then the case manager would locate others who need what the client has to offer and can provide what the client needs in exchange. The case manager can introduce the client to a reciprocal other with the hope of forming a "trade-unit." (Examples of trade-units are provided in chapter 7.) If a trade-unit was created, the case manager can proceed to phase 3, but if the client has no assets to trade for needed services or a trade-unit between individuals was not established, the work must stop.

LINKING

Once a plan is organized and service contract has been made, it is time to link the client with services/resources. These may be services and resources available from formal sources such as agencies, community centers, food banks, churches, or other institutionalized welfare providers, or from informal sources such as relatives, friends, neighbors, neighborhood associations, or other local projects. Such connections involve more than merely making referrals for clients to various agencies, as many clients are unable to make the necessary connections on their own. The case manager must do everything necessary to ensure that the client receives the needed services. For example, a case manager, herself, might take the client to the agency for an initial intake interview or transport the client to the health clinic. If the client is not able to get to the needed service locales, the case manager may have to find a volunteer to help the client on a regular basis. She must also keep in touch with the client to ensure that service delivery has begun as scheduled and as intended.

The process guide to case management in the linking phase shows the steps in connecting the client with the necessary services. There are two skills associated with the task of linking: (1) reconnecting with the client and service providers and (2) mediating between the client and service provider.

RECONNECTING WITH THE CLIENT AND SERVICE PROVIDERS Once the client and service providers have agreed to a referral date and a service delivery date, the case manager must reconnect with both the client and the agency to ensure that the client gets to the appointment and the agency is aware that the client is coming. To actualize this, the case manager telephones both the client and the appropriate agency staff member the day before the scheduled appointment.

MEDIATING BETWEEN CLIENT AND SERVICE PROVIDER If, for any reason, a service provider is reluctant to (or refuses to) honor a previously agreed upon service plan, the case manager takes the role of mediator and tries to help the client and the provider iron out their difficulty with each other. For example, Carla Le Croy, an abused woman, and her case manager arrived at Magdalene's House (a shelter for battered women). When the shelter worker who had agreed to help Carla discovered that Carla's abuser was another woman and that Carla was a lesbian, she initially refused to provide shelter for her. The case manager successfully mediated on Carla's behalf, and Carla was provided shelter.

PROCESS GUIDE IN THE LINKING PHASE Figure 11.3 shows how the case manger links the client with needed resources.

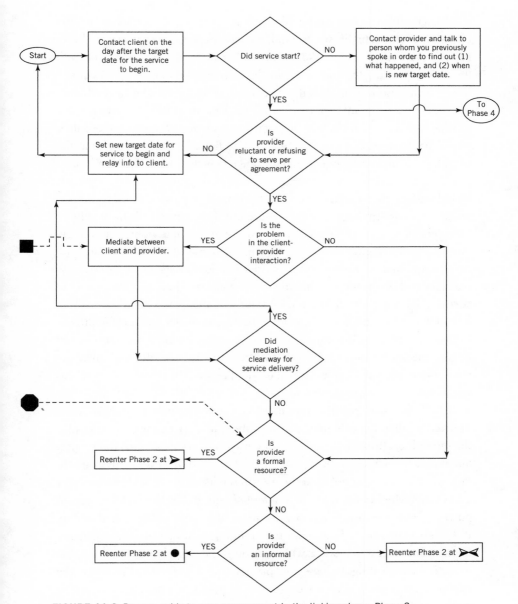

FIGURE 11.3 Process guide to case management in the linking phase: Phase 3

The day after a service is scheduled to begin, the case manager contacts the client to see if it actually did. If it did, the case manager moves to phase 4. If, for whatever reason, service *did not* begin, the case manager reconnects with the service provider to determine *why* the service did not begin as scheduled. If the given reason seems odd, the case manager seeks to understand whether the provider is reluctant to or is refusing to provide the agreed to service. If the provider is not reluctant to (or refusing to) provide service, a new target date is established, the case manager contacts the client, tells the client what the provider's problem was, and gives the client a new start date. Then the linking process begins anew.

If, however, the provider is reluctant or refuses to provide the agreed upon service, the case manager needs to figure out if the problem is in the client/provider interaction. If the answer is, "No, there is not a problem in the client/provider interaction," then the case manager asks herself whether the provider is a *formal* resource. If the provider is a formal agency, then the case manager and client reenter the process in phase 2, where the directive is to advocate for the client in the formal setting. If the service provider is not a formal but rather an *informal* provider, the case manager reenters the process in phase 2, where the directive is to advocate for the client in the informal setting. If the service provider is not an informal resource, the case manager reenters the process in phase 2, where the directive is to locate other clients whose assets match the client's needs.

If the case manager discovers there is a problem in the client/provider interaction, then the case manager takes the role of mediator to try to resolve the difficulties. If mediation cleared the way for service delivery, then a new target date for service implementation is set and the process begins again. If, though, mediation did not clear the way for service delivery, the case manager asks herself whether the resource is a *formal* one. If it is, then she reenters in phase 2, where the directive is to advocate for the client in the formal setting. If the provider is not a formal but rather an *informal* one, the case manager reenters the process in phase 2, where the directive is to advocate for the client in the informal setting. If the service provider is not an informal resource, the case manager reenters the process in phase 2, where the directive is to locate other clients whose assets match the client's needs.

MONITORING

The primary goal of monitoring is to ensure that the services being provided continue to be high-quality, timely, relevant, necessary, and sufficient for the client's current needs. Therefore, the case manager must maintain continuous contact with both the client and the service provider until all agree that the particular service being delivered is no longer required or no longer appropriate. Through monitoring, progress toward meeting the tasks outlined in the service contract can be evaluated. If necessary, monitoring will show when the contract should be modified to reflect a new objective or new arrangements for quality or delivery of services.

The process guide to case management in the monitoring phase (figure 11.4) outlines the way of monitoring task flows. There are two skills associated with this: (1) reconnecting with the client and service provider and (2) mediating between the client and service provider. These skills are identical to those used in the linking phase.

PROCESS GUIDE IN THE MONITORING PHASE Once the client and service provider have been linked and services have begun, the case manager needs to monitor the services. Three or four months after service delivery has begun, the case manager should reconnect with the client to ask how the service is going from the client's point of view. If the client is having a problem, then the case manager asks if the problem is between the provider and the client. If the answer is, "Yes, there is a problem between the client and the provider," the case manager reenters in phase 3, where the directive is to mediate between the client and provider. On the other hand, if there is no problem between them, the case manager reenters in phase 3, where the question is, is the provider a *formal* resource.

If there is no problem from the standpoint of the client, the case manager should reconnect with the service provider to ask how service to the client is going from their perspective. The case manager asks if there are any problems with provision of service to the client. If the answer is no, then the case manager reenters phase 4 in three or four months and continues to monitor service delivery. If the service provider indicates a problem exists, then the case manager mediates between the provider and client. If the mediation is successful, in three or four months, the case manager starts phase 4 again. If the mediation is not successful, the case manager must ask whether the service provider will continue to provide services to the client. If the resource and client are willing to continue, the case manager begins phase 4 once again. However, if the provider or client is not willing to continue service, the case manager reenters phase 3, where the question is, is the provider a *formal* resource.

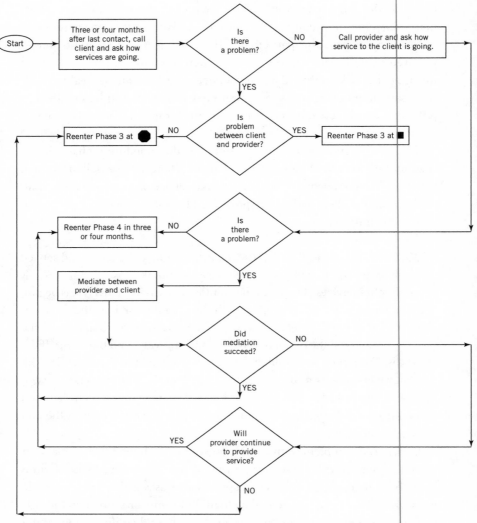

FIGURE 11.4 Process guide to case management in the monitoring phase: Phase 4

THE CASE MANAGER AS ADVOCATE

The case manager as advocate intercedes on behalf of the client (or clients) to assure equity for that client or for any larger group or class to which the client may belong. It is a special role used by the case manager in which the emphasis is on power and pressure used in the pursuit of particular outcomes, and in which the client alone is unable to negotiate a successful solution to a problem. This is accomplished through the use of strategic thinking and tactical actions. For the case manager, two different types of advocacy are possible. Case advocacy that focuses on influencing formal and informal service delivery systems on behalf or particular persons' needs (Quadrant C type activities) is the first. The second is class advocacy that focuses on influencing these systems in relation to their general functioning for the larger population in need (Quadrant B type activities).

The process guides for case management show that advocacy activities occur primarily in phase 2 when the worker is linking people with specific service needs to service providers. However, in *any* case management phase when there is a need for advocacy, it is not only an appropriate but also a mandatory role for the case manager. How often the case manager will have to employ the role of advocate is, in large measure, dictated by the range and wealth of resources in a given area and the unique needs of a specific client. Where there are more resources, advocacy may not be as necessary as when there are fewer available services.

DETERMINING THE WORK

Determining the work related to case management can be guided by two questions. The first asks whether there is an existing resource that can provide the necessary services. The second asks whether there is more than one person in the same situation. When a formal resource exists and there are no others in the client's situation, presumably those in need are being adequately served somewhere. However, when a formal resource exists and there *are* others in the client's situation, there may be obstacles to service delivery that must be addressed. If no formal resources exist and no others are in the client's situation, the case manager must find support from informal sources in the client's community for that particular client. When no resources exist and there are others in the client's situation, it is appropriate for the case manager to invite those persons to a meeting to see if they want to become a support group to help each other cope. Figure 11.5 depicts the case manager's choices.

Is There an Existing Resource?

	Yes	No
Yes	Eliminate barriers to make formal services available to all.	Help clients help each other.
No	Link client to appropriate formal resources.	Find supportive informal resources.

Are Others Similarly Situated?

FIGURE 11.5 The window of orientation

As figure 11.5 shows, the case manager must be involved with both the client and various formal and informal service networks simultaneously. This means that the case manager must be competent to perform all the roles and skills needed for working with the client and those required for doing the necessary work with formal and informal service providers. The following example illustrates some of the intricacies involved in case management.

Marcia, twenty-eight years old, has been hospitalized ten times in the past two years, jailed twice in the past four months, and treated in the mental health system for schizo-affective symptoms for the past six years (this diagnosis now appears questionable). Her true capabilities are not known, as they have been eclipsed by her dependency on illicit drugs, sexual promiscuity, violent temper tantrums, and paranoid beliefs. She has been "stable" for the past four months since being released from the mental hospital. She is showing signs of wanting to improve her life circumstances—she is tired of the frequent trips to jail and the mental wards, she longs for a relationship with her child, and values autonomy.

I met with her and helped her plan how to budget her SSI checks, find an apartment, apply for food stamps, and plan meals.

In this example, the case manager took the role of conferee in discussing the SSI checks, then moved into the role of broker when helping the client find an apartment. Moving back into the role of the conferee, the case manager helped Marcia apply for food stamps and plan her meals.

As the work continued, the worker continued to act as conferee as she helped Marcia get used to purchasing her own groceries.

I accompanied Marcia to the grocery store twice a week while she selected her food. I also helped Marcia think about what to do if there was money left over at the end of the month. What were her priorities? While this might have been naïve on my part (Marcia's monthly check was only $540), I helped Marcia think about simple budgeting.

In addition to the weekly trips to the grocery store, I was simultaneously looking for a drug rehabilitation program for Marcia. After speaking with several treatment programs staff members who "knew" Marcia, I was finally able to convince one of them to again accept her again. The proviso in accepting her was that I would try and help Marcia understand that medication alone would not solve all her problems. She would have to work hard and demonstrate a commitment to treatment. I reassured Marcia that I would continue to stand with her throughout the treatment program and beyond.

It was in the role of advocate that the case manager convinced the staff of the drug treatment program to give the client another chance, and in the role of conferee, she assured Marcia of her continued assistance. The role of conferee will also be used as the case manager discusses Marcia's behavior with her to help her stick out the treatment program that she will reenter.

As the example continues, because of Marcia's recurring problem with drugs, the case manager, in the role of conferee, accompanies Marcia to Narcotics Anonymous (NA) meetings. The case manager shifts from the role of conferee to the role of broker when she forms a self-help group for Marcia and others in a similar situation because none currently exists.

I agreed to attend two NA meetings with Marcia, and I also coordinated the development of a small self-help group for her and other agency clients with similar problems. Marcia had told me that she hated to be so "spread out," having to see five different workers, each trying to help her with a different aspect of her struggles. She was enthusiastic when I agreed to coordinate the services to provide her and others some "in-house" support and help with narcotics dependency. As a result, Marcia had only two professionals in her life that she had to talk to regularly—her psychiatrist and me.

I saw my work with Marcia as a combination of general counseling and teaching activities. I did this by giving Marcia feedback to foster her productive behaviors, and giving her supportive messages to bolster her nascent belief that she is a person of value and worth. But I did not seek to befriend Marcia, as that is inappropriate and unethical in a worker/client relationship. Rather, I tried to discuss and demonstrate the significance of being connected to others through friendship as a way of maintaining and reciprocating others' needs to maintain mutual self-esteem. I hoped this approach would begin to counter some of Marcia's long standing alienation from others. I was hoping to help Marcia find some compelling reasons for staying well that might sufficiently counter some of the perceived protections sickness brings (e.g., fewer family and financial worries, the guaranteed shelter of the hospital and jail).

The preceding example demonstrates the many complexities involved in case management by showing the many balls that a case manager must juggle in order to provide competent case management for a client. The needs of the client are linked with existing resources, previous client/service provider encounters, and current client need. The role of the case manager is to ensure that the client's *needs are identified* and that the client is then *appropriately connected* with requisite formal and/or informal resources. Once linked, the case manager must *continually monitor* the services unless and until all agree that there is no further need for them.

THE CASE MANAGER IN QUADRANTS A, B, AND C

To assist the case manager in coping with the complexities of her or his role, we have presented process guides. To facilitate understanding, we will refer to these as discussion of the case manager in each of the three direct-practice quadrants proceeds. Because the case manager moves from quadrant to quadrant, this discussion of the quadrants is integrated.

Figure 11.1 depicts the assessment phase. In this phase, the primary role of the case manager is that of conferee, and Quadrant A is the predominant locus of the work. The worker's interactional skills are directed toward reaching for information and attending to the client's feelings as they arise.

Having performed the assessment, the case manager moves into the planning phase depicted in figure 11.2. Because the client must play as prominent a role as possible in planning to meet her or his needs, the case manager shuttles between the role of broker in Quadrant C and the role of conferee in Quadrant A as she variously locates resources (Quadrant C) and then discusses them with the client (Quadrant A). As the process guide shows, it is in the planning phase that the case manager will sometimes need to take the role of advocate if and when existing resources refuse to accommodate clients in need.

Once a service contract that is consistent with the assessment and agreeable to the client and the worker has been made, the case manager moves into the linking phase (figure 11.3). While linking occurs primarily in Quadrant C, with the case manager in the role of broker, there are times when the worker may also need to take the role of mediator as well. Note, too, that there are also times when the case manager may need to return to the planning phase (Quadrants A and C).

The monitoring phase (figure 11.4) finds the case manager once again shuttling between two roles and two quadrants. As broker in Quadrant C, the case manager talks with service providers about how things are going from their perspective. And, as conferee in Quadrant A, the case manager talks to the client about how things are going. As in the linking phase, the case manager must be prepared to take the role of mediator if necessary and, when circumstances warrant, return to specific parts of the linking phase. The process is not merely linear. It often requires doubling back.

Few case management activities occur in Quadrant B save for class advocacy activities that focus on influencing formal systems in relation to their general functioning, that is, breakdowns in or nonexistence of services that affect whole populations in need. No case management occurs in Quadrant D. Case management primarily takes place in Quadrants A and C.

CONCLUSION

Since the 1970s, case management as a role for social workers has gained prominence. As the new century continues and services are reevaluated in terms of governmental versus private responsibility for public welfare, the role of case management will continue to be an important one.

12

THE GROUP WORKER

THE GROUP and the awareness of groups, critically important to the lives of individuals, are at the heart of structural social work practice. It is an extricable component of the principle of following the demands of the client task — particularly the directive to *look beyond the client to see if others face the same plight*. This directive immediately urges workers to consider more than a one-by-one approach to problem situations by working with individuals in their human contexts along with others who are similarly affected. The role of the group worker is essential when working with support groups, social groups, therapy groups, or advocacy groups. Workers work with groups in three of the four quadrants (Quadrants A, B, and C), and when they assume the role of group worker they use specialized group work skills to enable people to interact toward the ends specified in the service contract.

The principle of maximizing supports in the client's environment (often these supports are other persons or groups) emphasizes that the worker should "not occupy the central position in the helping process" but rather, change and create structures that can carry on without the worker. It is imperative that social workers have faith in the potential helpfulness of groups for their members and/or those who join groups seeking to help others in need.

In this chapter, social workers will gain an appreciation of groups and their workings and understand the skills involved in fulfilling the role of an effective group worker. The primary focus is on the tasks and skills related to group work with clients, but we also explore the tasks and skills related to group work on behalf of clients and others.

THE BASIC GROUP

Human beings are social beings. Most cannot exist for long in total isolation. Ordinarily, they long for the companionship of others. It is almost impossible to escape the ties that bind people together. In social work, the term *group* means people who come together because of some shared commonality of interest. It is no accident that the concepts *network*, the workings of a net of personal relationships that connect people with others, and *safety net*, something used to "catch" a falling person, are popular in social work talk. These concepts capture the usual need for connectedness of individuals, their need to be linked with others—not isolated and alone.

But *alone* must be distinguished from *lonely*. Some people relish alone time enjoying their solitude without being lonely. Others, though, can be lonely in the midst of a busy workplace, marriage, or set of social activities. While physical aloneness need not breed loneliness, prolonged aloneness can encourage loneliness by its separating quality. The popularity of cell phones and computer chat rooms attest to this.

TYPES OF GROUPS

When thinking about groups and social work with groups, it is important to conceptualize various types of groups. There are four types of groups in which social workers play a professional role: (1) support groups, (2) social groups, (3) therapy groups, and (4) advocacy groups.

SUPPORT GROUPS

Evolving from the settlement house movement, the support group has a long history in social work. Traditionally, such groups have focused on helping group members cope with problems related to common human needs. Aimed primarily at persons who are systematically stigmatized or disenfranchised, support groups are used for developmental, preventative, and enhancement purposes. The focus of the support group is interpersonal, helping participants to communicate with and help one another. That is, support groups are ventures in mutual aid.

Support group workers are professionals, direct service practitioners who encourage cognitive learning to supplement experiential awareness. These workers have a special "know-how" about working with groups and engaging them in problem-solving activity. Support groups are as varied as the problems of people and may include groups for survivors of suicide, survivors of woman battering, adults molested as children, children coping with the loss of a parent, children of divorce, and the like.

While support groups and self-help groups are often lumped together, self-help groups such as Alcoholics Anonymous do not involve professional intervention and are not within the purview of practitioners of direct social work. Many of these groups believe that "having been there" is a stronger basis for helping. When social workers attend meetings of self-help groups, they do so as members.

SOCIAL GROUPS

All groups are, by definition, socially constructed and related to society in some form or another. The most common in the North American culture is the family unit and is thought by many to be the cornerstone of society. It is a familiar one to social workers, and is easily conceptualized as a special type of group. Traditionally, the family has been defined as those who are biologically related in some way. However, today's family is more broadly defined to include those persons living together by choice whether there is a biological or legal connection. Such would include, among others, single parents, heterosexual married couples with or without natural or adopted children, gay/lesbian couples with or without children, those linked to one another emotionally and sharing living space, or fictive families of any description. In other words, defining today's family unit is not as easy as it may have been in 1950. In fact, merely being able to identify a family unit may require some detective work. And to solve any potential dilemma, the worker may simply want to ask the client to describe that client's family unit. Confusing as it may be to define any one family unit, the functions of the family as a social institution are for members to care for one another, socialize the young, and carry on traditional societal rituals.

Often families, functional or dysfunctional, move through life on their own without professional intervention, but there are times when family members require help. This occurs when they face situations that they or others seem to think they cannot manage on their own. It is at this point that social workers are likely to become involved with the family group.

In addition to the family group, there are countless other social groups where social workers, as group workers, play a role—groups formed because of similar needs. Such might include local church groups where social workers help elderly members do reminiscence work; staff a midnight basketball program for teens at an inner-city housing project; or facilitate groups at the local Jewish Community Center or YWCA aimed at providing parenting skills for teenage mothers, playgroups for children, and teen social activity groups.

Finally, there are social groups where social workers are not likely to intervene—groups formed because of similar likes or interests. Such might include church auxiliaries, bowling leagues, fraternities and sororities, bird-watching groups, Girl Scout troops, meditation circles, and countless others. These kinds of social groups do not usually require social work intervention.

THERAPY GROUPS

The social-work therapy group is an orientation to group work adopted by many social agencies as a component of their treatment plan. Some clinical social workers prefer group therapy to individual work, especially when the work focuses on family or related others whose support the client needs. Like support groups, the focus of the therapy group is interpersonal, helping participants to communicate with and help one another. It differs from support groups insofar as the focus is personal as well as interpersonal, and each individual may have different tasks to accomplish. The group process is transparent and is actively directed toward group members helping each other with forces in their daily living situations (jobs, children, housing, and the like), stress, interpersonal relations, and psychological struggles.

In social work, there is an emphasis on the individual and the group. The individual is seen in terms of the group—both as a participant in helping others in the group confront and resolve their problems and, by having others in the group confront and help to resolve the problems of the individual. The group as a holistic entity is guided by the professional group worker who ensures that the task of the group and its individual members are met (Schopler and Galinsky 1995).

In therapy groups, intimate details of people's lives are the content of talk; therefore, confidentiality is expected. The group therapist defines this expectation explicitly when the group is together for its first session.

ADVOCACY GROUPS

Advocacy groups are generally composed of people who want to obtain opportunities and resources they cannot get by themselves. Many of these people are undervalued, stigmatized, disenfranchised, or are concerned with particular issues or the welfare of people other than themselves. Such might include mentally ill persons, profoundly deaf persons, transgender teens, elderly persons, and so forth. Additionally, examples include disadvantaged groups such as women, minorities of color, and others who suffer the pangs of disaffection with their realities. Advocacy groups are frequently, but not always, constructed through some professional leadership where the aim is to deal with oppressive aspects of "the system." Advocacy groups employ a problem-solving approach, are action-oriented, and may be devoted to issues outside the participants (for example, social reform). They often use statistics and numbers in arguments, persuasion tactics, and demonstrations to pressure unresponsive government officials or bureaucrats in the private sector. Thus, the emphasis of advocacy groups is on changing some part of the social environment, not on personal or interpersonal relationships among members—except when intragroup struggles require the social worker to take the role of mediator as a temporary measure to challenge the obstacles and restore all members' ability to do the agreed-upon work.

In sum, while there are a variety of groups with which social work practitioners interact, the most prominent group work tasks require the social worker to focus on both the group as well as the individuals comprising it, and the emphasis is on interpersonal interdependence *and* on the environment. This connection of persons with others and with their outside environments is a hallmark of social work, especially important in the structural approach.

TASKS FOR WORKING WITH GROUPS

Irrespective of the kind of group a with which social worker is working, there are five tasks to which the worker must attend: (1) using a holistic approach, (2) intervening with groups, (3) sustaining groups, (4) comprehending group dynamics, and (5) facilitating interaction in groups. Embedded within each of these tasks are skills.

USING A HOLISTIC APPROACH

Group work in social work requires that the social worker apply a holistic perspective to the group process. In other words, the group is seen as a social system in which there are reciprocal relationships between members and a concern for what is outside the group. There are two cognitive skills associated with using a holistic approach: (1) thinking group and (2) viewing group.

THINKING GROUP Thinking group means having group concepts as a cognitive mind set that provides a frame of reference for what is happening in the group. It assures that the group as a unit is the primary focus of attention rather than the individual, and that the interests of group as an entirety must supersede the interests of one or more members (Middleman and Wood 1990).

In order to *think group*, the worker must understand group structure—the unseen framework that holds the group together and partially accounts for the regularities in members' behaviors. Group structure consists of roles, norms, and intermember relations. Roles refer to the various sets of behaviors taken on by group members as the group matures. These may include task leaders, social emotional leaders, and gatekeepers (these will be discussed in more depth later in this chapter).

Norms are the rules that describe the actions that should (prescriptive norms) or should not (proscriptive norms) be taken by group members, and serve as the standards by which group members regulate their own behavior. Intermember relations refer to the types of relationships that differentially link group members with one another. The three most important are authority relations, attraction relations, and communication relations. In terms of authority relations, though group members may all start out on an equal footing, soon certain members begin to coordinate the activities of the group, provide other members with guidance, or relay communications to various other members. Over time, these differences in authority, prestige, or power create a stable pattern of intermember relations that can be described as a hierarchy of authority within the group. Attraction relations refers to the stable pattern of liking or disliking that evolves over time between members as they interact with one another. Group members are also linked in a communication network that significantly influences the problem solving efficiency of the group, its leadership, and member satisfaction. *Thinking group* is a continuous skill the worker uses to understand the group's process. Its counterpart, *viewing group*, is also a continuous skill.

VIEWING GROUP Viewing group requires the group worker to look at the group analytically. This involves seeing the group not as two dimensional, but rather one with four dimensions and is conceptualized as follows:

me (the worker) looking at
us (the group with me in it), in
context (time and space; the here and now and the history) with a
purpose (support, social, therapy, advocacy).

These four components comprise a continuous transactional field of force that, when combined, makes up the specific group situation.

The *me* looking at *us* suggests that the worker is always mindful that she is seeing things through her own biases, cultural background, professional screen, and other filters that may cloud her judgment of what is going on; and that she realizes her presence in the group changes the group situation. The group itself is a continuously moving, changing entity. The *context* directs attention not only to what is happening in the moment but also to where the group is in its current process (at the beginning, near the middle, or ending). The context encompasses, too, previous experiences of the group as a whole and each individual's experiences with groups as pertinent to the here and now. Finally, the group's *purpose*, or why it has been formed, will have a major effect on all that happens within it.

Thus, the two skills required for a group worker to use a holistic approach are thinking group and viewing group—both skills that go on continuously when working with a group. In addition to these, there are other tasks and skills that must be employed by the effective group worker.

INTERVENING WITH GROUPS

Intervening with groups refers to the actual "doing" of group work. There are four skills associated with this task: (1) selecting group members, (2) creating goals and objectives, (3) implementing the contract, and (4) assessing the outcomes.

SELECTING GROUP MEMBERS The first skill associated with intervening with groups is that of *selecting group members*—identifying who will be in the group and for what purpose the group is being created. Various types of groups will have various types of members. The members, goals, and service contracts of support groups will vary from those of therapy groups and advocacy groups because of the basic nature of the group. Selecting and forming any group dependents on the purpose of the group, for that will be the focus of, and the primary variable for determining group membership. This is true for any type of group.

CREATING GOALS AND CONTRACTS Creating goals and contracts with groups is similar to formulating them with individuals—the key difference is that there is a group goal and contract that takes precedence over individual pursuits. Since groups are designed for specific purposes (that is, dealing with specific issues confronted by its members), it is assumed that the goals of the individual group member can be accomplished through the group experience. In keeping with the principle of accountability to the client, the group worker, in concert with group members, develops a service contract that will make explicit for all concerned what the group members and worker will try to accomplish. The second part of the service contract—that of a clear understanding of how the worker and group members would accomplish the task—must also be discussed at the first group meeting (although it may not be concluded in one session). In keeping with the six practice principles (see chapter 4), the worker and group members agree to how best to meet the goals set forth.

IMPLEMENTING THE CONTRACT Once the group goals and contract that embodies them have been agreed to, the real work of the group begins. Groups generally meet at the same time each week and continue for a specified amount of time. Sometimes open-ended group membership is necessary, and it is the worker's responsibility to orient incoming members so that the group does not need to go back to the beginning phase whenever new members join. At the group meetings, group members and the worker follow the agreed-upon service contract, and if changes are necessary, the group decides upon the new direction. Because groups are composed of unique individuals, the dynamics of the group process is ever in flux. Some groups arrive quickly at solutions while others labor. As membership changes, groups can shift from one to another. Regardless of the group's membership status—open-ended or closed—the group worker must be aware of where the group is at any given point in time. She must be prepared to go with the flow of the group as long as it is moving toward the desired outcomes and to redirect the process when the group moves away from its work.

ASSESSING THE OUTCOMES Assessing to what extent the goals of the group are being accomplished is an ongoing process. Such assessment can occur at each session, and it is important to have group members regularly share their perceptions on how well the goals are being met. Because groups are made up of individuals, each may differ as to their assessment. Ideally, all members achieve their own and the group's objectives by the end of the group process. Thus, the group worker must be alert to where each member is at all times. At the end of the agreed-upon time for termination of the group experience, the group members and the worker should fully discuss whether or to what extent their goals were attained and, if necessary, renegotiate for another set of group meetings.

SUSTAINING GROUPS

Sustaining groups is directly related to fostering cohesion within the group. It refers to the task of building the group across time and nurturing the group throughout its life. The cohesiveness of a group is the glue that holds it together and makes members want to keep coming back. Four skills are related to this task: (1) setting boundaries, (2) voicing group achievements, (3) preserving group history and continuity, and (4) encouraging the development of traditions and rituals.

SETTING BOUNDARIES Early in the life of the group, the group worker articulates boundaries for member behaviors. These boundaries help members conduct the business of the group in an orderly fashion. They are the rules that specify what group members may or may not do while in the group. Some of these are dictated by the agency under whose aegis the group meets (for instance, only pregnant teens are allowed in the hospital group), and others are dictated by generally accepted codes of conduct (respecting other members, not using profanity). Whatever they are, they need to be verbally stated early in the process of the group and repeated when necessary. If violated, the group and/or the group worker must confront the breach.

VOICING GROUP ACHIEVEMENTS Once the group has been formed and has met at least once, the worker can begin to voice group achievements. This refers to a verbal summary of individual and group goals that have been accomplished since the beginning of the group process. It also refers to the worker's voicing notable efforts on the road to achieving these goals—especially during the early sessions. Individual positive progress in the face of backsliding counts as an accomplishment and should also be mentioned. Giving voice to these positive movements helps keep the group on task, focuses on cohesion, and provides fodder for assessment. This benchmarking is done periodically across the lifespan of the group, and with every new achievement, additional or higher goals, if appropriate, may be set.

PRESERVING GROUP HISTORY AND CONTINUITY Preserving group history and continuity refers to the worker's need to remind the group of its past successes and efforts that were not successful. These reminders can be used to create smooth transitions between sessions. The continuity is seen as helping the group move into its present session by recalling what had been accomplished (or not) in its last session (or previous sessions). This linking from session to session not only preserves the history of the group but also serves as a way to begin the new session. Both the group worker and group members provide input into this activity. It is also possible for one or two members to be historians. They may keep a scrapbook of the group's journey together for the group to review periodically. It may contain group decisions, issues to be addressed, cards or notes from members, journal entries, or photographs. In groups where confidentially is expected, such documentation is eschewed.

ENCOURAGING DEVELOPMENT OF TRADITIONS AND RITUALS A group's special traditions and rituals tend to heighten group identity and loyalty. They evolve as the group matures, and they increase group joi de vivre, spirit, and pride. Some groups may begin each session with a tradition such as identifying who in the group is celebrating a special day (a birthday, an anniversary) or end each session by joining hands and reading a poem. The rituals and traditions that are developed by groups are as varied as the groups themselves. In a support group for battered women, a group ritual might include a brief sharing of each member's story since the last session and end with the group proclaiming, "I was not to blame!" In a therapy group, the closing ritual might be for each member to support the progress of others openly. A social group that is trying to identify new members might include, as an opening ritual, having old members share how many potential members they contacted since the last session. Advocacy groups who successfully get what they wanted might always have a planned celebration at the conclusion of their quest.

These traditions and rituals tend to create bonds between members and the social worker is encouraged to foster the development of these special rites that help support the group as it evolves. Some symbolic behaviors may even exist for members outside the group setting. For example, if a battered woman can recall the "It is not my fault" proclamation at the end of the session when she is away from the group, it might help her to believe that the battering is really not her fault.

COMPREHENDING GROUP DYNAMICS

A holistic approach to group work is enhanced by comprehending what goes on in groups—the dynamics of the group. Two skills are associated with comprehending group dynamics: (1) scanning group and (2) recognizing and managing role differentiation.

SCANNING GROUP Scanning group is a process that is constant when working with groups and refers to the group worker's looking at the group as a whole, with her eyes and listening to the group with her ears. It involves interpersonal, cognitive, and sensory skills related to communication — verbal and nonverbal communication and a "taking in" of what is happening in the group at all times. The process of consciously looking at and listening to each group member throughout each session enables the worker to build the group and to understand better the ongoing dynamics and role behaviors of group members. The skills of simultaneously being "in tune" with both the individuals and the group depend on comprehending group dynamics.

RECOGNIZING AND MANAGING ROLE DIFFERENTIATION Recognizing the role behavior of group members, its positive (and negative) influences on group dynamics and processes, and managing it across the life of the group is another group work skill. As mentioned previously, across time different group members assume different roles.

The first level of role differentiation is reached when most of the group members recognize one or more individuals as leaders. The first type of leader to emerge tends to be a person (or persons) concerned with accomplishing the task at hand who tries organizing the group to move toward attaining their agreed upon goal. This person may be called a *task leader*, and though various members may fill the role at various times during the life of the group (Bales 1950), initially it seems to belong to one person.

Even though a group needs task leadership to help move it toward its goals, tension in a group is unavoidable. Work on the task generates tension. As the tension of the group increases, *social emotional leaders* emerge to help maintain the emotional stability of the group by responding to individual's feelings. The function of a social emotional leader is to reduce interpersonal hostilities and frustrations and maintain some semblance of harmony. Task leaders dominate in the problem-solving area by giving suggestions and opinions, while social emotional leaders dominate in the emotive area by reaching for and getting with feelings and pointing out agreements between members.

In addition to these leadership roles, another important role sometimes emerges in groups. A group member may guard the gates of group process by allowing group discussion of difficult topics to occur only when she and the group seem ready to discuss the topic. Until that point, the topic is deferred. Some gatekeeping is necessary in any group, but some gatekeepers steer groups away from important work. For example, a gatekeeper in a group of female incest survivors did not let the group proceed into the topic of child molestation until her pattern of moving the group off point was brought to her attention.

These roles appear gradually as the group matures across time. Not all the roles are played or continuously played by all the same people. Although groups may make it difficult for members to change their roles, roles do shift. If the group worker notices that a pattern of behavior is getting in the way of the group then she must bring it to the group's attention. Ignoring disruptive behavior or monopolizing behavior, for example, may damage the group's process and development.

In order to manage behaviors that could have a deleterious effect on the group process, the group worker must first notice the pattern of behavior and then confront it during the group meeting. The identification and management of differing roles within the group is an important skill in understanding group dynamics and facilitating interaction in groups.

FACILITATING INTERACTION IN GROUPS

Facilitating interaction in groups refers to those skills related to understanding and encouraging communication among members. In addition to a constant awareness of group dynamics, group workers face the same challenges that confront workers dealing with individual clients—hearing and seeing what is being said on a variety of levels, verbally and nonverbally. Moreover, group work requires practitioners to master ten skills to facilitate interaction in groups: (1) setting the stage and fostering cohesion, (2) amplifying subtle messages, (3) softening overpowering messages, (4) creating empathic connections, (5) reaching for an information link, (6) redirecting messages, (7) inviting full participation, (8) turning issues back to the group, (9) reaching for consensus, and (10) reaching for difference (Middleman and Wood 1990).

SETTING THE STAGE AND FOSTERING COHESION Setting the stage and fostering cohesion refers to behaviors the social worker performs to launch and sustain the group experience. This includes the physical space in which the group meetings occur (room, seating, public/private area. temperature, and the like)—or the "stage" on which the group will dramatize its real life situations. This stage sets the tone for what the group views at its first and subsequent sessions and should be designed for member comfort and safety in discussing issues related to the purpose of the group. The setting should allow appropriate space for members to accomplish the tasks for which the group was developed. For example, if the object of a group was to discuss abortion with newly pregnant teens, holding such a group meeting in the lobby of a public building, if the group is small, or even in an overly large private room would be inappropriate. The place, along with the interpersonal relationships generated by the group worker with each member and with the group as a whole, paves the way for the development of group cohesiveness and will encourage members to want to come to future sessions. Although the group stage is set at the start of the group experience, fostering cohesiveness between members is a process that endures across the life of the group.

AMPLIFYING SUBTLE MESSAGES Amplifying subtle messages involves calling attention to verbal or nonverbal messages that have been sent by a group member, seen and understood by the social worker, but missed by other members of the group. The primary goal is to verbalize the subtle, overlooked message to those who missed it, not to the one sending the message. If, for example, all the members of the group are giggling about something, but one member's eyes swell with tears, a message has been sent. If the others who are involved in the giggling do not notice the message, the social worker would call attention to it by saying, for example, "Sophie is crying." Subtle messages need amplifying only when they are not noticed by other members of the group. Some subtle messages, such as a clenched fist or audible sigh, that other members have apparently seen or heard need not be amplified, even if members choose not to respond. Rather, the worker should direct her comments to the sender and *reach for that person's feelings.*

SOFTENING OVERPOWERING MESSAGES Softening overpowering messages refers to reducing the emotional power of messages that are verbalized in such a forceful manner that they cannot be easily taken in or accepted. This may include messages that are shouted, glares, or strident pacing around the room. In order for the sender of the message to be actually *heard* or dealt with, the overpowering message must be made easier to take in—or softened. Often words spoken in anger are hard for group members to hear and deal with. The affect of the message sender must be softened to a point where the message *can be heard.* Group workers must be able to soften the anger without trivializing the message or the validity of the powerful emotion in its delivery. This requires group workers to resend the message as a report, complete with a description of the forcefulness of the content and its attendant feelings. For example, one group member was extremely angry at having to park some distance from the group meeting. He brought this anger to the group and announced that if he ever had to park so far away again, he was going to quit coming to the meetings. He screamed that he was just as handicapped as other group members who got special parking privileges because of their disabilities. The worker softened his message by telling the group, "Bill is frustrated and furious about his parking situation," then *creating an empathic connection* by asking the group, "Can anyone connect with how Bill is feeling right now?" Later the group can be invited to make suggestions to help Bill deal with the very real problem that generated his powerful emotions.

CREATING EMPATHIC CONNECTIONS Creating empathic connections requires that the social worker ask group members to connect with a feeling that is being expressed by another. It is through these empathic connections that members are better able to appreciate and understand what another is feeling, plus support the other by expressing empathy. It can be likened to "walking in another's shoes" and sharing experiences with that other person. Asking members to connect with the feelings of another validates that group members do, indeed understand the other's inner experience and care about the feelings of another.

Every group member has the potential for empathic connections and the worker creates opportunities to have this demonstrated. It is as important for people to tap into their capacity for empathy, experience it, and express it as it is for them to experience genuine empathy from others. The group worker's effort to create an empathic connection is for the benefit of the person struggling with deep and sometimes confusing feelings. Her aim is not to provide the group with an exercise in flexing their emotional muscles. Nonetheless, empathic connections create benefits for both the group and the individual.

An example of *creating an empathic connection* occurred in a hospice group that was dealing with the impending death of a member. Group members realized a young member had never before experienced the death of a loved one and was noticeably upset. The worker created an empathic connection between other members and the person struggling with the first death by asking if anyone could imagine what it must be like to watch, for the first time, someone they felt close to dying. This invited group members to express empathic connections and provided support for the troubled young member.

REACHING FOR AN INFORMATION LINK Reaching for an information link means that workers (and group members) generate information from each other that will help accomplish the group task.

It requires the social worker to ask group members to connect with a verbal or nonverbal message that has been sent by another member. It seeks to clarify information from all group members and provide feedback to specific group members related to information that has been communicated. For example, at a group meeting related to how to obtain food stamps, a member stated that she had been denied food stamps only because she lived with her mother. The worker *reached for an information link* by asking if any group members had had a similar experience and could provide information. One group member who also lived with her mother but who had obtained food stamps asked whether the apartment was listed in the group member's name or her mother's name. This was an important question, because the answer could clarify the problem's solution.

REDIRECTING MESSAGES Redirecting messages refers to ensuring that communication specifically meant for someone is given and received by the person for whom it is intended. In other words, when a group member directs a comment meant for another member to the group worker (or another member for whom it is not ultimately intended), the social worker instructs the communicator to redirect the message to the person or persons for whom it was intended (whether that person is present). For example, a teenager in a substance abuse group told the worker that another member of the group was picking on her. Rather than falling into a trap that would force the worker to respond, the worker tells the group member to redirect the message to the member who was picking on her.

When a group member brings up difficult situations related to those outside the group with whom she or he is having problems, the social worker can appropriately ask the group member to discuss the situation with those outside the group with whom she is having a problem—thereby redirecting the message to the appropriate target. Once the group member has delivered the message, she then reports her experience back to the group.

INVITING FULL PARTICIPATION Inviting full participation refers to encouraging everyone in the group to participate in the process. The worker wants to ensure that all the voices of the group are heard and selectively asks (either verbally or nonverbally) for nonparticipating members' input. By hearing all participants, decisions are more inclusive, participation is better balanced, and all members feel as though, because they are, part of the process. For example, a retired union organizer had been part of an advocacy group for three weeks. He always came to meetings and would vigorously nod or shake his head at things, but never spoke. Others in the group tended to look at his nonverbal communication, but never ask what he might be able to contribute beyond his opinion of what others were saying. When the group worker asked, "Mr. Milgram, what have you been thinking?" after a moment of silence he voiced several thoughts about the issue under discussion. By inviting full participation, all members' voices have an important place in the group dialogue.

Because communication patterns may crystallize and roles solidify, it should be noted that the group worker must specifically invite silent members to speak very early in the life of the group. The longer one is silent, the harder it becomes for that person to participate verbally.

TURNING ISSUES BACK TO THE GROUP Turning issues back to the group refers to having the worker refuse to make decisions for the group. This is especially necessary early in the life of the group, when members expect the group worker to provide the direction. Whenever the group looks to the worker for solutions, she can say to the group, "What do *you* think? The problem belongs to the group." The group must reach its own conclusions about those things that are of importance to its purpose. Rather than provide what the worker thinks might be an appropriate ideas, the worker asks the members to examine whatever issue is at hand and help each other deal with it. This allows the group to use its collective expertise and creativity. For example, a support group dealing with eating disorders was having a difficult time with an issue related to body image. Various group members repeatedly asked the group worker for direction. After she provided information about eating disorders and body-image issues, the worker turned the issue back to the group for thought and discussion whenever she was asked for direction, thereby requiring the group members to help each other to devise coping strategies and not rely on her to do so for them.

REACHING FOR CONSENSUS Reaching for consensus refers to the worker's periodic checking with the group members to see if everyone is in agreement with the group's process. Consensus is a way to test for harmony and end minor and inconsequential disagreements between members. While consensus may involve some compromise, it can facilitate the work of the group to achieve mutually agreed upon goals. As the term is used here, consensus is achieved when *most* of the group members mutually agree upon a decision, even when it means some members modify their original positions for the good of the group. It is not a decision making process in which one

or two members can obstruct group process and bring progress to a permanent halt. As a decision-making requirement, consensus is subject to the
tyranny of the minority—especially a vocal minority—and decisions cannot
be made.

In reaching for consensus, the worker may take the role of the mediator to
help members hear and speak to each other with purpose and genuine feeling. For example, a support group of elderly nursing home residents wanted to
meet weekly for reminiscence work. At the first meeting, group members
decided they would do their work by recalling what happened in various
decades of the 1900s, and wanted to begin with the decade between 1910 and
1920. There was a bit of disagreement because some of the group members
had not been born until after 1920 and they wanted to contribute. Sensing the
discomfort with lack of consensus, the worker urged the members to discuss
the timetable again, and they did so. After some discussion and compromises,
members agreed that the reminiscing would begin in 1925, when all members
were old enough to recall important events in their lives. Once that decision
was made, the worker again reached for consensus in the group and found
that it was truly present.

REACHING FOR DIFFERENCE Reaching for a difference refers to helping
group members see things from a variety of perspectives. Hearing different
voices with different ways of seeing and doing things enables members to
explore various alternatives related to the same issue. Hearing all the possibilities allows for a more informed conversation and gives all members an
opportunity to have their say on whatever the issue. The worker encourages
group members to think "outside the box" and see not only black and white,
but also shades of gray. Doing so combats groupthink and, if consensus is
reached, enhances the possibility that the consensus is based on all information available to the group. For example, a settlement house advocacy group
was trying to determine the best way to get the local police to better patrol a
particular block in their neighborhood that was a haven for drug users. Members had various ideas, and the group worker reached for difference when she
encouraged members to hear and evaluate each idea before trying to arrive at
a decision.

It should be noted that it is very hard for some people to voice a dissenting
opinion when a majority of members take a strong position. It is even harder
when the group is cohesive with less tolerance of difference—even when the
different idea is valid and valuable. Thus, it is incumbent upon the group
worker to reach for the hesitant or unvoiced difference and encourage the

group to consider it before simply rejecting it because the majority have spoken and agreed.

THE GROUP WORKER IN QUADRANTS A, B, AND C

Group work activity takes place in Quadrants A, B, and C. Quadrant A work includes working with clients/members on their own behalf (social groups, support groups, therapy groups). Quadrant B work includes working with clients/members on behalf of themselves and others like them (client advocacy groups), and Quadrant C work involves working with others on behalf of a specifically identified client population who are suffering (nonclient advocacy groups, boards of parents setting policies for teenage activity groups). Quadrant D work, a macro-practice, involves working with others on behalf of an entire population in need and is rarely considered in micro-practice.

GROUP WORK IN QUADRANT A

Group work in Quadrant A involves working with clients/members on their own behalf. The example that follows is that of a support group for those struggling with clarifying their sexual orientation and coming out.

The Seneca Service Center (SSC) serves a large metropolitan area in the Midwest. Part of its catchment area is what has been called "The Hub"—a mile-square area of Victorian-era slums and recently rehabilitated grand old homes inhabited by a diverse group of people that includes young and old lesbians, gays, heterosexual couples, homeless persons, and various ethnic minorities. The local gay bar and what was, in the pre-AIDS era, the men's bathhouse are in the area; lots of small trendy shops run by those who live in the area; three churches (one Catholic, one Presbyterian, and one Unity); a synagogue, a mid-sized grocery store with a pharmacy, and a local grocery. It is a vibrant place with all the joys and dilemmas of city living.

Seneca Service Center itself is located on the fringe of the Hub, and many of its clients are lesbian, gay, bisexual, or transgender (LGBT). An ongoing issue that seems to be causing difficulty with many clients is their coming to terms with their sexual orientation and coming out. Because there were several clients with the same issue who had indicated it would be helpful to them if they could meet with others in the same situation, the social worker decided to try to form a support group to deal with "coming-out" issues. Because of the specialized focus of the group, group membership was limited to those who were grappling with sexual orientation issues related to something other than heterosexuality. Thus, the SOS (Sexual Orientation Support) group was born.

In the case of the SOS group, the overall goal was formulated before the group actually met to deal with helping each other struggle to understand their sexual orientation better. It was on this basis that the group was formed and the worker made it explicit to various individuals invited to join. It was therefore understood by all who were invited, as well as stated again at the first meeting, that the focus of the group would be on helping members cope with their struggles related to sexual orientation. The task was discussed at the first session. All members contributed and the specific group goal—to emerge from the group experience less confused about sexual orientation—was unanimously accepted.

The SOS group had five members, all of whom were at various stages in their life journey. Terry Lee, a twenty-four-year-old Asian American male, believed he was trapped in the wrong body—he was actually a woman. After the death of her husband, Allie Pellegrino, a fifty-eight-year-old mother of three, reawakened a thirty-year-old lesbian relationship with her former college roommate. Sylvia Dominique, a twenty-nine-year-old Cajun who had been in a convent for a decade, had decided that the life of a nun was not compatible with who she thought herself to be. Art Longknife, a thirty-three-year-old Native American, was seeking a more spiritual understanding of his homosexuality, and Bob Cowan, a thirty-eight-year-old, married trucker, engaged in same-sex activities while on the road. Each sought something slightly different, but for each there was a quest to become less confused about who they are when it comes to sexual orientation. They decided the group would last for twelve sessions, after which they would reassess whether it should be continued. The worker said she would help them talk and listen to one another's thoughts and feelings. All agreed to these terms, and a service contract was made.

Once the tasks and service contract that embodies them were agreed to, the real work of the group began. Using a holistic approach (thinking and viewing group), the worker set about the work of sustaining the SOS group. The meeting place of the SOS group was a cozy room with sofas, overstuffed chairs and a pleasant atmosphere. Free coffee and sodas were available and the space exuded a feeling of warmth and acceptance. The stage was set.

At its first meeting, the SOS group agreed that because of the nature of the group, no new members would be allowed to join during the initial twelve weeks. They decided that each member's voice would be honored, confidentiality would be kept, and they would be respectful of one another. They decided to begin each meeting by recalling something good that had happened to each one of them in the preceding week. In other words, they set group boundaries and began to establish group rituals.

During the process, the worker began to understand the dynamics of the group. The group was diverse. Members ranged in age from twenty-four to fifty-eight; there were two men, two women, and one transgender Asian. The two women, Allie and Sylvia, sat beside each other on the sofa; Art, the Native American, sat across from them in a straight-backed chair; Bob, the trucker, slouched in an overstuffed chair next to Art; and Terry, the transgender person, sat on an ottoman next to the women, somewhat separated from Bob.

As the worker watched the group members' interaction, she was struck by the nervous chatter emanating from Art and Bob. The women and Terry appeared more relaxed and anxious to get on with the business at hand, although Terry seemed very quiet and almost withdrawn. It was Allie who, in that first meeting, emerged as the task leader. She got the group to focus on its objectives and helped move the group toward its goal.

As the group matured and members became more comfortable and familiar with one another, other roles emerged. Art became the social emotional leader, Sylvia was a silent member, Bob assumed a gatekeeper role, and Terry tended to monopolize. Whenever Terry talked too much, Allie would try to steer him back to the topic, and Art would try in his quiet way to keep balance and harmony in the group while attempting to silence Terry.

During all group meetings, the worker facilitated interaction within the group. When Sylvia became teary-eyed at a discussion related to Bob's wife, no one in the group other than the worker seemed to notice. The worker told the group that Sylvia was tearing up. Group members then turned to her and asked what had touched her and how she was connected with it (amplifying subtle messages). Similarly, when Art was explaining his tribe's reaction to his two-spirited nature, the worker asked other members of the group if they ever had similar experiences (creating empathic connections). When Allie complained that her lover, Miranda, was not in touch with her own sexuality and needed to be in a group like SOS, she was encouraged to direct that message to her girlfriend—not the group (redirecting the message) and then come back and tell the group the process and outcome of her discussion with Miranda.

While continuously scanning the group, managing role differences, and contending with various group dynamics, the worker gave voice to the achievements of individuals in the group as well as achievements of the group as a whole. When Terry decided she was going to begin hormone treatments to move toward her goal of being a woman, the worker made a point of it. When Bob decided he was going to tell his wife of his risky sexual activities, she also noted that for the group. By the time Art proclaimed he was going on a vision quest to gain insight into his sexuality, group members spontaneously acknowledged his achievement. As a whole, each of these individual's movements contributed to the overall goal of the group, and the worker also voiced that as a group achievement. The worker engaged in these activities in meetings across the life of the group.

The group's agreed-upon twelve-week period came to an end quickly, and the worker along with the group assessed to what extent the original goal of the group had been met. While most felt that the original goal (feeling better about who they were in relation to their sexual orientation) had been well met, they also agreed that the group support was an awesome thing and that they wanted to continue to meet for an indefinite amount of time. The worker agreed to continue to meet with them, and a new service contract was negotiated.

GROUP WORK IN QUADRANT B

Group work in Quadrant B involves work with clients/members in behalf of themselves and others like them. Expanding the preceding example of the SOS group, the following example shows how the worker and two members of the SOS group created a group designed to promote Hub services for lesbian teens.

Midway into the SOS group process, the topic of problems related to the needs of LGBT teens was discussed. Allie, the middle-aged widow and mother who had her first lesbian experience as a teenager and Sylvia, the Generation X former nun, became quite engrossed in the discussion to the point that it continued well after the meeting ended. They began the next meeting with this topic and asked it they could discuss the creation of a group designed to challenge the stereotypes of LGBT teenagers. The others in the group pooh-poohed the idea as too big and something they were not interested in pursuing. They wanted to stick to the original task of the group (issues related to their own development).

Sylvia and Allie persisted for a brief time and then let the issue drop in the SOS meeting. Following the meeting, both approached the group worker and asked if she thought it possible to form a group that could advocate for its members and others. Allie and Sylvia, who had done their homework, bombarded the social worker with facts and figures related to the need for such a group in the Hub, especially focusing on young lesbian women in the Hub. They understood that if there effort were successful, later the group could be expanded to include gay, bisexual, and transgender persons, too. The three of them decided to meet as a group the following week to discuss what would be involved in starting and sustaining such an advocacy group. The group worker agreed to see if she could find a time and place for such a group and asked that Allie and Sylvia think about the specific issues they would want to address and why they thought them to be important. The worker also asked that they see if there were others like themselves who might like to become part of such a group. If others were identified, they would be welcomed at the following week's session.

The following week, the worker had set the stage for the new group by finding a quiet, cozy nook off the main meeting room. The space contained a table with six comfortable chairs around it and easy access to the kitchen where drinks and snacks were available. The space turned out to be just the right size because Sylvia brought two new possible members and Allie brought her daughter. Cassie, an eighteen-year-old college freshman, was involved with her school's LGBT caucus and adamant about changing the way some in the Hub treated young lesbian women. Bonnie, a nineteen-year-old high school graduate, had met Cassie during gay pride month and was particularly interested in how she and her cohort were treated by Hub merchants. She thought her spiked green and blue hair along with her motorcycle leathers and body piercings should not be reason for discrimination. Both knew Sylvia from attending worship services at the Unity Center. Doreen was Allie's twenty-one-year-old daughter, who had come out when she was in high school. Both she and her mom vividly remembered the anxiety, bullying, and self-esteem issues that Doreen had faced as an openly lesbian teenager attending the Hub's high school.

The group brainstormed and came up with two things they wanted to address: (1) how homophobia against lesbian teens was manifested in the Hub and (2) what social service agencies needed to know about working with lesbian teens. They agreed that the group size would expand to include anyone who wanted to join (as long as they were young lesbians), that they were going to need a larger space in which to meet, and that they would continue meeting as long as necessary. Because they wanted to be inclusive, they decided to call the group Hub Friends of Equal Rights (HFER) and they adopted a cow (the state animal) as their mascot. A service contract was made. Sylvia agreed to find a larger space for subsequent meetings and the group worker agreed to continue to meeting with them. Specific activities that would move the group toward its goals were identified, and members took responsibility for advancing the group's cause. In an effort to see what role homophobia played with storeowners, Doreen and Bonnie agreed to meet with the neighborhood merchants association, and Sylvia agreed to gather information from church members. Allie said she would get information on this issue from her partner, Justine, who was the director of the Hub's shelter for battered women, and Cassie agreed to gather data from her friends and faculty at college.

Gaining a good understanding of homophobia in the Hub was, as the group discovered, an enormous task that was not accomplished in a short amount of time. Thus, the group had to assess its progress from week to week and readjust goals accordingly. Some weeks after they began to unravel and understand the insidious nature of homophobia in the Hub (some merchants were terrified of persons who looked like Bonnie; many faculty members were heterosexist in their pedagogy; and the local battered women's shelter routinely refused to assist battered lesbians, fearing they might harbor the perpetrator and feared that housing a lesbian would harm other residents), the group members realized that addressing their second task (identifying what social service agencies needed to know when working with young lesbians) required more members and more commitment.

The group had originally agreed that while group membership could expand, they were going to allow only young lesbians to join. They agreed to this because they felt it would increase group solidarity and foster group cohesion. As the original five members continued to meet and their cause became prominent within the Hub, more persons joined. At its zenith, HFER had twenty-five active members, with another fifteen or so who would show up from time to time. In three months HFER had gathered what its members thought were adequate data related to their first objective (seeing how homophobia manifested itself in the Hub) and contemplated how they were going to make the Hub's assorted welfare agencies aware of the myriad social issues facing lesbian teens.

After brainstorming a variety of possibilities, the group members agreed that they would first try consciousness-raising within the agencies by creating a brochure that incorporated their cartoon cow mascot and detailed the most salient issues associated with being a lesbian teen (being scapegoated, bullied, or disenfranchised) and the outcomes of those (such as lowered self-esteem, high suicide rates, and increased substance abuse). The brochure also listed what agencies could do to help, such as avoiding heterosexist biases, promoting programs for lesbian teens, and sponsoring P-FLAG (Parents and Family of Lesbians and Gays) groups. The group worker and group members believed that this form of intervention was appropriate as a first step, but they did discuss the possibility of bargaining or even lobbying for the necessary services should it become necessary at some future time.

The group worker agreed to meet with various Hub agency personnel, distribute the brochures, and thoroughly discuss the issues raised by HFER. She did this at a series of Hub forums (regularly held meetings of Hub agency workers and supervisors). The outcome seemed to be a positive one. Agency workers were receptive to the group's suggestions and agreed to see what steps could be taken to implement them. Additionally, some agency heads agreed to invite HFER members to speak at agency colloquia.

As with the group process when working in Quadrant A, work in Quadrant B has a similar genesis and progression. In both Quadrants A and B a holistic approach is used; interventions are similar; and tasks used to sustain the group, comprehend group dynamics, and facilitate group interaction are identical. What differs are the persons with whom the worker works and the intended beneficiaries of the worker's efforts. In Quadrant A, the work is done with clients/members on their own behalf. In Quadrant B, the work is done with clients/members on their own behalf and the behalf of others like them; the population of intended beneficiaries is broader.

GROUP WORK IN QUADRANT C

Group work in Quadrant C involves working with others (not clients) in behalf of a specified client group. The following example builds on the previous examples and shows how the group worker moved from Quadrant B to Quadrant C work developing a resource group for the benefit of HFER members.

Wanting to promote better social services for HFER members, keeping in mind experiences of the SOS and HFER groups, the worker mobilized an advocacy group of social workers working in the Hub to talk with HFER members to begin understanding their special needs and work to promote better social services for them. To set this in motion, the worker first identified and invited potential group members who were social workers whose agencies operated in the Hub to an initial meeting. First she made a list of Hub agencies and identified two or three social workers and agency heads in each. She then created an information pamphlet about the need for an advocacy group, made several copies, and invited all on her list.

Although the worker had invited a small number of social workers and had no idea how many might actually come to the initial meeting, being optimistic, she found a room large enough to accommodate two-thirds of her invited guests. She was not disappointed when six agency social workers and two agency directors showed up. The local bakery had donated day-old baked goods, which she placed on a large tray, and a Hub soft-drink franchise had provided an assortment of sodas that she had chilled in a cooler of ice. The stage was set, and, after some socializing, the group worker discussed the purpose of the group (to understand and obtain adequate social services to meet the needs of HFER members). After much thought and deliberation, a service contract was agreed to. Group members agreed to first, address homophobia in each of their agencies and second, to identify specific workers in their agencies who would be available to other Hub agencies to speak for the needs of HFER members and act as resource persons for helping them to address the homophobia in their agencies that prevent HFER members form obtaining appropriate services.

Members of the advocacy group for HFER realized that if their goals were accomplished with HFER, they could expand their membership to include other Hub service providers and have the broader goals of (1) getting every Hub agency to include a written nondiscrimination clause in their mission that included LGBT persons; (2) having all of these agencies make a concerted effort to be LGBT-friendly; (3) changing written agency forms to erase heterosexist biases; and (4) having all the Hub agencies become more aware of LGBT service needs.

This expanded group with goals to benefit an expanded population would involve work in Quadrant D, where the work is done by others on behalf of an entire population in need—in this case, agency directors working and direct practitioners working on behalf of all LGBT persons in the Hub. Ordinarily, direct practitioners do not operate in Quadrant D. In this instance, though, the need for continuity requires the worker to do so.

As with other types of group work, work in Quadrant C (and Quadrant D) employs similar skills to accomplish the same requisite tasks as work in both Quadrants A and B. The only significant difference is that group work in Quadrant C involves work with others (nonclients) in behalf of a specified client group.

CONCLUSION

Group work involves identifying in what kind of group the group worker will be working and employing five tasks and their related skills to the group process. Group work is done primarily in three of the four quadrants, where the tasks and skills are similar.

13

THE COMMUNITY ORGANIZER

GRASSROOTS COMMUNITY organizing has a long tradition within professional social work; the early settlement-house movement, for instance, had at its heart the well-being of the community. Jane Addams and those associated with Hull House were community activists involved with social action designed to ensure that the social needs of those in the neighborhood were met. Historically, grassroots community organizing in social work has been wildly popular in some eras and in disrepute in others. During the early 1900s (the settlement-house era) and in the 1960s (the Great Society era), social work embraced social activism, political involvement, and community organizing. However, since the 1960s, political activism—and, with it, community grassroots organizing—has fallen on hard times. As Kahn (1995) asks, how many social welfare agencies would want to hire Jane Addams today? The reality is that community organizing should continue to play an important role in the social work profession, and this chapter argues that, like advocacy, community organizing is a critical part of social work in general and structural social work in particular.

This chapter describes the role of the grassroots community organizer and the tasks that comprise it. Examples of how social workers provide community organizing in all three direct practice quadrants (A, B, and C) are provided.

WHAT IS COMMUNITY ORGANIZING?

Communities are socially constructed, and community organizing is generally thought of as mobilization efforts taken on behalf of those in a specified community who are seen as victims of various social problems or injustices that affect them. The specific actions of grassroots mobilization involve grouping affected individuals, deciphering specific problems, and taking social action to mitigate these identified social injustices (Rivera and Erlich 1998). Communities, because of their ever-evolving nature and definitions, will differ in what members construe as problematic. For example, wealthy community members might believe that having a recently sold mansion used for a halfway house for the mentally ill was unacceptable because it would bring down property values. However, an inner-city neighborhood with too many vacant and boarded-up homes might welcome having a halfway house because the once-vacant drug haven would thereby be transformed. The lesbian/gay community might find it distasteful not to be able to enjoy all the benefits of marriage, while the heterosexual majority might regard discrimination against gays and lesbians as justifiable.

Community organizing has long been thought of as less a direct practitioner role than a role for advocates, administrators, or others in macro areas of social work. While some choose to differentiate between "community organizing" and "grassroots organizing," the distinction is spurious, and the terms are used interchangeably here. Because of its links to clients, grassroots organizing may be seen as an activity suited to direct practitioners.

The impetus for doing grassroots organizing arises at the client/social worker interaction level in accord with the principle of following the demands of the client task, and it includes a variety of direct practice skills.

THE TASKS OF THE COMMUNITY ORGANIZER

There are four tasks associated with grassroots community organizing: (1) identifying communities, (2) organizing communities, (3) planning for change, and (4) implementing change. Embedded within these four tasks are related skills.

IDENTIFYING COMMUNITIES

Identifying communities refers to differentiating between what is or is not a "community" and who is and who is not is a member of that community. Because the concept of community is socially constructed, it may be difficult to identify a community. For practice purposes, it is necessary to define two types of communities—those that are constructed by geography (such as neighborhoods with specific streets as boundaries) and those that are constructed by persons connected by similar interests, needs, or issues (for example, the lesbian/gay community). Because of their fluid nature, the second may be harder for the community organizer to identify. Irrespective of the type of community in which worker is working, the skills the organizer must master are the same.

First, the worker, as organizer, must recognize potential issues facing the community, and then she must locate community members. Identifying geographically defined communities is easier because of the rigidity of the boundaries (usually streets, county or state lines, rivers, and the like), but communities of persons beset by particular issues are also of importance to any community organizer. It is incumbent upon the worker to know the communities in which she works and to know the issues that press both geographically and humanly defined communities. Issues will always be present. The worker must be savvy enough to learn what they are from the clients with whom she works and to want something done about it. Two skills are required to identify communities: (1) recognizing issues and (2) locating community members.

RECOGNIZING ISSUES The first skill with which a social worker must grapple includes identifying issues that might affect community members. Recognizing issues refers to identifying problems with which a community is struggling. It starts with the social worker, as conferee, hearing from one or more of her clients that there is a neighborhood problem. For example, a client living in a waterfront housing project tells his worker that the area is beset by rats displaced by recent development along the river. The rats seem unafraid of people and several neighborhood children have been bitten. To determine the scope of the problem, the worker talks with other housing project residents. She then sets up a neighborhood meeting for all those concerned about the infestation. At that meeting, it becomes evident that rat control is necessary to protect neighborhood families.

LOCATING COMMUNITY MEMBERS After the worker comes to know the communities in which she works and, with the help of community members, has identified issues that are causing problems, she next needs to locate community members who may also be affected by them. Identifying members of geographically defined communities is easier than identifying members of oppressed groups because the worker knows where to look for community members. Maps, census data, telephone books, and neighborhood hangouts all may yield potential community members. If, however, the worker's transgender client is being battered by the police and knows of others similarly beset by this problem, the worker must first identify the population and then seek out members of the identified community. For example, if the worker, after conversations with a male-to-female (MTF) transgender client, became aware of the fear of police brutality in the transgender community, she would try to solicit from her client where she could find information about the "trans" community. The road to discovering members of oppressed groups can wind from client conversations to Internet chat rooms or local bookstores. It is up to the worker's creativity and intuition to discover the best way to identify sometimes invisible community members.

ORGANIZING COMMUNITIES

Organizing communities refers to those actions taken by the worker to facilitate interaction among community members. This involves two skills: (1) mobilizing community members and (2) learning from them what the real issues are that must be addressed and what needs to be changed.

MOBILIZING MEMBERS Mobilizing community members means refers to bringing members of the community together for face-to-face meetings. The same skills related to intervening with groups, as discussed in the previous chapter (selecting group members, creating goals and objectives, implementing the contract, and assessing the outcomes), apply when mobilizing community members for community organizing.

For example, residents of the West End of Louisville, Kentucky, experienced an increase in black on black homicides coupled with police brutality and racial profiling. Through conversations with an after-school teen group, a social worker in a West End community center was made aware of the issue. The worker asked if he could talk to others in the community and perhaps help mobilize community members to address these critical concerns. The teens themselves agreed to discuss this offer with their parents, friends, and neighborhood schoolteachers. After this, the social worker was able to arrange a neighborhood meeting where he had an opportunity to hear from a range of people the details of what the really troublesome issues were.

LEARNING THE NITTY-GRITTY OF TROUBLESOME ISSUES Once the worker manages to get community members mobilized, the work turns to getting at the heart of identified issues are and determining what, if anything, might alleviate the stress they are causing. While community members may have differing views on what the real problem is, there is usually some identifiable community crisis or problem that they agreed has brought them together in the first place. To identify troublesome issues, the worker uses the same tasks and skills as are presented in chapter 12 (sustaining groups, comprehending group dynamics, facilitating group interactions).

In the case of the homicides and racial profiling in the West End neighborhood, the specific issue that brought community members to the neighborhood meeting was the apparent racism on the part of some white police officers who were from the neighborhood precinct. At the initial community meeting, the worker discovered that there was a history of racial profiling in the neighborhood and that in less than three years, three community members had been killed by the police. Despite what community members believed to be compelling evidence against them, the police officers were never found guilty of any wrongdoing and continued to patrol the neighborhood. Community members were angry and wanted something done about it.

PLANNING FOR CHANGE

Planning for change involves all the strategies and activities necessary to prepare for proposed modifications. Because community organizing is complex and may involve many different constituencies, the planning stage is vital to the outcome. Four skills are related to this task: (1) analyzing policy, (2) identifying potential strategies for required changes, (3) creating alliances, (4) and mediating. Each skill has both a cognitive and an interactive piece.

ANALYZING POLICY Analyzing policy refers to exploring existing policies around the specific issue to determine whether policy that currently exists provides for what is needed and, if it does, whether it is being appropriately administered. If current policy and activities in accord with it do not ameliorate existing need, then changes have to be made to the current policy or its implementation. This is not easy to bring about. First, the social worker must have an understanding not only of the existing formal policy but also of how the policy is being implemented. "Policy" can refer to an existing statute or law, formalized procedure, or other standardized practice that is sanctioned by the formal organization implementing it. Such a policy may be as innocuous as signing in and out of the agency or as controversial as prayer in school. However large or small the scope of the policy, the social worker must be able to evaluate it in terms of whom it affects and where and how it does so (Tully 2002). The process of policy analysis is both a cognitive one done independently by the worker and an interactive one as the worker shares her analysis and related information with community members and learns more from them.

Because policies are socially constructed, it is important for the community organizer to use the views described in chapter 2 related to the postmodern perspective. Analyzing policy using this philosophical approach will enable the community organizer to view more holistically the community and its current situation.

In the example regarding racial profiling and police brutality, the social worker dug into newspaper archives, current police policies, and state law. She then held discussions with community members. The worker was able to use the newspaper archives, the manual of police procedures, and the code-book of state statutes because these are available in the public domain. Her analysis of newspaper articles revealed that on-duty police officers had been responsible for seven fatal shootings in the previous five years, and there were fourteen articles in the previous twenty-four months that indicated that police officers seemed to be involved in racial profiling. Conversations with those in the community indicated that there were many more instances of racial profiling that were not reported, but the number of shootings had been accurately stated.

While the police manual and state law prohibited discrimination on the basis of race, both seemed a bit more flexible on when an officer was allowed to discharge a service weapon. The guiding principle in this instance is related to fear of personal or public safety. This means that shooting someone then depends on the personal judgment of a police officer. Judgments, by virtue of their subjective nature, are often clouded by values, beliefs, and attitudes.

Those in the community believed that the white police officers were "racist" and "trigger-happy" because all the victims had been black men. The racial-profiling cases were a bit more confusing, inasmuch as white, Latino, and black men were being pulled over and harassed by both Caucasian and African American police officers. Those in the community had no real answer for this other than to say that young African American teens seemed to be targeted frequently with or without cause. With the information the worker gained from her own analysis and conversations with community members, she was ready to move to the next step.

IDENTIFYING POTENTIAL STRATEGIES FOR REQUIRED CHANGES Identifying potential strategies for required changes refers to both a cognitive process done by the worker by which she thinks of various ways that change might occur and to an interactive one by which the worker shares her ideas with community members and hears what ideas they have for ways to make modifications. Once the community organizer has analyzed carefully all potential policies related to an identified situation, she needs to hear community members' views on potential policy changes to ease the community crisis. She listens to community members' feedback and their ideas of possible ways to confront the community's dilemma. From these meetings, the worker and community members agree to a specific set of strategies designed to change existing policies or how the policies are being implemented.

For example, with respect to the racial profiling concern, the worker realized that while the policies related to nondiscrimination probably did not need to be changed, the way they were being implemented by the police did. To deal with racial profiling, the worker identified one possible strategy: a meeting between precinct police officers and concerned citizens could be held. The meeting could be conducted at the local community center in the heart of the neighborhood, and the initial purpose would be to open channels of communication between the precinct police officers and those who lived in the neighborhood, while the core focus to follow would be to discuss possible solutions mutually acceptable to both the citizens and the police. The worker discussed this possibility with members of the community and heard their suggestion to hold meetings as well with local youth who were being profiled. They thought that perhaps discussing how to deal with the police might be helpful. Thus, from the worker's cognitive and interactive processes, two possible strategies to stop racial profiling in the neighborhood were identified. Having identified strategies to create change, the worker and community members were ready to move forward.

CREATING ALLIANCES Creating alliances refers to identifying constituencies outside of those affected by the problem who believe that the problem requires change. The worker and members of the affected community brainstorm and create a list of all possible alliances that might help. Once this cognitive process is completed, the worker and members of the community reach out to possible allies. If the potential ally is agreeable, it becomes part of the community's effort to effect change.

In the racial profiling situation, for example, the worker and the community members met and, through a brainstorming session, identified several constituency groups as possible allies. All were seen as having a stake in the problem and included neighborhood associations in other primarily African American sections of the city, members of the city's governing organization who represented potentially affected districts, the local newspaper, and the Fraternal Organization of Police.

The worker and members of the neighborhood agreed to use whatever contact they had in each of the ally constituencies. The neighborhood is rich with resources—there are teachers, police officers, social workers, and city employees who live in it, and all are deeply concerned about racism. Using the resources at hand, possible allies were contacted, and most agreed to send at least one member to the next neighborhood meeting.

MEDIATING Mediating refers to those activities in which the worker engages to ensure that all those who are invested in solving the problem are all on the same page. Mediation as a grassroots organizer is identical to what was detailed in chapter 8.

Once the worker and community members have created an array of allies, there is a need to be certain that all members of the coalition agree to what the solution of the problem should be and how the change should be implemented. Without this, no service contract is possible. The process requires that the worker and the community members stay aware of various constituency groups' motivations for being involved, their values, and what they may see as possible outcomes. This cognitive process needs to be as meticulous as possible, because various allies bring various values and needs to the process. If one ally will not agree with another—a not uncommon occurrence—mediation must occur.

For example, when the white police representatives met with the very angry, mostly African American neighborhood members to discuss incidents of racial profiling, their complementary interests—that is, their common view that the police needed to carry out their mandate to protect the neighborhood, and that the neighborhood needed police protection—were almost completely obscured. The role of the social worker, as mediator, helped them remember their need for each other and begin to act on it. By the end of the meeting, compromises had been made on both sides and a mutually satisfactory approach to the problem was reached.

IMPLEMENTING CHANGE

Implementing change refers to actions taken by the grassroots organizer, community members, and allies to develop and implement policies and activities to resolve the problem. Three skills are associated with this task: (1) creating broader alliances, (2) initiating interaction with power brokers, and, if needed, (3) protesting en masse.

CREATING BROADER ALLIANCES In accord with the principle of following the demands of the client task, creating broader alliances refers to actions taken by the worker to look beyond the client community to see if other communities are facing the same problem. Therefore, the worker, community members, and members of allied groups reach out to still others to make larger numbers of people aware of the problem. It is likely that if one community has a problem, other communities will have the same or similar problems. Even if a community does not currently have the same problem, it could be of such a horrendous magnitude that they simply need to be made aware of it. Social consciousness also drives the need to create broader alliances.

For example, through the West End neighborhood's actions, some sections of the greater Louisville, Kentucky, area were aware of racial profiling, but little was known about the practice outside certain sections of the metro area. Because the problem was seen as being broader than in just the city's African American communities, members of the group that had been convened to discuss possible solutions (worker, community members, and allies) decided to increase their power base and try to benefit other communities by making the problem known to the greater Louisville metro community. Each group member agreed to become involved. Some opted to meet with people in a predominantly Asian community. Others agreed to meet with white people in East End neighborhoods; still others said they would meet with people living in older, racially integrated neighborhoods. As a result of these meetings, some people, regardless of whether racial profiling was going on in their neighborhoods, agreed to write letters to the editor; some agreed to be interviewed by local television reporters; and some agreed to speak at city government meetings. Through their actions and broader community support, racial profiling became a problem that was perceived not only by a small West End neighborhood as horrific and unjust, but was similarly viewed by many others in the city as well.

INITIATING INTERACTION WITH POWER BROKERS Initiating interaction with power brokers refers to conversations that the worker and representatives of the constituency group have with agency representatives whose organizational policy is at the heart of the problem. These conversations center on the identified problem and solutions that have been agreed to. Ideally, a representative from the agency whose policy is a problem has been involved in the solution. To keep things as nonconfrontational as possible, the principle of least contest should be followed as this interaction begins and progresses.

The target of the racial profiling resolution was not the policy of the police department; rather, it was the way the policy was being implemented. The worker and community members had involved the Fraternal Order of Police from the beginning of the grassroots organizing process, and police representatives had been helpful in crafting what appeared to be a feasible solution that was acceptable to the neighborhood community, the police, and the larger metro area. The worker, one community resident, and a police patrolman who had been working with the group were selected by the coalition to meet with the chief of police. Their mission was to articulate the problem that racism was having in their community through racial profiling and then to present solutions to which the group had agreed. One solution with two parts was to be proposed. First, in an effort to have teens become more aware of what to do if stopped by the police, community members would agree to hold monthly meetings between teens and local police where a dialogue could develop. Second, in an effort to lessen much of the anger in the neighborhood at teams of white police officers, the police would agree to split up the white teams and pair each white officer with an African American partner who knew and was known by the neighborhood.

PROTESTING EN MASSE Protesting en masse refers to actions taken by the grassroots organizer and her constituency group if the desired outcomes are not accomplished as a result of conversations with the power brokers. Sometimes conversations between power brokers and grassroots organizers yield unfavorable results, or no results at all. If this is the case, pressing for the needed change should occur. That is to say, the worker and constituents must "up the ante." This is when mass protests are an appropriate form of action. Protesting can take many forms—sit-ins, boycotts, picket lines, marches, letter-writing campaigns, telephone blitzes, email bombardments, blogs, mass mailings, media ads, door-to-door visits, and so on. The type of protest is determined by the principle of least contest, in that lesser pressures are applied before greater pressures. The type of pressure also depends on the problem, the policy that has created the problem, the reasons the solutions have not been implemented, and the resources available to the protesters.

For example, the chief of police, who was faced with charges of racism in relation to continuing racial profiling incidents, was presented with two necessary tasks related to a single resolution. While he was comfortable with having his patrol people meet with neighborhood teens on a regular basis, he balked at the thought of breaking up a set of partners. He announced that a white team would continue to patrol the neighborhood as it had done for the past year, adding that no amount of pressure would get him to change his mind. The worker, neighborhood members, and their allies were angered by this. At the meeting where they discussed their interactions with the power brokers, they decided to bring more pressure to bear on the chief. Again, members rallied and agreed to take on the situation through protests. Many of them had been alive during the civil rights era and knew how to protest. Because they had little money for television, radio, or newspaper ads, they relied on marches, frequent interviews with television media who covered them, letters to the editor, and testimony at city council meetings. It took only six weeks before the chief of police announced that in order to foster public and race relations in the department, he was initiating a system whereby black officers and white officers would be paired and that single-race partnerships would no longer exist.

THE COMMUNITY ORGANIZER IN QUADRANTS B AND C

Grassroots community organizing occurs when the worker is working with some clients on behalf of themselves and an entire group in a like situation. Therefore, grassroots community organizing happens primarily in Quadrant B. If the community organizer works with the client and others similarly situated, and then brings in allies (nonsufferers) to join in the action, talk with the allies is a Quadrant C task. When the work is with the mixed groups of clients and nonsuffering allies, the worker is situated at the corner of Quadrants B and C.

CONCLUSION

Grassroots community organizing involves identifying communities, organizing communities, planning for change, and implementing change. Identifying communities involves the skills of recognizing issues and locating community members; organizing communities involves mobilizing members and learning about troublesome issues. Planning for change involves analyzing policy, identifying potential strategies for change, creating alliances, and mediating disputes; and implementing change includes creating broader alliances, initiating interaction with power brokers, and protesting when necessary.

PART IV

CONTEXT

14

LEARNING THE ORGANIZATION

THIS CHAPTER explains why and how a social worker learns the formal and informal organizational arrangements for service delivery in the agency in which she or he works. It explores the physical dimension—exterior and interior design of the building, its location, and its impact on the worker and client, as well as the relative power/status structures of participants found in every organization (Nord 1972; Thompson 1967). We discuss how the worker can pragmatically comprehend the setting in which she or he practices structural social work and move through the organization, and we elaborate on learning to identify the key questions that determine what happens to clients at each choice point in the organization.

THE STRUCTURES OF ORGANIZATIONS

All organizations are socially constructed—that is, they are determined by persons in power to be socially or politically desirable or necessary. Thus, they are created by humans to serve specific functions. While some organizations are created to build or manufacture things, like the Philip Morris plant in Richmond, Virginia, others are created to deal with selected aspects of the human condition. Though some social workers do find employment in organizational settings where "things" are the product (for instance, in Fortune 500 companies where they may work in employee-assistance programs or human resource departments), this chapter focuses on organizations designed to work with and serve people—human service organizations or agencies.

In the United States there are thousands of such agencies—governmental ones including those at the federal, state, and local levels, as well as nongovernmental ones such as church-based services, mental health clinics, or family agencies. In these social service organizations, goods and services are usually provided and delivered directly to clients themselves. While these organizations run the gamut in size from larger human service organizations such as the Social Security Administration to very small organizations such as a local area settlement house, they share many similar traits. All are physically housed within some type of building and have both formal and informal power and communication arrangements, written policies and procedures, budgets, philosophies, designated populations to serve, and accountability methods. Every organization also has goals beyond providing services to the populations that are presumably their raison d'être (such as survival of the agency and the jobs of its employees, attraction of grant monies, production of research, and organizational growth).

THE PHYSICAL DIMENSION

The first thing that clients see when they seek services from a social agency is a building and its location in physical space. Geography plays a silent but salient role in both client and community members' perceptions of the agency. This section discusses the ecological organization and "culturescape" as well as time-distance-cost factors and territoriality associated with the agency as a physical entity (Dahlke et al. 1980; Goffman 1961; Korda 1973; Seabury 1971).

ECOLOGICAL ORGANIZATION

Ecological organization refers to the building itself and the physical space around the building (Dahlke et al. 1980; Seabury 1971). This includes the building's location—downtown, neighborhood, suburbs—and its physical surroundings—sidewalks, alleys, parking lots, vacant lots, nearby buildings, and so on. These features speak to people. For example, the public welfare office located in an urban slum rife with foul graffiti is an indication of how our culture views social welfare and the people who require it. Some buildings are austere and lead clients to feel small and insignificant. Some buildings, despite crumbling bricks and mortar, are festooned with banners that announce available services or neighborhood events that lend warmth to an otherwise bleak facade. Clients take in all of these sensory data as they encounter the building and its outside surroundings. Once approached and entered, the building provides another set of sensory experiences that generate further, perhaps more significant emotions.

CULTURESCAPE

While the employee has no control over physical layout of the internal part of the building, including how halls are constructed and where offices, bathrooms, or snack areas are located (that is, the internal ecological organization), the worker may have some control over common areas of the agency such as the waiting room and does have some control over how her office will look. The term *culturescape* means how the internal space of an agency can be arranged to maximize positive client comfort and interaction (Korda 1973).

Since the first thing a client usually sees inside the agency is a waiting room, this area should be made user-friendly. Many agency waiting rooms consist of rows of molded plastic chairs or walls lined with them, tables with dog-eared old magazines, bulletin boards with agency regulations in small print, receptionists behind glass partitions with narrow vertical slits between the panels to allow conversation between receptionist and client, and an occasional dying potted plant. Some agencies have locked security doors where the client must be buzzed through to enter the reception area, and in some public buildings, clients may have to pass through metal detectors. A few agencies have colorful airy reception areas with bright rugs, fish tanks, comfortable chairs in private seating cul-de-sacs, current magazines, informative pamphlets, and bulletin boards covered with client artwork or easily readable pertinent agency and neighborhood information. However, such user-friendly, comfortable waiting rooms tend to be found less frequently than the more austere, institutionalized ones. Waiting rooms, like offices, need to reflect an atmosphere that projects an air of professionalism, safety, and comfort. Although it is perhaps impossible to remove the glass partitions, providing current magazines, pamphlets that explain agency services, several healthy plants, a play area with toys for children, private seating areas with comfortable chairs, and decorative art can make reception areas far more user-friendly.

After the waiting room, the next space a client is likely to encounter is the office of the social worker. Because it does provide a set of visual cues available to the client, how one chooses to decorate one's office space is important. The office should be designed both to reflect a sense of who occupies it and to provide a sense of welcome and safety for the clients. The office decor should also reflect a place where serious and intimate talk can occur in a professional setting. Tastefully displaying one's professional license and professional degrees may provide the client with a sense of well-being. The office decor should not impart the message that the worker views clients as children or friends, nor should it be so austere as to frighten or belittle clients. Items on a desk that reflect who the worker is may provide a sense of comfort, a small rug on the floor adds color to an office, and having small candy available adds warmth.

How the office furniture is arranged plays an important role in how clients will perceive the social worker and the agency (Korda 1973). Where the client is physically positioned in relation to the worker conveys a lot about how the worker views her status and the status of the client. For example, if the worker physically positions herself behind a large desk with the client seated squarely opposite (where the client and worker are at 180 degrees), the desk provides a physical barrier that may convey a sense of distrust and power imbalance. If, on the other hand, the office is small and the worker must sit at the desk, having the client sit on the short side of the desk (where the worker and client are at 90 degrees) where the corner of the desk provides a workspace, provides a more intimate setting and one that is more equal. If possible, it is always nice to have space in an office that allows the worker and client to converse without having to contend with the awkwardness of a desk, but that is not often possible. Figure 14.1 illustrates various placement options for furniture in an office.

It is best to be seated in the most intimate arrangement possible. In addition to being the most intimate situation, the knee-to-knee position in A is also the one that suggests the least power differential between worker and client. In situation C, on the other hand, power is vested in the person behind the desk, and this direct face-to-face position is a setup for confrontation and conflict.

Yet there are certain circumstances where the safety of the worker must take precedent over comfort levels. Sometimes workers encounter clients who may pose a danger to them—for example, a paranoid schizophrenic woman who is not taking her medication or an angry Gulf War veteran wearing a Bowie knife. In such instances, it is prudent to ensure that if the client becomes hostile the worker has an identified exit route.

FIGURE 14.1 Office seating arrangements

Some offices are equipped with under-the-desk silent-alarm buttons that alert the police that there is an emergency. If that is not the case, the best solution is to position the desk and the worker's chair close to the door so that the worker will not be in danger of being trapped in an office with no escape route.

The culturescape presented by the agency and the offices within the agency do provide powerful visual hints about how the agency and its workers view clients. Because the culturescape is something that can be manipulated by the employees (as opposed to the ecological organization), we encourage social workers to make agency waiting rooms and personal offices as welcoming as is possible, given the opportunities and limitations of the organizational setting.

TERRITORIALITY

Territoriality (or catchment area) refers to the geographic area that the social service organization is designed to serve (Dahlke et al. 1980). For example, a state agency on aging is designed to provide policies and procedures for an entire state, whereas local area agencies on aging provide actual services to specific geographically defined areas (often defined by existing county, town, or parish structures).

CLIENT TIME-DISTANCE-COST FACTORS

Factors related to time-distance-cost are those that involve how long it takes clients to get to the agency, how far away are they located from the agency, and what the actual costs involved in an agency visit are (Dahlke et al. 1980). These factors often account for missed appointments as well as reluctance to seek needed services at all and may be seen as barriers to effective service delivery. For example, if a client lives at the edge of the catchment area (or territory) that the agency serves, and if she has three preschool-age children, it will take more time and cost her more money to get to the agency than if she lived a couple of blocks away. As costs in and of themselves, time and distance are interrelated—the farther away the agency site, the longer it will take clients to reach their destination.

Time also enters the equation at another point. Besides how long it takes to get to the agency, how long it takes for the client to receive services once at the agency is another factor. Monetary cost enters the picture if the client has to use some type of transportation (automobile, bus, taxi, streetcar, train). Using one's own car requires money for gas and parking. Using public transportation requires money to pay the roundtrip fare. The client may have to pay for child-care or eldercare when making an agency visit, and if the client must take time off from employment, lost wages also must be factored in as a cost the client bears. Additionally, should the client be required to return to the agency several times in order to receive services, then the monetary costs are multiplied.

LEARNING THE FORMAL AND INFORMAL ARRANGEMENTS OF THE ORGANIZATION

In learning the organization, it is important that the worker learn about not only the formal arrangements as defined in organizational charts and policy manuals and the informal arrangements that are operative, but also the bases for decisions that affect how clients move through the organization. A dynamic balance exists between the formal and informal arrangements in any organization. This section examines the ongoing relationships between these formal and informal organizational arrangements and how and why decisions are made. The framework that supports the formal and informal arrangements content is depicted in table 14.1.

ORGANIZATIONAL MISSION, BOUNDARIES, AND SERVICES

Formal organizational structures are socially constructed for the purpose of doing something (Selznick 1957; Thompson 1967) such as providing mental health services or safe housing for battered women. Each social service organization has a specified mission, identified boundaries, and specific services to offer. It is created to meet social service needs generally defined as a *social problem*. Some social service organizations are federal (Social Security Administration); some are state (state department of public health); and others are local (mental health clinic). While each agency may have a slightly different mission (the state public health department's mission is broader than that of the local mental health clinic's mission), they may be tied to each other by, for example, federal funding and all are ultimately governed by administrative law that define policies and procedures that, in turn, define organizational mission, boundaries, and services.

For example, the United States Department of Health and Human Services (DHHS) is mandated by federal law to provide various social services—for instance, services related to diseases, safety and wellness, families and child

TABLE 14.1 Formal and informal organizational arrangements

FORMAL ORGANIZATIONAL ARRANGEMENT	INFORMAL ORGANIZATIONAL ARRANGEMENT
Has a defined orgaizational mission, boundaries, and services designed for specific populations.	Has a defined orgaizational mission, boundaries, and services designed for specific populations.
Has a set of "legitimate" policies/procedures.	Has a set of "legitimate" policies/procedures.
Requires workers to follow policies/prcedures without question.	Requires workers to follow policies/prcedures without question.
Organizational control based on legitimae, reward, and coercive power is exerted through a top-down hierarchical system.	Organizational control based on legitimae, reward, and coercive power is exerted through a top-down hierarchical system.
Has sepcific horizontal and vertical divisions of labor (roles) that do not change.	Has sepcific horizontal and vertical divisions of labor (roles) that do not change.
Has formal horizontal and vertical channels of communication.	Has formal horizontal and vertical channels of communication.
Tends to make people's needs fit the system.	Tends to make people's needs fit the system.
Tends to be concerned about contact hours and records of service, etc.	Tends to be concerned about contact hours and records of service, etc.
Reacts slowly to proposed organizational change.	Reacts slowly to proposed organizational change.
When forced to change, tends to place priority on system maintenance often to the detriment of the client population.	When forced to change, tends to place priority on system maintenance often to the detriment of the client population.

welfare, aging (DHHS 2003). Thus, their mission, boundaries, and services blanket the entire country. Smaller, regional, state, and local organizations have been created to fulfill the mission of DHHS. As the related agencies decrease in geographic area of responsibility, their boundaries and services grow progressively narrower and more specific. State and local departments of public welfare have smaller boundaries or catchment areas and more specific services to provide than DHHS.

This formal structure is top-down and rigid, whereas the informal structure of organizations, while bounded by laws, policies, and procedures that create and maintain the formal structure, often stretches the boundaries defined in the mission statement and the services for which the agency was developed. For example, while the formal organizational structure of the public health department does not identify handing out condoms or sterile needles as one of their services, the informal structure identified these as needs and ensured their dissemination.

POLICIES AND PROCEDURES

Embedded within the formal organizational arrangement is a set of policies and procedures designed to regulate the functioning of the agency. Such policies are often created as a result of administrative law—legal procedures or programs created by various governmental bodies such as federal, state, county, or city governments (for example, Medicaid or Social Security). For example, figure 14.2 outlines this formal paper trail of agency policy development and clarifies what may be construed as "givens."

The policies that flow from administrative law detail the formal procedures by which workers shall carry out their duties. These may include the number of hours and days an agency is open, eligibility requirements for clients, the number of times a client may be seen, and the amount and kinds of paperwork required for each client or how many bus tokens are given to each client. Related to the worker, polices include such things as salary scales, job descriptions, numbers of vacation days allowed in any given year, number of clients a worker is expected to have, or how many workers share an office. The formal

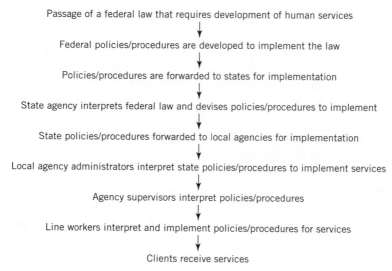

Passage of a federal law that requires development of human services
↓
Federal policies/procedures are developed to implement the law
↓
Policies/procedures are forwarded to states for implementation
↓
State agency interprets federal law and devises policies/procedures to implement
↓
State policies/procedures forwarded to local agencies for implementation
↓
Local agency administrators interpret state policies/procedures to implement services
↓
Agency supervisors interpret policies/procedures
↓
Line workers interpret and implement policies/procedures for services
↓
Clients receive services

FIGURE 14.2 Typical formal policy paper trail through a formal organizational structure

organizational policies are often viewed as "givens" and not subject to change. As such, workers are required to obey them.

In the informal organization, what are viewed as "legitimate" policies or procedures may be implemented, modified, subverted, or at least called into question if it is in the best interests of the client. For example, a formal organizational policy might state that a client is only eligible for twenty free work-related bus tokens a month. In mid-month, however, a client's child has a medical emergency for which she uses some of her work-related tokens to get to the doctor. This leaves her short of tokens to get to work. The agency's formal policies do not permit free bus tokens to be issued for medical appointments, but the client needs them. Using the informal system, the worker can talk with the person who has responsibility for distributing tokens and make a case on behalf of the client. Usually, the tokens will be forthcoming. Then the worker has to begin raising the issue of tokens for medical emergencies with peers and supervisors escalating slowly up the formal system in accord with the principles of *least contest*.

THE TOP-DOWN HIERARCHICAL ARRANGEMENT

In the formal organizational arrangement, organizational control is generally exerted through a top-down hierarchical system that tends to define the organizational arrangement for accountability and collegiality—line and staff relationships. It is that formal arrangement with which most workers are familiar and is generally available in chart form (see figure 14.3), but, if it is not, a few questions to one's supervisor and another worker or two should yield enough information to create such a chart. In this vertical view of the organization, the director or chief administrator is seen as being the most important person and the client—the ultimate consumer of the services provided—is seen as less important than everybody else in the agency. Service workers—those who do the basic work with the clients—are viewed as less important than their supervisors—middle-level managers who link service workers with administrators, and agency directors, as those at the top are the ones who make strategic, long-range decisions. Support staff—those who provide indirect services such as information processing, filing, secretarial support—while vital to the efficient operation of any organization, are frequently seen as less important than other employees of the bureaucratic structure. This hierarchy is evident not only in the organizational chart, but also in the salary earned at each level. Workers at the top tend to have higher salaries than those of workers at the bottom. The lowest-paid positions are those of support and custodial staff. The hope of

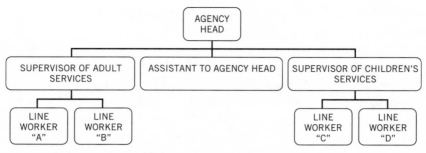

FIGURE 14.3 Typical hierarchical formal organizational structure

hierarchy is that each of the bureaucratic entities will work together in a harmonious balance to meet the stated objectives of the agency and serve the needs of the clients. Working together has a different look when the "informal" arrangement of the organization is considered.

The real life of the agency is at the informal level by the relationships workers have with each other and their clients. Informal arrangements in organizations tend to vest organizational control in an alternative system formed by shifting interpersonal interactions across time that are based on legitimate, expert, reward of coercive power between organizational colleagues and clients. Legitimate power refers to power that is vested in the position which gives the holder of that role the right to prescribe the behavior of subordinates (French and Raven 1959). For example, it is generally agreed that the director of an agency has *legitimate power* in relation to issues affecting the organization. Expert power is based on the perceived expertise of a person irrespective of that person's assigned position in the organization. For example, an agency supervisor may call on the expertise of a subordinate in determining the best course of action when the worker's knowledge of a particular topic is far greater than the supervisor's. Attraction power refers to influence based on interpersonal liking. For example, staff members may support views held by those they like and esteem. Reward and coercive power refers to a person's ability to assess and apply rewards and punishments.

The informal structure of the organization is best described as those relationships that emerge within any agency irrespective of worker placement on the hierarchical organizational chart. For example, relationships blossom around the water cooler, in the cafeteria, in the parking lot, or in the gym and develop over time. These relationships, while work-related, are not defined by supervisor/worker guidelines. Workers of a similar rank may find that their supervisors approach similar situations differently, or administrators and line workers may have an opportunity to discuss agency issues over lunch.

As noted in figure 14.4, while the organizational chart stays the same in the formal organization, the relationships identified on the informal chart differ, and are not hierarchical. In this particular example, the supervisor of adult services has an informal relationship with the assistant to the agency head because they attend the same church and their two families go to brunch together every Sunday. Line worker A has an informal relationship with line worker D because they eat lunch together at the agency cafeteria and were hired the same month.

Line worker C is in the most powerful position because he has informal relationships with the agency head as well as with the supervisor of adult services and line worker B. From the moment line worker C walked into the office of the agency head and announced that he wanted to meet and talk with the man he was working for, the agency head liked him. The agency head had thanked line worker C for coming in and told him he valued his input, that he liked to know what line workers were thinking and feeling. After that, line worker C bumped into the agency head at the diner where both started their day. Over breakfast, the agency head and worker chatted and discovered that line worker C's five-year-old attends the same private school that the agency head attended and that line worker C was currently in the same doctoral program from which the agency head had graduated. The agency head sees a lot of himself in this bold and upwardly mobile young man, and, because the two ate at the same diner, he began to mentor the worker informally over breakfast.

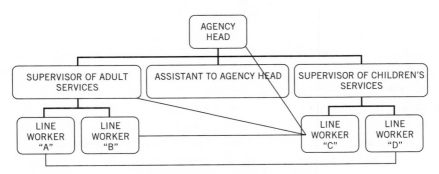

FIGURE 14.4 Sample of a possible informal organizational arrangement

Line worker C and the supervisor of adult services share a dislike of the supervisor of children's services and frequently complain to each other about her. Mutuality led to drinks after work, with more talk and agreements on other work- and nonwork-related issues and ultimately a personal friendship. Further, there are benefits for both in that the supervisor of adult services has informal access to assistant to the agency head and line worker C has informal connections to the agency head. Thus, both have opportunity to influence top administrators and to hear privileged information about the entire agency.

Line worker B's informal relationship with line worker C puts her in a position to hear what is going on from line worker C and have some input into his thinking. Line worker B cultivated this relationship by serving with line worker C on the annual Toys for Tots Campaign and by showing an interest in and flattering him.

These relationships and conversations should not be construed as office gossip or mere chat. Rather, they should be viewed as an important part of working with people in an agency setting. Informal structures exist in every organization and provide a dynamic part of the overall organizational structure. They are fertile ground where the seeds of organizational change are sown and nurtured before being sent forward to the formal structure for implementation.

HORIZONTAL AND VERTICAL DIVISIONS OF LABOR AND COMMUNICATION PATTERNS

The formal organizational structure defines vertical and horizontal divisions of labor and communication patterns. These channels have been previously identified as the organizational arrangement for accountability and collegiality — line and staff relationships. Labor at the top is more administrative in nature while labor at the lower rungs of the organizational chart is directed toward the provision of services to clients. Middle rungs tend to be managerial with respect to service provision. Formal communication patterns tend to move up and down this hierarchy. In addition to the top-down pattern, there is a horizontal pattern of labor and communication. For example, supervisors at the same organizational level (like the three supervisors or the direct service workers in figure 14.3) are seen as organizationally equal and have formal lateral or horizontal functions about which they are required to communicate with one another.

When role-holders — that is, employees in various organizational positions — change, the formal structure of roles and role relationships does not change. In the informal structure, these arbitrary patterns of labor and communication are constantly shifting based on changes in personnel and the interpersonal attraction network. Use of the informal system is driven by the needs of the clients and the workers themselves. For example, direct-line social workers may have informal discussions about agency services with various supervisors or others outside the context of the formal structure—in the cafeteria or hallway—that can affect service delivery to specific clients. Further, when needed, supervisors may provide direct services. These informal arrangements can change across time, but they are always vital to the effective provision of services.

THE CLIENT AND THE FORMAL AND INFORMAL ORGANIZATIONAL ARRANGEMENTS

Persons in power have designed the formal organizational arrangement for specific purposes with a one-size-fits-all philosophy. Hence, the specific needs of the client tend to be force-fit into the categorical needs of the system—a major need being assurance that the system sustains itself. To that end, formal organizational arrangements tend to be quite concerned with specific policies and procedures that detail such things as number of client contact hours, completion of agency forms from which appropriate data can be collected and documented, and up-to-date, adequately completed paperwork. In this formal arrangement, the unique needs of the client may be overlooked in favor of the requirements of the organization.

It is through the informal organization that individual needs of the client come to light and are dealt with. The informal organization tends to adapt the system to meet the needs of both the client and the worker and is more concerned with client satisfaction than rigid adherence to timelines and paperwork. That is not to say, however, that social workers are immune from keeping adequate case notes and adhering to agency policies. It is to say that skilled workers can work around the system both to meet the expressed needs of many clients and to comply with policy. For example, a client in a rural setting has court-ordered supervised visitation with his children. The children are supposed to be seen weekly in the local welfare office, which is a three-hour drive for the father and a two-hour drive for the worker to pick up the children and bring them to the office. To enable the visits with fewer costs to the parent, the children, and the worker herself, she agrees to meet the parent at a neighborhood McDonalds that is only an hour's drive for each of them. The meeting place is a public one, yet the visit is structured and supervised. Moreover, the father is now able to be with his children in a setting that is more natural than a welfare office.

ORGANIZATIONAL CHANGE

Formal organizations are loath to change, and when changes do occur, they occur at a glacial pace. Changes, when they do happen, may be the result of a crisis that threatens the existence of the organization. For example, when major tobacco companies were forced to remove their advertising from television, a crisis occurred that required them to rethink how to sell their product. A more salient example might be that of the March of Dimes, which was created to fight infantile paralysis (polio in children). When a preventative vaccine for polio was developed in the 1950s, the organization faced extinction. This crisis of extinction led it to shift its focus to the welfare of all children with birth defects.

In general, the informal organization tends to be more responsive to the perceived needs of the client and may identify and influence formal organizational changes of benefit to workers and clients. For example, direct-line workers in a mental health agency were confronted with a waiting room that was not in the least bit client- or worker-friendly. Drab plastic chairs were lined along two walls, torn and tattered magazines were outdated, windows were grimy, and there were no living plants or colorful wall decorations. Clients, when asked about the ambience of the place, reflected the depression of the setting. Direct-line workers and supervisors agreed that something should be done to make the waiting area more welcoming and joined forces to convince the agency director (who held the organizational purse strings) to refurbish it. What emerged was a brightly lighted, well-appointed waiting room with colorful wall decor and rugs, private seating areas with padded chairs, several healthy potted plants, and current magazines. Clients noticed the changes immediately and were noticeably pleased with the new surroundings.

Both formal and informal organizational arrangements play a significant role in the life of any social service agency. Social workers must be cognizant of both and know how to work in and with both entities. Not knowing the intricacies of both the formal and informal could jeopardize the effective provision of services to clients.

CHOICE POINTS IN THE ORGANIZATION: GETTING FROM POINT A TO POINT B

Concern for clients requires the social worker to learn the bases for every agency decision that affects them. From admission through termination of services, there are many choice points, many times when employees and related others make key decisions regarding services and interventions. What are the available options and on what do decision makers (intake workers, service workers, supervisors, treatment teams, and so forth) base their choices among these available options? These are things the social worker needs to know. At some point, the social worker may have to raise questions about fuzzy criteria at consequential choice points and work within the agency to increase the clarity and specificity of significant questions and reliability among decision makers' responses. Moreover, the worker may find it necessary to work toward increasing currently available options. Ways of doing this are discussed in chapters 4 and 7. This section provides a method for analyzing agency decision making regarding clients and a method for identifying choice points and unearthing the criteria embedded in each without ruffling too many feathers in the process of gathering relevant information.

As in analyzing direct practice, the easiest way to identify an organization's choice points, options, and criteria for selecting among options is to begin at the beginning, with the client's application for services, and chart a process view of the questions decisions makers at each choice point ask themselves in order to select the *appropriate* option. It should be noted that this chart (figure 14.5) is in useable form—especially for later, when the worker identifies where there are fuzzy criteria (or no criteria) in order to discuss and resolve these anomalies. Figure 14.5 elaborates this content and can be referred to help clarify the process.

The first action occurs when persons arrive at the agency. Persons who become clients of human service agencies do so because they (or someone else with greater clout, such as parents or courts) believe the individual has some need that can be met by the agency. In the case of voluntary applicants, it is the person herself or himself who determines whether to apply for agency services. However, for involuntary applicants, a powerful someone outside the individual (often a judge) determines whether services from a particular agency are appropriate. Irrespective of the route people take to become involved with a human service agency, newcomers are first confronted by the physical entity (ecological organization and culturescape) that houses the services they are seeking. They have to deal with time-distance-cost factors associated with receiving the services and cope with formal and informal policies of the agency. In sum, all human service organizations share commonalities, including formal and informal organizational structures that provide the glue to hold the agency together and facilitate its functioning. However, while the applicant is viewed as the consumer of the agency's services, that applicant

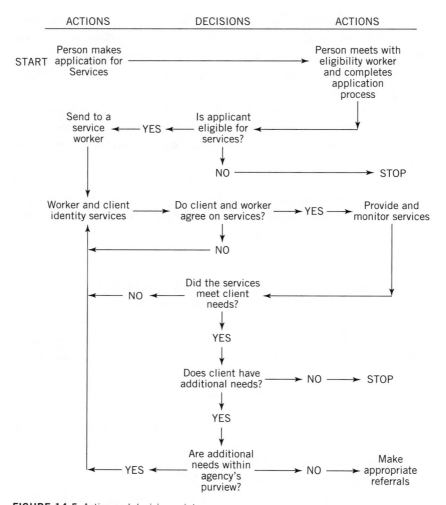

FIGURE 14.5 Action and decision points

may have little say in what is done to or for her or him in the name of these services.

The next first action occurs at intake where the worker meets with the client and all relevant application forms are completed. The length and type of application will vary from agency to agency, as will the requisite documentation necessary to ensure eligibility.

The first decision that will affect the applicant is made at intake, where the worker, using information from the applicant, makes a determination about whether the applicant is, in fact, eligible for the services provided by the agency. Eligibility for services is determined by the policies of the agency that are often handed down from federal, state, and local laws and monies.

Once a client has made an application for services, if there are eligibility requirements, the first decision point relates to determining this. An intake worker who examines the applicant's relevant documents and interviews her or him generally determines eligibility. Based on the information gleaned from this process, it is generally this worker who must answer the question, "Is this person or family eligible for services provided by this particular agency?" If the answer to the question is, "No," then no services other than possible referrals to more appropriate agencies are provided, and the person's interaction with the agency terminates. For example, if a woman with a teenage child applies at an agency whose only function is to provide food for infants, the applicant will not be eligible for services even though she and her child are hungry.

If, however, the answer to the question is, "Yes, the applicant is eligible for services from the agency," then the applicant becomes a client and is sent to a service worker. Based on input from the intake worker, the service worker and the client work to identify what specific needs the client has and what services are required. This is not necessarily a one-session enterprise. Often, identifying client need is complex and emotional. It takes both the worker and the client time to understand the troublesome situations and then translate these into service requirements.

For example, an eight-weeks-pregnant college sophomore who was a victim of date rape is unsure of what she wants to do about her pregnancy. She applies for counseling services at the Metricom Family Planning agency. Once she has completed required paperwork and has met with an intake worker, she is found to be eligible. Her intake file is forwarded to a service worker who meets with the client to identify her concerns, feelings, and needs and to discuss her various options. Because the client is confused and the service options complicated and emotionally charged, this initial session ends with both the client and worker agreeing to meet again in order to complete a service plan.

The next decision point comes when needs and appropriate services are identified. The question to be asked is, "Do both the client and the worker agree that the identified needs and services are appropriate?" If the answer is, "No," then continued exploration, understanding, and identification of services are necessary. If the answer is, "Yes," then a service contract is made. This contract gives the worker the client's permission to perform the agreed-upon services (case management, mediation, therapy, and the like). Once the contract has been negotiated, then the specific services and interventions can be provided and monitored.

Using the example of the pregnant college student from above, the client and the worker meet a second time in order to identify a course of action agreeable to the client. The client decided that she wanted to keep the baby, needed prenatal counseling, and would probably benefit from parenting classes. She also agreed to accept a referral to the health clinic where she could receive regular checkups during her pregnancy. The worker informed her of agency policies related to informed consent and confidentiality and created a service contract that outlined the work they would do together.

When agreed-upon services have been provided—or at some point during their provision, if they are being delivered over time at regular intervals—the services and their delivery are assessed. Thus, the next question is, "Did/do the services meet the client's needs?" If the answer is, "No," the client and the worker return to an identification of needs and services. They will also explore ways in which the service or its provision were unsatisfactory or not appropriate vis-à-vis need and will pursue further details of the client's struggle. From this exploration and in light of a newly conceptualized aspect of need, an effort to match services more precisely will be made.

For example, our pregnant college student agreed to a variety of services, and the worker agreed to provide those services. At regular intervals, the client and the worker discussed how their work was going and whether they were making progress toward meeting the client's expressed needs. Along the way, they made necessary minor changes as indicated by these discussions. One of these minor changes consisted of rescheduling the client's prenatal counseling appointments to coincide with the day of her weekly parenting classes.

If the answer is, "Yes, the provision of services did meet the client's needs," another question arises: "Does the client have additional needs?" The worker probes to discover whether the client has needs to which attention has not been given. If no additional needs come to the fore, that is, the answer is "No," then the worker and client summarize and terminate their work together, the client leaves the agency, and the case is closed.

For example, seven months later, the social worker's delivery of services to her pregnant client as specified in the initial service contract—prenatal counseling, parenting classes, and a referral to the health clinic—were concluded. In their assessment meeting, both the client and the worker agreed that the client's needs had been met. Following the baby's birth, the client again met with the worker, and they summarized their time and work together. It was determined that the client had no more service needs, and, following a termination process, her case file was closed.

If the answer is, "Yes, there are additional needs for which services are necessary," there is still another question: "Are the newly identified needs within the purview of the agency?" If the answer is, "No, the client's needs are outside the agency mandate," then referrals to appropriate organizations are provided, the client's interaction with this particular agency is terminated, and the case is closed.

If after our pregnant client gave birth she unexpectedly needed financial support for the child and indicated this in her postnatal meeting with the worker, this would constitute an additional need, but Metricom Family Planning does not provide financial assistance to clients. Thus, the agency is unable to assist the client other than providing her with a referral to a public welfare office. That done, the termination process occurs, and her case file is closed.

If, however, the answer is, "Yes, there are additional needs for which the client is eligible and such services are within the purview of the agency, then the client and the worker revisit the action where needs are explored, defined, and matched with services. A new service contract is negotiated and the newly agreed-upon services are monitored and assessed.

Assume again that our pregnant college student needed postnatal services she had not considered before. Perhaps she now realizes that if she is going to continue with her college career, she will need daycare services. The client and worker then revisit the box where needs are explored, defined, and matched with existing agency services. Metricom Family Planning offers daycare services, and the client is eligible for them. Thus, a new service contract is created, and the services are provided and monitored and assessed as before.

As we look down the center column of figure 14.5 (Decisions), the critical questions that govern service delivery leap out. Their clarity and specificity or their fuzziness and lack of specificity are exposed. It is these critical decision points that govern who is eligible to receive services; whether the client and the worker agree on identified need and choice of services; whether the delivered services met or meet client need; whether the client has additional needs; and, given additional needs, whether these services are within the agency's purview.

CONCLUSION

Social work is essentially a bureaucratized profession, and there is ample evidence to demonstrate that the context in which social work is practiced seriously affects the type and effectiveness of social services and the impact they can have on clients. The best direct practice skills in the world can be eclipsed by aversive organizational policies and practices. Most social services agencies have fixed jurisdictions; policies and procedures established by some governmental entity and rooted in administrative law; hierarchical command structures; job classifications systems based on performance, education, examination, or longevity; and work that is broken into small units. However, the status quo need not remain so. Organizations are made up of human beings and should never be seen as fixed in time or space. They should be viewed as socially constructed, permeable systems that are capable of being moved and changed.

15

WORKING IN THE ORGANIZATION

THIS CHAPTER examines how workers actually work within an organizational setting. It is divided into three sections. The first section, on the self principle, parallels the structural approach to practice with clients, but it is focused on the worker in the organization as the primary beneficiary. The second section, on changing the organization from within, discusses the use of the principle of least contest in the organization and details what the worker can do to negotiate the agency setting in order to accomplish organizational change. The final section, on metawork, explores the work, other than work with clients, in which the worker must engage to function effectively within an organizational setting.

THE SELF PRINCIPLE

The self principle directs social workers, in their organizational contexts, to apply the direct practice principles (see chapter 4) to themselves. That is, the direct practice principles form the foundation of processes for carrying out the self principle. While the self principle parallels the structural principles for work with clients, it is the worker rather than the client who is the ultimate intended beneficiary. The processes for carrying out the self principle include (1) being accountable to and for oneself; (2) alleviating one's own struggles to serve clients; (3) maximizing potential supports for workers in the organization; (4) deconstructing oppressive cultural discourses that circulate in the organization; (5) exerting the least pressure needed to accomplish organizational change; and (6) increasing worker strategies for maximizing positive experiences for self and minimizing negative ones.

PROCESSES FOR CARRYING OUT THE SELF PRINCIPLE

BE ACCOUNTABLE TO AND FOR ONESELF

Accountability for and to oneself refers to a worker's concern that her or his professional needs are being met within the organization—for instance, that the worker has access to a helpful supervisor who knows the "ropes," or that the worker is responsible for a caseload that is of a manageable size—while at the same time ensuring that the worker is satisfying the legitimate requirements of the job in the organization, such as paying attention to client needs and completing required paperwork in a timely manner. Accountability to and for oneself also involves voicing concerns regarding policies of the agency that seem to interfere with the best interests of clients as well as worker efforts to meet client need. This requires practitioners to work from an active, well-honed social conscience. Workers must always question any agency policy that causes or increases unnecessary stress for any employee, any client, or any oppressed population and advocate for new, diverse, and nontraditional roles and rules. Although there is ideological diversity within the profession (as in any profession), it is agreed that good social workers continue to be animated by a belief in the dignity and worth of all persons. This means colleagues as well as clients. Thus, it is expected that social workers maintain ongoing engagement with unpopular, as well as popular workers and in potentially conflictual, as well as predictably agreeable situations. In addition to having compassion for clients, caring and compassion must be the guiding values that characterize social workers' interactions with colleagues and superordinates. This means that no matter what the circumstances, the social worker must treat all other agency employees equally, ethically, and with sensitivity even during necessary confrontation. The receptionist and the supervisor deserve the same level of respect and compassion. All are equal as persons and are equally entitled to be treated with dignity and genuine concern, regardless of the positions they occupy or the stands they take on issues. Obviously, working from a social conscience is not always easy.

ALLEVIATE PERSONAL STRUGGLES TO SERVE CLIENTS

Alleviating one's own struggles to serve clients includes looking beyond the self to see if other workers are struggling with similar problems. This is essential for determining whether a structural change is needed. If many workers are trying to cope with the same situation, structural change is needed. If only one worker is struggling with it, a special accommodation to the specific situation is necessary. For example, if a worker finds that the seat of the old desk chair he has been given and on which he must sit for several hours a day has sunk in the middle, aggravating his lower back, a special accommodation (such as padding the seat) would be appropriate. If, on the other hand, old, misshapen desk chairs are causing or exacerbating lower back problems for many workers, then a structural solution (replacing all of the old desk chairs with new ones) is required.

Work in all four quadrants is also necessary to alleviate workers' struggles to do the job. The worker should step into Quadrant A to work on her or his own behalf, such as, for example, pursuing continuing education activities. In Quadrant B, the worker can work with some colleagues to benefit all colleagues in the agency by engaging some co-workers to develop groups for support and peer supervision for all co-workers. When in Quadrant C, the worker works with others on behalf of self, as in advocating with agency administrators for a salary increase commensurate with one's level of expertise and caseload size. In Quadrant D, the worker works with others, such as lobbying agency administrators for additional health benefits for all agency employees.

Alleviating one's own struggles to serve clients also demands that the worker take different roles at different times. Specifically, the roles of conferee, broker, mediator, and advocate are necessary. In the role of conferee, the worker discusses differences with colleagues. In the role of broker, the worker can refer a "wounded" colleague (a co-worker with depression, burnout, or a substance abuse problem, for example) to appropriate resources for help. When colleagues are at odds with one another, the worker can assume the role of mediator and stand between them, helping them to hear each other and articulate their concerns. Acting as an advocate in a child-protective-services setting, the worker can try to enable workers to have more time to spend with clients who are in potentially harmful situations by arguing with state officials for reducing caseload size by increasing the size of staff.

MAXIMIZE SUPPORT FOR WORKERS IN THE ORGANIZATION

Maximizing potential supports for workers in the organization refers to modifying or creating structures to benefit workers. This occurs on two levels. First are the supports that have a direct impact on the individual worker. Such might include ensuring that adequate office supplies are available, that adequate time for one-to-one supervision is provided, or that the workload is equitably distributed. Second are supports and changes that will occur within the organization itself and will benefit all employees. Such might include instituting an agency exercise with built-in times to participate; establishing regular forums for interacting with administrators to expose problems and discuss solutions; and providing regularly scheduled professional development events. As these innovations endure across time, they become institutionalized and a regular part of the organization.

DECONSTRUCT OPPRESSIVE CULTURAL DISCOURSES THAT CIRCULATE IN THE ORGANIZATION

The deconstruction of oppressive discourses that circulate within the organization refers to the worker's responsibility to challenge and debunk beliefs and actions deleterious to clients and co-workers (for example, negative attitudes toward poor people, African Americans, lesbian/gay/bisexual/transgender persons, aged people, and so forth). This can be done by identifying the oppressive discourses (reified psychiatric labels, offensive characterizations of members of minority groups), loosening them by introducing multiple realities, discovering who benefits from them, and undermining deleterious beliefs thought to be the truth. The worker tries to influence others to stop believing in these widespread hurtful myths and stop replicating them in the organization. Deconstruction aims at shifting concepts and challenging attitudes, that is to say, destruction of the myths that stigmatize and dehumanize entire populations.

EXERT THE LEAST PRESSURE NEEDED TO ACCOMPLISH ORGANIZATIONAL CHANGE

It is a basic law of physics that for every force there is an equal and opposite force. The principle of least contest applies to this. Consistent with this also is the process of having the social worker exert the least pressure needed to accomplish organizational change. Using less pressure will presumably reduce the counterpressure that the social worker's efforts at change will generate. One must approach change deliberately, in keeping with generating the least pressure. Similarly, the worker should escalate issues slowly. Rather than storm into the director's office, the worker should first discuss change with colleagues, perhaps bringing them on board; next with supervisors, possibly garnering additional support; and so on, moving up the hierarchy, the formal organizational structure.

Further, also consistent with exerting the least pressure, the worker would take the role of conferee before acting as a mediator and would act as a mediator before becoming an advocate. This means that discussion on an issue always comes first. If arguments ensue and the worker is not a party to them, she can stand between and help those arguing to hear each other and think about what they are hearing. But even when the worker believes there is a clear conflict of interest, discussion always precedes an argument, no matter how well founded.

In terms of the quadrant model, a worker who wanted to initiate organizational change would engage in Quadrant A and C activities before engaging in Quadrant B activities. For example, she would discuss issues with her peers and then superordinates before resorting to such actions as organizing staff to confront administrators. But, if it is necessary, she would do the latter, provided she has exhausted her range of alternatives.

INCREASE WORKER STRATEGIES FOR MAXIMIZING POSITIVE EXPERIENCES FOR SELF AND MINIMIZING NEGATIVE ONES

In order to maximize positive workplace experiences and minimize negative ones, a worker must maintain pivotal readiness. Pivotal readiness implies a posture of alert, poised-for-action responsiveness that is free to move in a variety of directions. A prerequisite for this is having a variety of ways to react in relation to agency situations.

A pivotal readiness stance emphasizes contingencies, expects the unfamiliar, and is ready to cope with whatever happens with sensitivity, a sense of tentativeness, and a tolerance for ambiguity. The emphasis is on being ready to do something, even with awareness that there may be some negative outcomes: do and doubt—but do. Pivotal readiness implies that thorny situations should not mire one down in self-doubt, but rather be seen as opportunities to learn, shift one's strategies, and again do something in relation to the troublesome situation.

CONNECTING THE CONSCIOUS USE OF SELF WITH THE DELIBERATE USE OF SELF

To have a conscious understanding of oneself requires insight related to who you are. This may include knowledge of such things as ethnicity, family history, gender identity, sexual orientation, spiritual beliefs, cultural/personal biases, lived experiences, and emotional sensitivity. These are aspects of oneself and will better inform and help the social worker monitor work done with clients and colleagues. Moreover, conscious understanding of oneself in the workplace (of, for instance, motivation, attitude, competence, potential) and of one's position in the interpersonal dynamics of the organization (such as roles, norms, communication patterns, and interpersonal attraction networks) will have a direct bearing on one's ability to use the processes evoked by the self principle. As indicated in figure 15.1, the processes flow from a conscious understanding of self and provide the basis for the worker's deliberate use of self. The deliberate use of self feeds back to the conscious understanding of self and provides a continuous feedback loop that enhances professional growth.

CHANGING THE ORGANIZATION FROM WITHIN

Working in an organization requires an understanding of how to create organizational change. While effecting organizational change refers in part to the process of least pressure noted above, being a change agent also involves specific means of creating and managing change. There are four key concepts to creating organizational change: (1) positioning oneself to be influential, (2) stretching organizational norms, (3) questioning unethical agency practices, and (4) raising taboos.

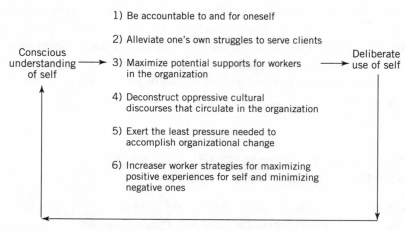

1) Be accountable to and for oneself

2) Alleviate one's own struggles to serve clients

Conscious understanding of self → 3) Maximize potential supports for workers in the organization

Deliberate use of self →

4) Deconstruct oppressive cultural discourses that circulate in the organization

5) Exert the least pressure needed to accomplish organizational change

6) Increaser worker strategies for maximizing positive experiences for self and minimizing negative ones

FIGURE 15.1 Processes for carrying out the self principle

POSITIONING ONESELF

Positioning oneself refers to the deliberate garnering of influence by building positive relationships within the organization. These relationships are seen as being helpful to the worker in negotiating the formal and informal organizational arrangements (see chapter 14). Positioning oneself primarily occurs in the informal organizational arrangement and might include, in addition to doing one's job competently and fully, inviting the director to lunch, empathizing with a supervisor's struggles (work-related or personal), volunteering to assume some of a vacationing colleague's cases, or offering to emcee the office talent show. While some may see these acts as brown-nosing, they pay off. Having positive affect and a will-do attitude wins the worker lots of brownie points that have value in a variety of situations. For example, workers with positive attitudes who have positioned themselves favorably within the organization are seen as more credible than others with negative attitudes (though perhaps correct ideas), and credibility leads to influence when making suggestions or commenting on upcoming decisions.

STRETCHING ORGANIZATIONAL NORMS

Stretching organizational norms refers to the accomplishing of organizational change by pushing the limits of what was once thought of as a given. This involves getting an organization to move from point A to point B by using a strategy that seems to threaten even greater movement from point A to point Z. For example, an agency norm has been that of limiting service delivery to day hours (8:00 a.m. until 5:00 p.m.) despite the reality that the agency serves employed people, most of whom are unable to get to the agency for services during the day. This norm had been in place for decades, although there were some staff members who thought the agency should have evening hours to accommodate the population being served. To influence a normative change in hours, some of the workers who favored evening hours suggest that the agency to be open all five weeknights as well as weekdays, and that working hours for all employees be staggered to meet the new hours of operation. While this idea was angrily argued in a staff meeting and was opposed by the agency administrator, the administrator compromised by having the agency open two evenings a week. To the benefit of many previously underserved people, the original norm had been stretched.

QUESTIONING UNETHICAL PRACTICES

Questioning unethical practices refers to the social worker's ethical obligation to ferret out and expose any agency or individual worker's practice that is unethical (see chapter 3). Unethical practices are usually covert, for it is unlikely that an overtly unethical agency would not survive governmental or professional scrutiny. But social norms change, and what may have been considered ethical years ago (for instance, child labor) is no longer considered so. To ensure that unethical practices are unmasked and confronted, the social worker must be alert to subtle practices such as institutional racism or homophobia.

For example, in a local homeless shelter the unwritten policy is not to accept individuals who are overtly homosexual or visibly transgender. Those with a sexual orientation or gender identity that deviates from the conventional heterosexual norm are told to go elsewhere for shelter. While this is an obvious unethical practice, those committing it for whatever reason—religious, ideological, or personal—do not see it as such. The social worker has a responsibility to identify the unethical practice and try to change it.

RAISING TABOOS

Raising taboos refers to identifying and confronting those agency secrets that get in the way of service to clients. These are the things most agency workers know about but will not discuss. For example, there is a worker who has been with the organization for more than two decades and who simply does not want to retire. The man has been unable to make the transition from paper and pencil to computer, is not capable of getting his work done on a timely basis, and relies on the goodwill of his co-workers to bail him out. He is an affable guy, tells great jokes, and has a sad home life. Every one knows about his situation, and they know how his clients suffer, but no one is willing to say it aloud.

Similarly not discussed is the hyena-like laughter emanating from the office of a female supervisor who is having a sexual relationship with the agency's grantwriter. The two of them hang out in the supervisor's office, and their noise disturbs the entire first floor of the agency, workers and clients alike. Because the supervisor is perceived as being vengeful—she has actually fired workers and staff who disagree with her views—no one is willing to chance a confrontation. The social worker should break the code of silence by discussing the deleterious noise with affected staff members and then speak privately with the supervisor to report the effect of the noise level on clients and staff and ask that she rectify it.

Although raising taboos may come at a cost to the worker, these damaging situations must be addressed, and more brownie points can still be earned over time. Any taboo that gets in the way of providing effective services to clients cannot be allowed to endure.

THE METAWORK

Metawork refers to everything the worker does when not directly engaged in work with or for the client. In a sense, metawork is work about the work. When the rationale for being involved in a particular activity is that it is a response to the client's understanding of what is happening on her or his behalf, this is the work of direct service delivery. It may occur directly with the client (interviews) or indirectly on behalf of the client (telephone calls to people other than the client). All other work that is once-removed from direct engagement with or on behalf of clients is metawork—these are activities that may enhance direct service delivery but are aside from it. There are two major components related to metawork: the tasks associated with it and time management. The five tasks are (1) doing paperwork, (2) dealing with technology, (3) participating in supervision, (4) attending meetings, and (5) participating in professional development. Time management refers to how a worker uses time in relation to these five tasks. These tasks are required to maintain organizational integrity and include all the behind-the-scenes supportive work that is necessary to sustain the agency and to ensure quality service to clients.

PAPERWORK

Paperwork refers to written documents that may be required by the agency, the state, or the federal government. Such documentation is related to clients and the services provided to them. This written documentation begins when the client initially seeks services (intake). Figure 15.2 chronicles a typical paperwork trail that is created by the client/worker relationship.

While written documentation may vary from agency to agency, some form of records exists in every organization. In addition to records that detail client/worker interactions and what is done with and on behalf of clients, organizations require agency paperwork—for example, paperwork that is related to state or federal funding requirements, time studies, accreditation, statisti-

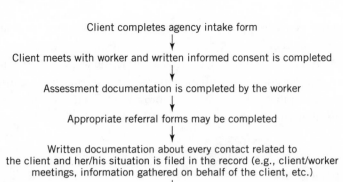

Client completes agency intake form

↓

Client meets with worker and written informed consent is completed

↓

Assessment documentation is completed by the worker

↓

Appropriate referral forms may be completed

↓

Written documentation about every contact related to
the client and her/his situation is filed in the record (e.g., client/worker
meetings, information gathered on behalf of the client, etc.)

↓

Summary of termination is documented

FIGURE 15.2 Typical paperwork trail created by the client/worker relationship

cal reports, and so forth. Keeping current with paperwork consumes enormous quantities of time. Ordinarily, much of it is central to organizational functioning.

TECHNOLOGY

Related to paperwork is the rapidly expanding technology used to create and disseminate paperwork. Gone are the days of meeting with a client and then dictating the verbatim interview for a member of a stenography pool to type and return for corrections and then put in the client's record. Gone are the days of filling out forms by hand and inserting them into the case file. Gone are the days of sending various consent forms by mail and waiting for a mailed return. Computers have replaced the steno pool, and fax machines and emails have replaced the traditional postal system. Because technology has become such an integral part of agency life, it is vital that workers are proficient with various programs (Word, Access, and so on), various search engines (Google, Yahoo), various operating systems (Windows XP, OS X), as well as various virus protection programs (Norton, McAfee). These computer skills, coupled with an understanding of how to use email, are required for most, if not all, current undergraduate students (many of whom grew up with computers), so we need not belabor the point that such skills are important for the social worker.

What may not be so easily understood are the ethical implications associated with the use of technology in the social welfare organization. The primary issue related to the expanded use of technology is that of client confidentiality. Sensitive case material must be considered as it relates to computers, faxes, email, and voicemail. Once entered into a computer, data becomes almost impossible to remove—yes, it can be erased from your program files, but it usually remains, forever hidden deep in the bowels of your hard drive. Faxing client release forms or any other documentation to various places probably should not be done. This is because errors can occur when entering the fax number (many times we have received faxes sent to the wrong number) or the receiving fax machine may be in a place where several people have access to it (the one in our office is in a public hall). Email creates infinite chances for breaches of confidentiality and should never be used in connection with client documentation. We have all seen what can happen when that innocent email is forwarded around the globe by well-wishers. Similarly, leaving messages with client-related material on answering machines must be done with the utmost caution. Be certain you know who has access to the messages and that no confidential material is ever divulged.

Similarly, social workers must be cautious when printing case-record materials created by computer. Where are the documents actually printed? If the social worker has a printer in her office, documents are more secure than if they are routed to a shared printer down the hall or on another floor. Since client confidentiality is paramount, hard copies of sensitive documentation must be safeguarded at all times and the social worker must be responsible for providing that document safety net.

So, although technology can be viewed as a laborsaving device and seems to fit into our "there is never enough time to do the task" mentality, using such technology must be done with thought and consideration. Even though the technology exists, there may be times when the old-fashioned way is preferred.

SUPERVISION

Supervision is the guidance that a social worker's designated mentor provides for the development of the worker's job skills and the monitoring of job performance in all areas. The worker spends time with a supervisor discussing client's and service provision to them, learning agency procedures, or going over paperwork. Regular meetings with one's supervisor are a vitally important part of the worker's metawork, and if such meetings are not held on a regular or sufficiently frequent basis, the social worker should request that they be part of weekly routine. It is during these meetings that a worker can talk about difficult clients, get tips on various clinical techniques, find out how the supervisor would have handled a particular situation, connect agency protocols with actual work situations, describe troublesome issues with co-workers, challenge oppressive agency discourses, advocate for various things, and get an ongoing sense of how well she or he seems to be doing the job. Supervisory conferences provide the worker with an excellent chance to practice the processes for carrying out the self principle.

MEETINGS

While engaging in supervision may be called a meeting, as the term is used here refers to all of the group activities in which co-workers, staff, and/or other employees gather for a common purpose. These may include unit staff meetings, departmental meetings, employee retreats, or any other activity an employee is generally expected, though not required, to attend (such as office picnics, Christmas parties, and retirement dinners). Depending on the organization, these may take a lot of time (weekly staff meetings and monthly departmental meetings) or practically no time at all (meetings are held on an as-needed basis only). No matter the amount of time required for meetings, they do take away from one's direct contact with clients and must be considered in the workload equation.

PROFESSIONAL DEVELOPMENT

Professional development refers to continuing education for social workers beyond the specific requirements of the job. These educational experiences are designed and expected to contribute to a worker's ongoing personal and professional growth as a social worker. They may include attending national conferences given by various professional groups, state or regional conferences offered by groups such as the Council on Social Work Education (CSWE), National Association of Social Workers (NASW), and Marriage and Family Therapy Institute, or local workshops and training activities such as those offered by the American Red Cross or by university continuing education programs. Many of these educational opportunities are approved for continuing education units (CEUs) required for maintaining state licensure. Some organizations allow time to be given by the organization for workers to attend these activities, and some may even defray a portion of the cost. In Kentucky, the Cabinet for Families and Children currently requires that every new employee take some master's-level social work courses offered at one of three universities in the state. The tuition costs and time to take the courses are provided by the Cabinet. The organization thereby gains employees who are better trained, and the worker gets free master's-level coursework and time away from the office to complete the classes. This tends to be a win/win situation for all concerned.

TIME MANAGEMENT

Time management is the way in which a worker manages time in relation to all of the tasks required by the worker's job description. Time is a quixotic element; tasks expand to fill the time available for them, and tasks are sometimes so numerous that they exceed the available time. If tasks routinely exceed the forty-hour workweek, the problem is a structural one—the worker is expected to perform too many tasks. Sadly, when an organization does not recognize that the problem is structural, there are two possible outcomes: individuals may spend evenings and weekends catching up, or they may try to handle the task within the allotted time, find they cannot, and be nailed to the wall by their supervisors for work left undone. Neither of these two outcomes is justifiable. Sometimes, thought, the problem is not structural—time allotted for requisite tasks is reasonable, and most workers handle their job responsibilities well. But a few do not. These workers need to develop better time-management skills. Ideally, required tasks should not exceed the time available for them, and workers should be held accountable for completing them in a timely manner. As before, there are five particular areas to which the worker must attend: (1) doing paperwork, (2) dealing with technology, (3) participating in supervision, (4) attending meetings, and (5) participating in professional development.

PAPERWORK

Paperwork includes the creation and management of all documents associated with service provision to clients and required for audits or other agency needs. While it could be argued that completing intake assessment forms and the like is direct work with clients, we will make a distinction here between paperwork and interviews where information is collected to complete the paperwork. Some paperwork is completed during direct client contact; other paperwork has a life of itself beyond client/worker interactions. For example, some forms need to be completed jointly with the client (intake forms, confidentiality forms). During worker/client conversations, workers should do as little writing as possible and indicate aloud what they are writing when they do it. For example, the worker might say to the client, "What you just said is complicated. Do you mind if I take a few notes?" Once the notes have been written, the worker should check out their accuracy with the client by reading the notes to the client and asking something like, "Does this capture what you were just explaining to me?"

Anecdotal evidence from social workers indicates that completing required agency paperwork consumes a lot of time. One worker reported that completing all of the required forms for just one client takes more than three hours. Thus, one must factor in adequate amounts of time not only to engage in direct work with clients, but also to complete the paperwork associated with each client encounter. It should be noted that time required for paperwork should decrease some as the worker's familiarity with each form increases and the worker develops parsimony in writing case notes. However, given the size of one's caseload and required number of contacts with each client within a specific timeframe, or the expectations of a certain number of billable hours, this can be a delicate juggling act.

TECHNOLOGY

While touted as a time-saver, often technology takes more time — time required to learn how to use the technology; time taken to read, delete, and respond to a host of email messages and attachments; time spent waiting for the fax to arrive; time waiting on hold for the next available assistant; time taken trying to unclog the paper jam in the touchy copier; time spent copying requisite forms. Managing technology's time consumption is especially difficult because one never knows how long each learning, waiting, or unclogging will actually take. But these are realities of organizational life, and time for each must be expected and managed.

SUPERVISION

The time required for supervision is far easier to determine than time required for either paperwork or dealing with technology for scheduling supervisory sessions can be done in advance, for weeks or even months at a time and each session assigned a finite block of time. Getting these sessions scheduled with dates and times clearly marked on one's calendar makes time related to supervision more easily managed. However, it must be realized that even regularly scheduled meetings should be flexible—less time taken when needed or more time taken for thorny situations. Also, there will be unscheduled supervisory times when urgent events—client or organizational—arise and demand immediate decisions that are outside the scope of agency protocols or worker authority.

MEETINGS

Because meetings, like supervisory sessions, are often put on the organizational calendar weeks or months ahead of time, these too, tend to be easily planned for. If one knows that each Monday from 3:00 to 4:00 p.m. there will be a unit staff meeting where all new cases are discussed, personal schedules can be arranged around this set time slot. There are, of course, those inevitable emergency sessions to deal with potentially difficult organizational issues (what to do about an impending hurricane, how to cope with the unexpected death of the agency administrator) for which one must carve out time to attend. But meetings, like other organizational activities, must become part of the time-management process of the worker.

PROFESSIONAL DEVELOPMENT

Of all the activities in which a worker engages, the one that is probably the simplest to deal with from the perspective of time is related to professional development. One knows precisely when agency training is to be held, when classes occur, or when professional meetings are going to happen. Knowing when an event will occur and attending that activity are only part of one's management of time. For, in order to be able to attend professional development events, the worker must be certain that other organizational tasks are taken care of so one's absence does not generate chaos and frantic catch-up work. In order for a worker to attend professional development activities paperwork must be current, meetings that will be missed must be covered, difficult case situations must be discussed in supervision, and colleagues who are acting on the worker's behalf must be briefed.

TIME-MANAGEMENT STRATEGIES

Time management can be problematic to the new worker or even an experienced worker in a new agency or a new job. Some basic strategies may help one get a hold on time management. Such would include the following tips:

- Get and use an appointment book/portable digital assistant (PDA) or similar calendar
- Even if you think you remember, constantly refer to your calendar and check off things as you finish them
- Write/enter all givens (list meetings, supervisory sessions, seminars, and such) on your calendar
- Schedule times for direct service contacts
- Complete the necessary paperwork on each client contact as soon after the contact as possible
- Stick to a schedule as rigidly as is possible and, when unavoidably interrupted, return to your schedule as soon as is possible
- Do not waste time: do not visit co-workers for reasons that are not job-related, play computer games on agency time, wander the halls, email cartoons to friends, flirt with co-workers, or engage in other activities that are not related to the position
- Group similar tasks (phone calls to other agencies, completion of various forms)
- Allocate some time each week to work on the self principle and to build relationships to garner influence, mediate disputes, and advocate for change

CONCLUSION

This chapter provided strategies related to the self principle for social workers as employed by organizations, described various methods of creating organizational change from within, and analyzed the construct of metawork. Each of these sections examined how social workers actually work within an organizational setting.

16

A PARADIGM DILEMMA

A MAJOR STRUGGLE involved in the current people-changing arena involves recent enthusiasm for an idea embedded in modernism—evidence-based practice (EBP). Some of those who embrace it tend to suggest that only those practices that have been "found to be effective" through quantitative research should be used, without considering the idea that what counts as "evidence" is socially constructed. Evidence has everything to do with who determines what constitutes it, and this fact makes the debate a political one. Even concepts and their operational definitions are socially constructed. While this debate continues, the following four factors should be kept in mind. The first of these is that evidence, like social work practice itself, is socially constructed. The second is that practice should not be limited by the limits of research methodology. The third is that all outcomes should not be determined in advance. The fourth is that the nuances in a helping relationship cannot be quantified nor controlled across practitioners in actual practice.

1. *Evidence is socially constructed*. Social work itself is a social construction. So is evidence. The privileging of one form of evidence over another is strictly a function of the power of the dominant group to stifle the voice of the less dominant group; but this does not prove that it is ideologically or methodologically better. As Thomas Kuhn (1962) makes clear, when a new paradigm appears, it threatens the old paradigm, and many will cling to it for fear of invalidating the very hard work they have done in accord with the old one. While quantitative methods fit easily with the old positivist paradigm, qualitative methods hold out the promise of learning within the new, postmodern paradigm, learning that could not be obtained within the limits of quantitative research under the old paradigm. Qualitative methods accept that researchers

are subjective participants with clients in a relationship they construct through their interaction.

2. *Practice should not be limited by the limits of research.* Some of those who believe that quantitative evidence of efficacy is required do not accept that what cannot yet be measured should still be done. The idea that practice should be limited by the limits of quantitative research is misguided. People continue to experience help from methods that cannot yet be measured. Qualitative inquiry, which has great potential for capturing the essence of practice, is still in its infancy, but increasing numbers of scholars are turning to it and developing it.

3. *Desired outcomes should not always be determined in advance, and they cannot always be defined in behavioral terms.* When a social worker in direct practice engages a client, the client decides what she or he wants to talk about, not accomplish. It often takes a while to come to a tentative decision even on a global, desired outcome. The client wants to feel better, for example, and cannot even begin to determine what that will look like at the beginning of the process. Moreover, the client's choices about the shape of "feeling better" frequently change over time. Further, the complexities and nuances of the client/worker relationship play a large part in the reality they construct together. It is neither possible nor desirable to standardize them.

The client has the right to participate fully in the helping process, and ultimately to determine her or his own destiny. This is a hallmark of social work. Social workers should not do things to, with, or for people that people do not want done to, with, or for them, nor talk them into changing their desires to match the worker's.

For example, when working with a battered woman, should the goal be predetermined? Should that goal be to leave the batterer? Many practitioners believe that it should be. But if so, the client has no choice other than to be deemed a failure if she does not want to leave the abusive man. She is once again being oppressed, this time by the would-be helper. Moreover, women are most vulnerable to being killed when they try to leave or succeed in leaving and are later tracked down and killed by their batterers. Should the woman not have a say in whether her own goal is to leave?

What if the client wants to change her goal during the course of therapy? As she gains insight into the institutional supports for woman-battering and how she has been recruited into believing that she is complicit in what the man does to her, if she chooses to take her knowledge and leave therapy, is her decision "evidence" of a satisfactory outcome if she herself considers it so?

4. *Complexities cannot be quantified.* The fourth major factor is that the worker/client relationship is at the core of the helping process. This relationship is complex, heavily nuanced, and uniquely co-constructed with each different client. There is no way to quantify this. Elements of it may be accessible, but if reduced to a few elements, the unique helping relationship is represented neither accurately nor fully. Even precisely defined interactional skills (Middleman and Wood 1990; Shulman 1983; Wood and Middleman 1987) are differentially used by different practitioners, and by the same practitioner with different clients. Differences in facial expression, which carry more than 60 percent of a message, and tone of voice, which carries over 30 percent of it (Davitz 1964; Davitz and Davitz 1959; Mehrabian 1968, 1969; Scheflen 1964), make quantifying such integral data virtually impossible.

Worker and client nuances cannot be captured with numbers, nor can they ever be generalizable. Qualitative methods may be able to shed light on what some social workers and clients generated in some conversations with each other, as well as how it happened. But the nature, complexities, and nuances of the helping relationship cannot be controlled across practitioners—nor should they be.

In sum, the paradigm dilemma facing contemporary social work professionals is which epistemology to follow in practice: to limit oneself to those practices for which there are quantifiable data, or to follow an epistemology that emphasizes the unique qualitative nature of the worker/client relationship.

REFERENCES

American Psychiatric Association. (1973). *Diagnostic and statistical manual of mental disorders.* 3rd ed. New York: American Psychiatric Association.

Anderson, H., and H. Goolishian. (1988). Human systems as linguistic systems: Preliminary and evolving ideas about the implications for clinical theory. *Family Process* 27 (4): 371–393.

Anderson, J. (1981). *Social work methods and processes.* Belmont, Calif.: Wadsworth.

Anderson, W. (ed.). (1993). *The truth about the truth: Deconfusing and reconstructing the postmodern world.* New York: Putnam.

Bales, R. F. (1950). *Interaction process analysis: A method for the study of small groups.* Reading, Mass.: Addison-Wesley.

Barker, R. L. (1999). *The social work dictionary.* Washington, D.C.: NASW Press.

Berger, P., and T. Luckmann. (1967). *The social construction of reality.* London: Penguin.

Bertolino, B., and B. O'Hanlon. (2002). *Collaborative, competency-based counseling and therapy.* Needham Heights, Mass.: Allyn & Bacon.

Bosanquet, B. (1916). The philosophy of casework. *Charity Organization Bulletin* 7 (10): 120–132.

Brown, R. (1992). From suspicion to affirmation: Postmodernism and the challenges of rhetorical analysis. In R. Brown (ed.), *Writing the social text,* 219–227. New York: Aldine de Gruyter.

Bruner, J. (1990). *Acts of meaning.* Cambridge, Mass.: Harvard University Press.

———. (1991). The narrative construction of reality. *Critical Inquiry* 18: 1–21.

Butler, J. (1992). Contingent foundations: Feminism and the question of postmodernism. In J. Butler and J. Scott (eds.), *Feminists theorize the political,* 3–21. New York: Routledge.

CASRO (Council of American Survey Research Organizations). (1999–2004). Code of standards and ethics for survey research. Retrieved February 1, 2005, from http://www.casro.org/codeofstandards.cfm.

Chambon, A. (1999). Foucault's approach: Making the familiar visible. In A. Chambon, A. Irving, and L. Epstein (eds.), *Reading Foucault for social work,* 51–81. New York: Columbia University Press.

Charmaz, K.C. (2005). *Grounded theory: Methods for the 21st century.* Thousand Oaks, Calif.: Sage.

Christensen, D.N., J. Todahl, and W. C. Barrett. (1999). *Solution-based casework.* New York: Aldine de Gruyter.

Collins, R. (1975). *Conflict sociology.* New York: Academic Press.

Craib, I. (1992). *Modern social theory from Parsons to Habermas.* 2nd ed. New York: St. Martin's Press.

Crozier, B. (1974). *A theory of conflict.* London: Hamish Hamilton.

Dahlke, H.O., T.O. Carlton, C. Itzkovitz, and T. M. Madison. (1980). *A foundation for social policy analysis.* Rev. ed. Lexington, Mass.: Ginn Custom.

Dahrendorf, R. (1959). *Class and class conflict in industrial society.* Palo Alto, Calif.: Stanford University Press.

Davitz, J. (1964). *The communication of emotional meaning.* New York: McGraw-Hill.

Davitz, J., and L. Davitz. (1959). The communication of feelings by content free speech. *Journal of Communication* 9:6–13.

DeJong, P., and I.K. Berg. (1998). *Interviewing for solutions.* Pacific Grove, Calif.: Brooks/Cole.

Derrida, J. (1976). *Of grammatology.* Baltimore: Johns Hopkins University Press.

Devore, W., and E. Schlessinger. (1981). *Ethnic-sensitive social work practice.* St. Louis: Mosby.

———. (1985). *Health care social work.* St. Louis: Mosby.

DHHS (United States Department of Health and Human Services). (2003). Online. Retrieved February 7, 2005, http://www.hhs.gov.

Dodson, L. (1999). *Don't call us out of name.* Boston: Beacon Press.

Dolgoff, F., R. M. Loewenberg, and D. Harrington. (2004). *Ethical decisions for social work practice.* 7th ed. Belmont, Calif.: Wadsworth.

Emerson, R.M. (1972a). Exchange theory, part I: A psychological basis for social exchange. In B.Z. Anderson (ed.), *Sociological theories in process,* 2:38–57. Boston: Houghton Mifflin.

———. (1972b). Exchange theory, part II: Exchanger relations and network structures. In B.Z. Anderson (ed.), *Sociological theories in process,* 2:58–87. Boston: Houghton Mifflin.

Farris, B., and J. Marsh. (1982). Social work as a foreign body in late capitalism. *Journal of Applied Behavioral Science* 18 (1): 76–94.

Flax, J. (1990). Postmodernism and gender relations in feminist theory. In L. Nicholson (ed.), *Feminism/postmodernism,* 39–62. New York: Routledge.

Foucault, M. (1978). *The history of sexuality: An introduction.* New York: Vintage Books.

———. (1980). *Power/knowledge.* New York: Pantheon Books.

———. (1985). *The use of pleasure.* New York: Vintage Books.

———. (1986). *The care of the self.* New York: Vintage Books.

———. (1995). *Discipline and punish.* New York: Vintage Books.

Freedman, J., and G. Combs. (1996). *Narrative Therapy.* New York: Norton.

Freeman, S. J. (2000). *Ethics: An introduction to philosophy and practice.* Belmont, Calif.: Wadsworth.

French, J., and B. Raven. (1959). The bases of social poser. In D. Cartwright (ed.), *Studies in social power,* 150–167. Ann Arbor: Institute for Social Research.

Gergen, K. (1999). *An invitation to social construction.* London: Sage.

Germain, C. (1983). Technological advances. In A. Rosenblatt and D. Waldfogel (eds.), *Handbook of clinical social work,* 26–57. San Francisco: Jossey-Bass.

Goffman, E. (1961). *Asylums.* New York: Doubleday.

Goldberg, G. (1974a). Macro-level intervention: A frame of reference and a practice model. *Journal of Education for Social Work* 10 (3): 25–29.

———. (1974b). Structural approach to practice: A new model. *Social Work* 19 (2): 150–155.

Hall, E. T. (1963). A system for the notation of proxemic behavior. *American Anthropologist* 45: 1003–1026.

History of research ethics (n.d.). Retrieved February 1, 2005, from Indiana University–Purdue University Indiana: http://www.iupui.edu/%7EresgradHuman%20Subjects/ethics#3A.html.

Hutcheon, L. (1989). *The politics of postmodernism.* New York: Routledge.

Johnson, A. (1955). Educating professional social workers for ethical practice. *Social Service Review* 29 (2): 125–136.

Kahn, S. (1995). Community organization. In R. L. Edwards (ed.), *The encyclopedia of social work,* 19th ed., 569–576. Washington, D.C.: NASW.

Korda, M. (1973). Office power: You are where you sit. *New York Magazine* (January), 35–44.

Kuhn, T. S. (1962). *The structure of scientific revolutions.* Chicago: University of Chicago Press.

Kurland, R., and R. Salmon (eds.). (1993). *Group work practice in a troubled society: Problems and opportunities.* New York: Haworth.

Lee, J. (1994). *The empowerment approach to social work practice.* New York: Columbia University Press.

Levine, M., and A. Levine. (1970). *A social history of the helping professions.* New York: Appleton-Century-Crofts.

Linzer, N. (1999). *Resolving ethical dilemmas in social work practice.* Boston: Allyn & Bacon.

MacKinnon, C. (1994). Feminism, Marxism, method and the state: Toward a feminist jurisprudence. In P. Bart and E. Moran (eds.), *Violence against women: The bloody footprints*, 201–227. Newbury Park, Calif.: Sage.

Mattison, M. (2000). Ethical decision making: The person in the process. *Social Work* 45 (3): 201–212.

Mehrabian, A. (1968). Communication without words. *Psychology Today* 2 (9): 52–55.

———. (1969). Significance of posture and position in the communication of attitude and status relationships. *Psychological Bulletin* 71:359–372.

Merton, R. K. (1968). *Social theory and social structure*. New York: Free Press.

Middleman, R., and G. Goldberg. (1974). *Social service delivery: The structural approach to social work practice*. New York: Columbia University Press.

Middleman, R. R., and G. G. Wood. (1990). *Skills for direct practice in social work*. New York: Columbia University Press.

Morgan, A. (2000). *What is narrative therapy?* Adelaide: Dulwich Centre Publications.

Myers, R. (1969). Some effects of seating arrangements in counseling. Ph.D. diss., University of Florida, Gainesville.

NASW (National Association of Social Workers). (1960–67). *Code of ethics*. Washington, D.C.: NASW Press.

———. (1979–80). *Code of ethics*. Washington, D.C.: NASW Press.

———. (1996–99). *Code of ethics*. Washington, D.C.: NASW Press.

Nord, W. (1972). *Concepts and controversy in organizational behavior*. Pacific Palisades, Calif.: Goodyear.

O'Connor, G. G. (1988). Case management: System and practice. *Social Casework* 69 (2): 97–106.

Parsons, G., and S. Holloway. (1978). *Changing human service organizations: Politics and practice*. New York: Free Press.

Parsons, T. (1967). *Sociological theory and modern society*. New York: Free Press.

Reamer, F. G. (1993). *The philosophical foundations of social work*. New York: Columbia University Press.

———. (1994). *Social work malpractice and liability: Strategies for prevention*. New York: Columbia University Press.

———. (1995). *Social work values and ethics*. Washington, D.C.: NASW Press.

———. (1998). *Ethical standards in social work: A critical review of the NASW code of ethics*. Washington, D.C.: NASW Press.

———. (2001a). *Social work ethics audit: A risk management tool*. Washington, D.C.: NASW Press.

———. (2001b). *Tangled relationships: Managing boundary issues in the human services*. New York: Columbia University Press.

Reid, P. N., and P. R. Popple. (1992). *The moral purposes of social work: The character and intentions of a profession*. Chicago: Nelson-Hall.

Rivera, F. G., and J. L. Erlich. (1998). *Community organizing in a diverse society*. 3rd ed. Boston: Allyn & Bacon.

Rose, S. M., and V. L. Moore. (1995). Case management. In R. L. Edwards (ed.), *The encyclopedia of social work*, 19th ed., 335–340. Washington, D.C.: NASW Press.

Ryan, W. (1961). *Blaming the victim*. New York: Pantheon Books.

Saleebey, D. (1997). *The strengths perspective in social work practice*. 2nd ed. New York: Longman.

Scheflen, A. (1964). The significance of posture in communication systems. *Psychiatry* 27:316–331.

Schopler, J. H., and M. J. Galinski. (1995). Group practice overview. In R. L. Edwards (ed.), *The encyclopedia of social work*, 19th ed., 1129–1142. Washington, D.C.: NASW Press.

Schwartz, W. (1971). The use of groups in social work practice. In W. Schwartz and S. Zalba (eds.), *The practice of group work*, 3–24. New York: Columbia University Press.

Seabury, B. A. (1971). Arrangement of physical space in social work settings. *Social Work* 16:43–49.

Selznick, P. (1957). *Leadership in administration*. Evanston, Ill.: Row Publishing.

Shulman, L. (1979). *The skills of helping individuals and groups*. Itasca, Ill.: F. E. Peacock.

——. (1992). *The skills of helping: Individuals, families, and groups*. 3rd ed. Itasca, Ill.: F. E. Peacock.

Smith, D. *The everyday world as problematic: A feminist sociology*. Toronto: University of Toronto Press.

——. (1990). *The conceptual practices of power: A feminist sociology of knowledge*. Toronto: University of Toronto Press. (1987).

Thompson, J. D. (1967). *Organizations in action*. New York: McGraw-Hill.

Tully, C. T. (2002). Social policy and resilience. In R. Greene (ed.), *Human Behavior Theory: A Resilience Orientation*, 321–335. Washington, D.C.: NASW Press.

von Glasersfeld, E. (1984). An introduction to radical constructivism. In P. Watzlawick (ed.), *The invented reality*. New York: Norton.

Wald, L. D. (1915). *The house on Henry Street*. New York: Henry Holt.

Walton, R. E., and R. B. McKersie. (1965). *A behavioral theory of labor negotiations: An analysis of a social interaction system*. New York: McGraw-Hill.

Weil, M., and J. M. Karls. (1985). *Case management in human service practice: A systematic approach to mobilizing resources for clients*. San Francisco: Jossey-Bass.

Weingarten, K. (1995). Radical listening: Challenging cultural beliefs for and about mothers. In K. Weingarten (ed.), *Cultural resistance: Challenging beliefs about men, women and therapy*, 7–23. Binghamton, N.Y.: Harrington Park.

White, M. (1991). Deconstruction and therapy. *Dulwich Centre Newsletter* 3:21–41.

——.(1995). *Re-authoring lives: Interviews & essays.* Adelaide: Dulwich Centre Publications.

——. (2000). *Reflections on narrative practice.* Adelaide: Dulwich Centre Publications.

——. (2004). *Narrative practice and exotic lives: Resurrecting diversity in everyday life.* Adelaide: Dulwich Centre Publications.

White, M., and D. Epston. (1990). *Narrative means to therapeutic ends.* New York: Norton.

Wood, G. G., and R. R. Middleman. (1987). *I-view skills.* Forest Park, Ill: OUTP ST Software.

——. (1991). Advocacy and social action: Key elements in the structural approach to direct practice in social work. *Social Work with Groups* 14 (3–4): 53–63.

Wood, G. G., and S. E. Roche. (2001a). An emancipatory principle for social work with survivors of male violence. *Affilia* 16 (1): 66–79.

——. (2001b). Representing selves, reconstructing lives: Feminist group work with women survivors of male violence." *Social Work with Groups* 23 (4): 5–23.

——. (2001c). Situations and representations: Feminist practice with survivors of male violence. *Families in Society* 82 (6): 583–590.

Wood, J. B., and C. L. Estes. (1988). "Medicalization" of community services for the elderly. *Health and Social Work* 13 (1): 35–41.

Yalom, I. D. (1985). *The theory and practice of group psychotherapy.* 3rd ed. New York: Basic Books.

INDEX

accountability: to client, 44–49, 79; to and for oneself, 250; in organizations, 237, 240

actions: in quadrant model, 10–12; social work defined in terms of, 7–8

activism, 1, 3, 216

Addams, Jane, 216

advise and consent, 147–49; informed consent, 35–37, 93

advocacy: basis for, 141; beneficiary of, 141–42; case, 187; defined, 139–41; groups, 192, 195–96

advocate, 51, 139–54; and advise and consent, 147–49; and alleviating workers' struggles, 251; case manager as, 176, 178, 181, 187, 189; and deconstructing issue, 145–47; and identifying groups, 143–44; and identifying issue, 144–45; intervention of, 149–53; and least contest, 69; and organizational change, 253; in Quadrant A, 153; in Quadrant B, 96, 153–54, 187; in Quadrant C, 93, 96, 154, 187; in Quadrant D, 154; in task phase, 93, 96

agencies: and NASW Code of Ethics, 30; role of, 22. See also organizations

alliances, creating, 222–23, 224

alone vs. lonely, 193

American Psychiatric Association, 161

answering machines, 259

arguing, 152–53

assessment, 171–74; of agency's services, 246; process guide of, 172–74

attending, 46; examples of, 48, 107; and radical listening, 156–57

attraction power, 238

attraction relations, 197

authority relations, 197

bargaining, 150–51

beneficence, 32–33

beneficiaries: of advocacy efforts, 141–42; categories of persons at risk as, 9; of deleterious discourses, 146–47; intended, 9, 10; self as, 249

Blaming the Victim (Ryan), 21

Bosanquet, B., 27–28

brainstorming, 147–48

broker, 51, 115–26; case manager as, 189; in contract phase, 82–83; and learning community, 116–18; and least contest, 69; in Quadrant A, 91, 123–25; in Quadrant B, 125–26; in Quadrant C, 89–90, 91, 120–23; in task phase, 89–92; and using community, 118–20; and workers' struggles, 251

Cabinet for Families and Children (Kentucky), 260–61

case advocacy, 187

case conferences, 170

case management: defined, 169; evolution of, 169–71

Case Management Society of America, 171

case manager, 51–52, 169–91; as advocate, 176, 178, 181, 187, 189; and assessment, 171–74; determining work of, 187–90; and linking, 181–84; and monitoring, 184–86; and planning, 174–81; in quadrant model, 190–91

change: implementing, 223–26; and organizations, 242, 252–57; planning for, 220–23; strategies of, 147–48, 221–22. *See also* environmental change

charity organization societies, 2, 169

Charmaz, K. C., 106

class advocacy, 187

clients: and access to information, 34; accountability to, 44–49, 79; assessment of services to, 246; attributes and skills inferred from counteracts, 167; and decision making, 109; eligibility for services, 245; help with reaching out by, 132–37; and informal organization of agencies, 241; informed consent of, 36, 93; as intended beneficiaries, 9; looking beyond, 50, 143–44, 224; maximizing supports for, 56–62; as persons engaged, 9; powerlessness of, 45, 147; protection of rights of, 141; reconnecting with, 182, 185; services needed, 245–46; standing with, 159; storyline of, 167–68; and termination of service contract, 111–12; and time-distance-cost factors, 233–34, 243

client task, following demands of, 49–54, 79; example of, 52–54; roles used in, 50–52

Clinical Social Work Federation, 28

Code of Ethics, NASW, 29–30; confidentiality in, 33–34

coercion theory. *See* conflict theory

coercive power, 238

collaborative language systems, 14

collegiality, 237, 240

Combs, Gene, 155

common ground, identifying, 128–32; example of, 130–32

communication patterns, 240–41

communication relations, 197

communities: identifying, 217–19; learning, 116–17; members of, 218–19; organizing, 219–20; types of, 217–18; using, 118–19, 181

community organizer, 52, 216–26; and co-ops, 125; in quadrant model, 226

community organizing, defined, 216–17

conferee, 50–51, 105–14; case manager as, 189; in contract phase, 80, 105–6; and decision making, 109–11; identifying needed tasks, 106–8; and organizational change, 253; in Quadrant A, 93, 98, 105, 114, 120, 123; in task phase, 92, 93; in termination/recontracting phase, 98, 111–13; and workers' struggles, 251

confidentiality, 33–35; *vs.* privileged communication, 34; and technology, 259; and therapy groups, 195

conflict theory, 15

consciousness-raising, 149–50

consensus, reaching for, 207–8

consensus theory. *See* systems theory

consent. *See* advise and consent

continuing education, 260–61

contract phase, 80–88; with group, 87–88; with one client, 84–87

cooperating, tapping into motives for, 128–29

cooperatives, 125
Council on Social Work Education, 260
counteracts: defined, 163–64; roots of, 166–67; seeking, 163–65

Dahrendorf, R., 15
"daughters' work" ideology, deconstruction of, 75
decision making, facilitating, 109–11; example of, 110–11
deconstruction, 17–18, 25; defined, 160; of issue in advocacy, 145–47; of oppressive cultural discourse, 72–76, 79, 160–63, 252; as political process, 163
Diagnostic and Statistical Manual (DSM), 161
discourses, oppressive: deconstruction of, 72–76, 79, 160–63, 252; defined, 18, 25–26; examples of, 160–61; identifying, 145–46, 162–63; internalized, 20, 161–63; in organization, 252
Dolgoff, F., 28

email, 259
empathic connections, 46, 56–57; example of, 108, 131–32; within groups, 205
empowerment approaches, 14
empty-chair work, 159
Encyclopedia of Social Work, 37
engagement with empathy, 106
environmental change, 43; and advocacy groups, 196; vs. changing people, 2; as first choice, 3, 16, 21; social workers as agent of, 21
essentialism, 16, 19–21
ethical absolutism, 28–29; and NASW Code of Ethics, 31
ethical relativism, 29
ethics, 27–39; beneficence, 32–33; cognitivist vs. non-cognitivist view of,

28–29; confidentiality, 33–35; defined, 27–29; honesty, 37–38; informed consent, 35–37; justice, 37; professional codes of, 28, 29–31, 33–34; questioning of, 256; respect for individual, 32; and structural approach, 31–39; and technology, 258–59
evidence-based practice (EBP), 265
exceptionalism, doctrine of, 20
expert power, 238

fairness, 37
family unit, 194
faxes, 259
feedback, 47; example of, 49
feelings, getting with, 46, 57, 58; and broker, 121; and case manager, 172–73; and conferee, 106, 107; examples of, 48, 107, 121, 130; and mediator, 130, 134
feelings, reaching for, 46, 57, 58, 66; and broker, 119; and conferee, 106; examples of, 48, 64, 107, 119, 131; and mediator, 130; and preconceptions, 109
feminist critique, 14
Freedman, Jill, 155

gatekeepers, 202–3
Germain, C., 8–9
grassroots organizing. *See* community organizing, defined
groups: creating goals for, 198–99; defined, 193; dynamics of, 201–3, 220; facilitating interaction in, 203–9, 220; full participation in, 206–7; history and continuity of, 200–201; relations within, 197, 201; role differentiation within, 202–3; selecting members of, 198; setting boundaries within, 200;

groups (Continued)
  sustaining, 200–201, 220; traditions
  and rituals of, 201; turning issues back
  to, 207; types of, 193–96; voicing
  achievements of, 200
group structure, defined, 197
group worker, 52, 192–215; and group
  dynamics, 201–3; and holistic
  approach, 196–98; and interaction in
  groups, 203–9; intervention of, 198–
  99; in Quadrant A, 91, 209–11; in
  Quadrant B, 209, 211–14; in Quadrant
  C, 209, 214–15; in Quadrant D, 209,
  215; sustaining groups, 200–201; in
  task phase, 91, 92
guiding questions: in contract phase, 81–
  84, 85; in task phase, 88–89, 92–95;
  in termination/recontracting phase,
  98–99

harm: defined, 33; duty of social worker
  to do no, 32–33
Harrington, D., 28
Health and Human Services, U.S.
  Department of, 234–35
hierarchy, formal organization and, 237–40
honesty, 37–38
Hull-House (Chicago), 216
Hutcheon, L., 17

immersion, 157
implementation dates, 177–78
inadequacy, 20–21, 77, 122
independence fostering, 112
individual, respect for, 32
inferences, checking out, 46; and broker,
  119, 121; and confronting preconceptions, 109; examples, 53, 63, 119, 121
information, giving, 133; examples of, 86
information, reaching for, 46–47; and
  broker, 121; and conferee, 106, 107;

examples of, 48, 53, 64, 86, 107, 108,
  121, 130; and mediator, 130
information link, 205–6
informed consent. See advise and
  consent
intervention: in advocacy, 149–53; with
  groups, 198–99; least contest principle
  and point of, 69–70
issues. See problems

justice, 37

Kahn, S., 216
Kuhn, Thomas, 265

least contest, principle of, 68–72, 79; and
  broker, 115; example of, 70–72; and
  organization change, 252–53; and
  protesting en masse, 225; during task
  phase, 90
line relationships, 237, 240
linguistic shift, 158–59
linking, 181–84; and process guide, 182–84
Linzer, N., 27
listening: to client's story, 143; radical,
  156–57
lobbying, 152
Loewenberg, R. M., 28
lonely vs. alone, 193

macro-practice, 23–25, 209
marginalization, 3, 18
Marriage and Family Therapy Institute,
  260
mediating, defined, 127
mediator, 51, 127–38; case manager as,
  182; community organizer as, 223;
  helping clients reach out, 132–37;
  identifying common ground, 128–32;
  and least contest, 69; and organizational change, 253; in Quadrant A,

93, 137; in Quadrant C, 93, 138; in task phase, 93; and workers' struggles, 251

meetings, 260; and time management, 263

messages: amplifying subtle, 204; redirecting, 206; softening overpowering, 204–5

metawork, 257–61; defined, 257; meetings, 260; paperwork, 257–58; supervision, 259–60; technology, 258–59

micro-practice, 23–25

minimax principle, 77–79; and self, 253; and task phase, 96

monitoring, 184–86; process guide for, 185–86

mutual compassion, developing, 133–34

narrative collaboration, 155

narrative therapy, 14

NASW. See National Association of Social Workers

National Association of Black Social Workers, 28

National Association of Social Workers (NASW): Code of Ethics of, 28, 29–31, 33–34; and continuing education, 260

obstacles, confronting, 129–30

offices, 231–32

organizations, 229–64; accountability in, 237, 240; boundaries of, 234; catchment area of, 233; and change, 242, 254–57; charity, 2, 169; choice points in, 242–47; and clients, 241; communication patterns in, 240–41; culturescape of, 231–33, 243; decision making in, 242–47; ecological organization, 230, 243; formal structures of, 234–37; hierarchy in, 237–40; informal structures of, 235–36, 238–40; mission of, 234; oppressive cultural discourses in, 252; physical dimension of, 230; services provided by, 234; as social constructs, 229; stretching norms of, 255; territoriality of, 233. See also agencies; working in organizations

outcomes: of advocacy, 148–49; assessing, in groups, 199; indetermination of, 266–67; translating needs/problems into, 172

Oxford English Dictionary, 27

paperwork, 257–58; and time management, 261–62

patterns, looking for, 144–45

persons engaged, 8–10

perspectives, multiple, 72–76, 163; within groups, 208–9; and reinterpretation of experience, 79

persuading, 151–52

philosophical base, 14–26

pivotal readiness, 253

planning, 174–81; process guide, 178–81

policies and procedures: and formal organization, 236–37; and informal organization, 237

policy analysis, 220–21

positioning, 45–46; examples of, 86, 107, 121; and office furniture, 232–33

postmodernism: and policy analysis, 221; on power, 18–19; and social work practice, 14, 17

power: balancing, 150; and informal organization, 238–40; interaction with brokers, 224–25; legitimate, 238; and postmodernism, 18–19

preconceptions, confronting, 109

pressures translated into tasks, 106–8

privileged communication, 34

problem definition, 26; in advocacy, 145; in case management, 171–72; and choice, 21; in psychological terms, 20; solutions affected by, 19–20

problems: within communities, 218, 219–20; exploring, 160; externalizing, 157–60; identification of, 143–45; separation from client, 159

process model, 80–101; contract phase, 80–88; task phase, 88–98; termination/recontracting phase, 98–101

professional assignment, 21–22, 26

professional development, 260–61; and time management, 263

protesting en masse, 225–26

Quadrant A, 8, 10; advocate in, 153; broker in, 91, 123–25; case manager in, 190–91; conferee in, 93, 98, 105, 114, 120, 123; and contract phase, 80; group worker in, 91, 209–11; and maximizing support, 56–60, 62–68; mediator in, 93, 137; and micro-practice, 23; and organizational change, 253; and workers' struggles, 251

Quadrant B, 8, 10–11; advocate in, 96, 153–54, 187; broker in, 125–26; case manager in, 190, 191; community organizer in, 226; group worker in, 209, 211–14; and maximizing support, 60; and organizational change, 253

Quadrant C, 8, 11; advocate in, 93, 96, 154, 187; broker in, 89–90, 91, 120–23; case manager in, 191; community organizer in, 226; group worker in, 209, 214–15; and maximizing support, 60–61; mediator in, 93, 138; and organizational change, 253; and resources creation, 120–23; and workers' struggles, 251

Quadrant D, 8, 11–12; advocate in, 154; group worker in, 209, 215; and macro-practice, 23; and workers' struggles, 251

quadrant model, 7–13; and demands of client task, 49–50; and least contest principle, 68–69; and maximizing potential supports, 55–68; research value of, 12; and specialization, 23–24

qualitative inquiry, 266

quantification, 267

radical listening, 156–57

Reamer, F. G., 28

recontracting phase. See termination/recontracting phase

referrals, 118–19; defining date of, 177–78

research: limits of, 266; and quadrant model, 12

resources, creating, 119, 120–23; and case manager, 177; and co-ops, 125; in Quadrant A, 123–24; in Quadrant B, 125–26; and trade units, 124–25

resources, formal, 117; and case manager, 187–88; identification of, 174–75, 178

resources, informal, 117; and case manager, 187–88; identification of, 176–77, 181; prescreening of, 118–19

reward power, 238

Rock, Chris, 161

roles, 50–52, 102–226; and least contest principle, 69. See also advocate; broker; case manager; community organizer; conferee; group worker; mediator; therapist

Ryan, William, 21

scanning group, 202

self, use of, 253–54

self-help groups, 194

self principle, 249–54; processes for, 254

self-subjugation, 18–19; and social beliefs, 72–73, 161–62

service contract, 65; and accountability to client, 44–45; in case management,

174; and conferee role, 105; with groups, 198–99; skills used to establish, 45–47; termination of, 98, 111

service providers: and case management, 169; contacting, 175–76; organizations as, 234; reconnecting with, 182, 185

settlement houses, 2; and community organizers, 216; social workers as brokers in, 115; and support groups, 193

social change. *See* environmental change

social constructionism, 19–21; and evidence, 265–66

social emotional leaders, 202

social groups, 192, 194–95

Social Work Dictionary, 37

solution-focused practices, 14

specialization, 22–24, 26

staff relationships, 237, 240

stage, setting, 203

stereotypes, 161

stigmatization, 161

strengths-based practices, 14; *vs.* structural, 15

strengths perpective, 14

structures: creation of, 55; defined, 25

supervision, 259–60; and time management, 262–63

support groups, 192, 193–94

supports, maximizing, 55–68, 79, 91; in client's environment, 56–62; and group worker, 192; in institutional setting, 62–68; in Quadrant A, 56–60, 62–68; in Quadrant B, 60; in Quadrant C, 60–61; using community for, 118–19; for workers in organization, 251–52

systems theory, 15; and NASW Code of Ethics, 30

taboos, raising, 256–57

task leaders, 202

task phase, 88–98; example of, 97–98; initial intervention in, 91–97

technology: and ethics, 258–59; and time management, 262

termination/recontracting phase, 98–101; conferee role in, 98, 111–13; example of, 100–101, 112–13

therapist, 52, 155–68; and counteracts, 163–65; and deconstructing oppressive discourses, 160–63; externalizing problem, 157–60; radical listening, 156–57

therapy groups, 192, 195

thinking group, 197

time management, 261–63; strategies for, 263–64

trade units, 124–25, 181

victim-blaming mentality, 77, 122

viewing group, 197–98

waiting rooms, 231

Webster's Ninth New Collegiate Dictionary, 27

White, Michael, 155, 157

working in organizations, 249–64; and alleviating workers' struggles, 250–51; and changing organization, 254–57; and metawork, 257–61; and self principle, 249–54; and taboos, 256–57; and time management, 261–63; and unethical practices, 256